Santa Fe

Hot & Spicy Recipe

Hot new recipes from Santa Fe chefs

by
Joan Stromquist

Tierra Publications

Tierra Publications
2801 Rodeo Road
Suite B-612
Santa Fe, New Mexico 87505
(505) 983-6300

Other books in this series by Joan Stromquist:
Santa Fe Lite & Spicy Recipe
Santa Fe Recipe
Taos Recipe
Southern California Beach Recipe

Additional copies may be obtained by contacting Tierra Publications. For your convenience, an order form is included in the back of the book.

Book Design by Carl Stromquist

Cover by James Finnell

Drawings by Larry Caldwell

Library of Congress Catalog Card Number:
93-60022

ISBN: 0-9622807-5-5

Printed in the United States of America

Author's Notes

To the innovative, talented and generous chefs of Santa Fe, I give my sincere thanks for the time and effort they spent in supplying me with these delicious, hot and spicy recipes. As always, without their contributions this book would not be possible.

Also, I would like to thank Susan Mootry, my right-hand person, whose intelligence and skill were an enormous help in the production of this cookbook. I also want to thank our courier "Kona" (a Golden Retriever) who cheerfully carried corrected copies of the manuscript up and down the stairs to our different offices, knowing she would be rewarded with a freeze-dried liver treat at the end of each journey.

Finally, I thank Jim Finnell for the beautiful cover, Larry Caldwell for his creative drawings, and Sonya Moore for her excellent proofreading.

Joan Stromquist

Chile Pepper Guide

About Chile Peppers

Americans have discovered the excitement of hot and spicy foods, and as a result, the use of chile peppers (genus *Capsicum*) has exploded in popularity. There are up to 200 identified varieties of chiles, each one with a unique taste and quality of heat. Chiles can be purchased fresh, dried, frozen, canned, crushed, and powdered. When working with any form of chile peppers, remember to be careful about touching your eyes with your hands because the heat will burn them. Many people use rubber gloves when handling chiles. If you eat a bite of food that is too hot, the best antidote for the heat is a dairy product such as milk, yogurt or ice cream, or a starch, such as rice or bread. Contrary to popular opinion, cold beer and water do not work.

For those of you who do not have access to the different chile peppers and Southwestern ingredients called for in these recipes, some mail order sources are listed on page 351. For more information on chile peppers, two excellent books that you can purchase are **The Whole Chile Pepper Book** by Dave DeWitt and Nancy Gerlach, and **The Great Chile Book** by Mark Miller.

How to Roast Chile Peppers

Place the peppers on a rack over a gas flame, on a grill, or under a broiler. The skin should blacken and blister all over. Do this quickly, so the flesh won't burn. Then place the peppers in a bowl, cover it with plastic wrap, and let the peppers "sweat" for about 10 minutes so that the skin loosens. Pull the skin off with your fingers. If the skin sticks, gently scrape it off with the back of a knife blade. Don't wash the peppers. Remove the seeds with a spoon or the tip of a knife.

Types of Chile Peppers

Anaheim: Long, green chile, similar to the New Mexico green chile, only milder and not as sharply defined in flavor. Excellent roasted. Good stuffed, in stews, and sauces. Widely available. Mild heat.

Ancho: A dried red-ripe poblano chile, 3 to 5 inches long and 2 to 4 inches wide. Reddish brown in color and very wrinkled. The most commonly used dried chile in Mexico. Sweet, with a fruity flavor of cherries and dried plums. Medium hot.

Arbol: Small dried red chiles, usually serrano, but sometimes cayenne or Thai chiles. Good toasted. Widely available. Extremely hot.

Bell, green: Bright green, sweet, and mild. Good stuffed and baked, grilled, or roasted. Available everywhere. No heat.

Bell, red: Very sweet and crisp. Good raw, grilled, and roasted. Almost always available. No heat.

Bell, yellow: Sweet, crisp; and fruity. Usually available. No heat.

Cascabel: Dried version of a Mexican chile, which, when ripe, looks like an Italian cherry pepper. Nutty-sweet flavor. Good toasted whole in oil. Medium hot.

Cayenne: Bright red dried pepper, 2 to 4 inches long and ½ inch across. Pungent heat. Can be used whole in soups, stews, and sauces, but usually are sold ground as a seasoning powder. Very hot.

Chile Caribe: Crushed dried New Mexican red chile peppers. In supermarkets it comes packed as "crushed red chile flakes." Varies in flavor and heat.

Chile Molido: Ground dried New Mexican red chile peppers. Varies in flavor and heat.

Chimayo Red Chile Powder: Ground dried red chiles from Chimayo, New Mexico. Highly prized for its excellent flavor. Hot, smoky, sweet, and nutty. Mild to hot.

Chipotle, dried: A smoked jalapeño, 2 to 4 inches long, light dusty brown in color. Good toasted. Used in soups and salsas. Very hot.

Chipotle, in adobo sauce: Canned, dried, smoked jalapeños that are simmered in a tomato-vinegar sauce. Widely available. Very hot.

Green (New Mexico): Fresh, related to the Anaheim, but with a much fuller flavor. Wonderful roasted. Used in sauces, stews, soups, or just eaten plain. Comes frozen or canned in most markets, but fresh is far superior. Frozen is preferred to canned. Also known as "Hatch." Mild to hot heat.

Guajillo: Dried red chile, about 4 inches long and reddish brown in color. Nutty-rich flavor. Good in salsas and moles. Mildly hot.

Habanero: Fresh, dark green to orange to red. About 2 inches long and 1½ inches wide. One of the hottest chiles in the world. Distinct flavor. Goes well with tropical fruits and tomatoes. Fierce heat!

Jalapeño: Fresh, dark green chile, about 2 to 3 inches long. The most popular chile in the United States. Readily available. Excellent raw or roasted. Comes in red and yellow as well. Medium to high heat.

Japone: Small, thin dried red chiles with a unique, sharp heat. Thai or arbol chiles may be substituted. Very hot.

Morita: A type of dried, smoked jalapeño with a sweet, smoky flavor. Used in soups and salsas. Medium high heat.

Mulato: A type of dried poblano. Dark brown with a slight licorice and tobacco flavor. Used in moles, sauces, stews, and soups. Low to medium low heat.

Pasado: A New Mexico or Anaheim chile which has been roasted, peeled, and dried. About 4 inches long and 1 inch wide. Sweet, toasty, dusty flavor. Good for flavoring stews and soups. Medium hot.

Pasilla: Dried chile, also known as "chile negro." About 5 to 7 inches long and 1 inch wide, with dark and wrinkled skin. Sometimes the fresh poblano or the dried ancho and mulato are mistakenly called "pasillas." Deep, rich, almost cocoa-flavor. Used in moles and salsas. Low to medium heat.

Pequin: Tiny dried red chiles. Fiery, sharp, sweet and nutty flavor. Easy to find. Very hot.

Poblano: Fresh, dark green and purple-black chile, 4 to 5 inches long and 3 inches wide. Always roasted or cooked. Good for rellenos or made into sauces and moles. Rich and meaty. Low heat.

Red Chile Powder: Ground dried red chiles. Varies in quality of flavor and heat.

Sambal Chile: Asian chile. Comes in paste form. Can be found in Asian stores and larger markets. Extremely hot.

Serrano: Fresh green small chile with a clean, sharp heat. Extremely easy to find. Very hot.

Tabasco: Fresh or dried chiles from Louisiana. Used to make tabasco sauce. Very, very hot.

Thai: Thin, fresh green or dried red chiles, about 1½ inches long and ¼ inch wide. Used in Southeast Asian cooking. Found in specialty stores. Very hot.

Table of Contents

Restaurant Addresses

Adobo Catering
1807 2nd Street, #7
Santa Fe, NM 87501
(505) 989-7674

Bishop's Lodge
Bishop's Lodge Road
Santa Fe, NM 87501
(505) 983-6377

Cafe Pasqual's
121 Don Gaspar Ave.
Santa Fe, NM 87501
(505) 983-9340

Casa Sena
125 E. Palace Ave.
Santa Fe, NM 87501
(505) 988-9232

Celebrations
613 Canyon Road
Santa Fe, NM 87501
(505) 989-8904

Coyote Cafe
132 W. Water St.
Santa Fe, NM 87501
(505) 983-1615

El Farol
808 Canyon Road
Santa Fe, NM 87501
(505) 983-9912

El Nido
P.O. Box 488
Tesuque, NM 87574
(505) 988-4340

The Evergreen
Hyde Park Road
Santa Fe, NM 87501
(505) 984-8190

The Galisteo Inn
HC 75, Box 4
Galisteo, NM 87540
(505) 982-1506

Geronimo
724 Canyon Road
Santa Fe, NM 87501
(505) 982-1500

Grant Corner Inn
122 Grant
Santa Fe, NM 87501
(505) 983-6678

Guadalupe Cafe
313 S. Guadalupe
Santa Fe, NM 87501
(505) 982-9762

Harry's Road House
Old Las Vegas Highway
Santa Fe, NM 87505
(505) 989-4629

Imperial Wok
731 Canyon Road
Santa Fe, NM 87501
(505) 988-7100

Inn at Loretto
211 Old Santa Fe Trail
Santa Fe, NM 87501
(505) 988-5531

Inn of the Anasazi
113 Washington Ave.
Santa Fe, NM 87501
(505) 988-3030

La Plazuela
100 E. San Francisco St.
Santa Fe, NM 87501
(505) 982-5511

La Tertulia
416 Agua Fria
Santa Fe, NM 87501
(505) 988-2769

La Traviata
95 W. Marcy St.
Santa Fe, NM 87501
(505) 984-1091

Mañana
234 Don Gaspar Ave.
Santa Fe, NM 87501
(505) 982-4333

Old House
309 W. San Francisco St.
Santa Fe, NM 87501
(505) 988-4455

Old Mexico Grill
2434 Cerrillos Road
Santa Fe, NM 87501
(505) 473-0338

On Water
100 W. Water
Santa Fe, NM 87501
(505) 982-8787

Ore House
50 Lincoln Ave.
Santa Fe, NM 87501
(505) 983-8687

Paul's Restaurant
72 W. Marcy St.
Santa Fe, NM 87501
(505) 982-8738

**Peppers Restaurant
& Cantina**
2239 Old Pecos Trail
Santa Fe, NM 87505
(505) 984-2272

Piñon Grill
100 Sandoval
Santa Fe, NM 87501
(505) 988-2811

Pranzo Italian Grill
540 Montezuma
Santa Fe, NM 87501
(505) 984-2645

Rancho Encantado
Route 4, Box 57C
Santa Fe, NM 87501
(505) 982-3537

Restaurant Thao
322 Garfield
Santa Fe, NM 87501
(505) 988-9562

**San Francisco St.
Bar & Grill**
114 W. San Francisco St.
Santa Fe, NM 87501
(505) 982-2044

Santacafe
231 Washington Ave.
Santa Fe, NM 87501
(505) 984-1788

Santa Fe Market
1441 Paseo de Peralta
Santa Fe, NM 87501
(505) 988-3159

The Shed
113½ Palace Ave.
Santa Fe, NM 87501
(505) 982-9030

Staab House
330 E. Palace Ave.
Santa Fe, NM 87501
(505) 986-0000

Steaksmith
Old Las Vegas Highway
Santa Fe, NM 87505
(505) 988-3333

Tecolote Cafe
1203 Cerrillos Rd.
Santa Fe, NM 87501
(505) 988-1362

Tortilla Flats
3139 Cerrillos Rd.
Santa Fe, NM 87501
(505) 471-8685

Zia Diner
326 S. Guadalupe
Santa Fe, NM 87501
(505) 988-7008

Food Categories

8

Salads

Salad Dressings

Sauces, Dips & Condiments

Fish & Shellfish

Fowl

Meat

Side Dishes

Potpourri

Desserts

Restaurant Table of Contents

Santa Fe

Hot & Spicy Recipe

*"Santa Fe is great, but its green
chile is even greater. That's
why I moved here.....for the
chile experience!"*

Rubin Rodriquez, Guadalupe Cafe

Appetizers

Santacafe Onion Rings
with Chipotle Ketchup

Santacafe Onion Rings

4	large red onions, sliced into ½" thick rings
1	quart buttermilk
2	cups flour
½	cup cornmeal
⅛	cup red chile powder
½	tablespoon salt *(or to taste)*
6	cups vegetable oil
	Chipotle Ketchup *(recipe on next page)*

In a large bowl place the red onions and cover them with the buttermilk.

Cover the bowl with plastic wrap and refrigerate the onions overnight.

In a medium bowl place the flour, cornmeal, red chile powder, and salt. Stir the ingredients together.

Dredge the onion rings in the flour mixture so that they are well coated.

In a large, heavy pan place the vegetable oil and heat it until it is 375°. Fry the onion rings for 2 to 4 minutes, or until they are golden brown. Drain them on paper towels.

Serve the onion rings with the Chipotle Ketchup on the side.

serves 4

"These are really delicious onion rings. By soaking them in the buttermilk some of their flavor is mellowed and they get a creamy texture. These are especially good with the Chipotle Ketchup."

Kelly Rogers
Santacafe

"I love to be in the restaurant business.....it just fits me to a 'T'. I love to cook, I love reading cookbooks, and I love the challenge of running a successful business."

Judy Ebbinghaus
Santacafe

Chipotle Ketchup

¼	cup olive oil
1	small yellow onion, chopped medium
2	tablespoons fresh garlic, finely chopped
3½	pounds Roma tomatoes, halved
3½	ounces chipotle chile peppers *(in adobo sauce)*
2	tablespoons brown sugar
2	tablespoons honey
2	tablespoons molasses

In a large saucepan place the olive oil and heat it on medium high until it is hot. Add the yellow onions and garlic. Sauté them for 7 to 10 minutes, or until the onions are golden brown.

Add the remaining ingredients and bring them to a boil.

Reduce the heat and simmer the ingredients for 30 minutes.

Place the ingredients in a food processor and coarsely purée them.

Place the ketchup in a bowl, cover it with plastic wrap, and refrigerate it.

makes approximately 1 quart

Red Chile Salmon Hash Patties with Cilantro Hollandaise Sauce

Red Chile Salmon Hash Patties

1	pound salmon fillet, skin and bones removed
2	large potatoes, peeled, finely diced and blanched
2	tablespoons red bell peppers, finely diced
2	tablespoons yellow bell peppers, finely diced
1	egg, lightly beaten
1	cup fresh bread crumbs
1	tablespoon fresh parsley, chopped
2	tablespoons chile caribe *(crushed red chile peppers)*
1½	teaspoons salt *(or to taste)*
3	tablespoons clarified butter
	Cilantro Hollandaise Sauce *(recipe on next page)*

In a food processor place the salmon and coarsely purée it.

In a medium bowl place the puréed salmon, blanched potatoes, red and yellow bell peppers, egg, bread crumbs, parsley, chile caribe, and salt. Mix the ingredients together well.

Divide the mixture into 8 equal portions. Form each portion into a patty.

In a large sauté pan place the clarified butter and heat it on medium high until it is hot. Add the salmon patties and sauté them for 5 minutes on each side, or until they are golden brown.

On each of 4 individual serving plates place two of the patties. Serve the Cilantro Hollandaise Sauce on the side.

serves 4

"This is a very tasty, simple dish to make. Just make sure your ingredients are really fresh and go from there."

"I believe that visual presentation is important because people do eat with their eyes. However, I also know of a restaurant in France which serves pressed duck that looks like a pool of mud, and yet the flavor is incredible. A lot of foods in Mexico are like this also, where the concentration is not on looks, but rather on flavors."

Mark Kiffin
Coyote Cafe

Cilantro Hollandaise Sauce

5   **egg yolks**
3   **tablespoons lemon juice, freshly squeezed**
½   **teaspoon salt** *(or to taste)*
1   **pound butter, melted and then cooled to room temperature**
2   **tablespoons fresh cilantro, finely chopped**
1   **pinch cayenne pepper** *(or to taste)*

In a medium bowl place the egg yolks, lemon juice, and salt. Whisk the ingredients together.

Place the egg mixture in the top of a simmering double boiler. While whisking constantly, cook the mixture for 5 minutes, or until it begins to thicken slightly.

While continuing to whisk, slowly dribble in the melted butter.

Add the cilantro and cayenne pepper, and stir them in.

makes approximately 3 cups

Picaditas

1   **pound corn masa dough** *(follow manufacturer's instructions)*
4   **cups vegetable oil**
2   **cups cooked black beans, drained**
1   **pound boneless chicken breast, skin removed, cooked and diced medium**
1   **bunch fresh cilantro, chopped**
2   **cups Pico de Gallo** *(recipe on page 70)*
½   **pound manchego cheese, grated**

Divide the masa dough into small amounts *(about the size of a golf ball)* and press them out into tortillas that are ⅛" thick. In a hot, dry sauté pan place the tortillas and cook them for 2 minutes on each side. Remove the tortillas from the pan and bend the edges up to form a small lip.

In a large, heavy pan place the vegetable oil and heat it on high until it is very hot. Deep-fry each tortilla for 1 minute, or until it is crisp. Drain them on paper towels.

On each tortilla place some of the black beans, chicken breast, cilantro, Pico de Gallo, and manchego cheese.

serves 6

"This is a simple hollandaise recipe which has some cilantro and cayenne pepper in it to add a Southwestern accent. It is wonderful with vegetables, egg dishes, or as a meat garnish for filets."

*"Mark Miller is the owner and founder of Coyote Cafe, and he is quite famous, both as a chef and as a cookbook author. He has written the popular **Coyote Cafe Cookbook** and the **Great Chile Book**. Together he and I are working on a new book called **Coyote's Pantry**. All the books are published by Ten Speed Press."*

Mark Kiffin
Coyote Cafe

"Picaditas are similar to tortillas, except that they are thicker. They form their own little pizza-shaped dish that you can fill with different goodies. These are a great thing to serve as appetizers."

Kimo Castro
San Francisco St. Bar & Grill

Flash-Fried Calamari with Habanero Mint Aioli

Flash-Fried Calamari

2	**cups flour**
1⅛	**cups corn meal**
½	**cup red chile powder**
1½	**teaspoons salt** *(or to taste)*
1½	**teaspoons black pepper** *(or to taste)*
1	**pound calamari, sliced into ¼" rings**
4	**cups peanut oil**
	Habanero Mint Aioli *(recipe on next page)*

In a large bowl place the flour, corn meal, red chile powder, salt, and black pepper. Stir the ingredients together.

Dredge the calamari rings in the flour mixture so that they are well coated.

In a large, heavy pan place the peanut oil and heat it on high until it is 375°. Fry the calamari rings for 45 seconds, or until they are golden brown. Drain them on paper towels.

Serve the calamari with the Habanero Mint Aioli on the side.

serves 4

"If you want to splurge on something really decadent and tasty, this is it. People universally love it. This is our favorite dish to 'comp' to customers who might have had to wait too long for a table, or for whom something may have gone wrong with the dinner or service. It has the power to turn an angry person into a very grateful, happy person."

"When I was eighteen years old I ran away from home and married a cowboy. We lived in the northeastern part of Nevada, where there was absolutely nothing but ranches and open spaces. I learned to cook for twenty men on a haycrew. An older woman who worked the chow wagon taught me to cook with limited ingredients, very few of which were fresh, and we never wasted a single ounce of food. She could make the best cole-slaw out of a two-month-old head of cabbage! If we butchered a cow we used up every single part, from the milk to the liver. I have carried this concept of total food utilization with me ever since, and employ it in the restaurant as well as at my home. Food is very precious and to waste any part of it drives me crazy!"

Judy Ebbinghaus
Santacafe

Habanero Mint Aioli

1	dried habanero chile pepper, stem removed, and ground into a powder
2	egg yolks, lightly beaten
1½	teaspoons honey
1½	teaspoons Dijon mustard
½	cup lime juice, freshly squeezed
¼	cup rice wine vinegar
3	cloves fresh garlic, finely minced
1	teaspoon salt
1	large bunch fresh mint, chopped
1¾	cups olive oil

In a food processor place the ground habanero chile pepper, egg yolks, honey, Dijon mustard, lime juice, rice wine vinegar, garlic, and salt. Blend the ingredients together so that they are smooth. Let the sauce sit for 5 minutes.

Add the mint to the mixture. With the food processor constantly running, slowly dribble in the olive oil.

makes 2½ cups

"The habanero chile is one of the hottest chiles in the world. Its heat is counteracted somewhat with the mint, so you get a wonderful balance between hot and cool. Other chile peppers may be used instead. You can use this aioli with almost anything, and it will be delicious."

Judy Ebbinghaus
Santacafe

Chile Roasted Pecans

1½	cups olive oil
⅛	cup Kahlua liqueur
¼	cup Chimayo red chile powder
⅛	cup sugar
1	tablespoon salt
3	cups whole pecans, shelled

Preheat the oven to 300°.

In a medium bowl place the olive oil, Kahlua, red chile powder, sugar, and salt. Mix the ingredients together. Add the pecans and toss them so that they are well coated with the mixture.

Spread the pecans on a flat sheet. Bake them for 20 to 30 minutes, or until they are crispy *(stir them frequently)*.

makes approximately 3 cups

"These pecans make wonderful munchies for a party, and are especially good with beer. We also use them on salads, instead of croutons."

"The only trick to roasting the pecans is to keep turning them as they are browning. A pastry knife or stiff spatula works really well, because the nuts get rather sticky and you have to scrape them off the pan."

Laura Taylor
Cafe Pasqual's

Salmon Cakes
with Yellow Curry Paste

Salmon Cakes

2	pounds salmon, poached rare and flaked
1	cup fresh bread crumbs
1	bunch scallions, finely chopped
1¼	cups mayonnaise
¼	cup Yellow Curry Paste *(recipe on next page)*
2	egg yolks, well beaten
1	teaspoon baking powder
1	ounce tamarind water *(see chef's comments on this page)*
2	tablespoons vegetable oil *(or as needed)*

In a large bowl place all the ingredients *(except for the vegetable oil)* and mix them together well with your hands.

Form the mixture into small patties.

In a large sauté pan place the vegetable oil and heat it on medium high until it is hot. Add the salmon patties and cook them for 5 minutes on each side, or until they are golden brown.

serves 8

"These salmon cakes have a wonderful curry flavor that makes them different from the typical American salmon cakes. The tamarind water also gives them a unique flavor."

"To make the tamarind water, take a small amount of tamarind and water, boil them, and strain the liquid. This also makes a very refreshing drink if you add a sweetener to it."

Patrick Lambert
Restaurant Thao

"The Thai are very passionate and fun loving people, and I think this is evidenced by their cuisine. The food is light, and just explodes with delightful flavors."

Ron Messick
Restaurant Thao

Yellow Curry Paste

3	tablespoons galangal *(see chef's comments on page 61)*
18	cloves fresh garlic, coarsely chopped
¾	cup shallots, coarsely chopped
2	lemon grass stalks, bottom ⅓ coarsely chopped
1½	bunches fresh cilantro, chopped
3	tablespoons ground turmeric
¾	cup peanut oil
¼	cup dried Thai chile peppers
1½	tablespoons cumin seeds
5	tablespoons coriander seeds
1	tablespoon black peppercorns
3	tablespoons shrimp paste
3	tablespoons lime juice, freshly squeezed
1	teaspoon salt *(or to taste)*

In a food processor place the galangal, garlic, shallots, lemon grass, cilantro, turmeric, and ½ of the peanut oil. Coarsely purée the ingredients together *(leave them in the food processor)*.

In a dry sauté pan place the Thai chile peppers, cumin seeds, coriander seeds, and black peppercorns. Sauté the ingredients for 3 to 4 minutes, or until their fragrance is released.

To the food processor add the sautéed ingredients, shrimp paste, lime juice, and salt. Purée the ingredients together so that they are smooth.

Add the rest of the peanut oil and blend it in.

makes approximately 2 cups

"A curry is a blend of spices, and there are hundreds of different kinds. This recipe takes a little time to prepare, but it is really worth the effort. Once it's made it will keep for a long time in the refrigerator, and you can use it with so many different things. If you add some coconut milk and a little fish sauce, you will have an elegant, truly remarkable sauce."

"The whole theory behind my cooking is that the food must be balanced. It is based on five elements..... sweet, sour, salty, bitter, and hot. In each dish one of these elements will be dominant, with one or more of the others backing it up. This theory comes from Taoism, and is over two-thousand-years old. I have a tremendous respect for the deep, spiritual knowledge of the Oriental people."

Patrick Lambert
Restaurant Thao

Red Chile Seared Tuna
with Teriyaki Glaze

Red Chile Seared Tuna

1   **cup red chile powder**
½   **cup coriander seeds, ground** *(see chef's comments on page 248)*
1   **pound tuna loin, cut into 2 long, narrow pieces that are approximately 1" to 2" thick**
¼   **cup olive oil**
     Teriyaki Glaze *(recipe follows)*

In a small bowl place the red chile powder and coriander, and mix them together.

Dredge the tuna pieces in the spice mixture so that they are well coated.

In a medium sauté pan place the olive oil and heat it on medium high until it is hot. Add the tuna pieces and sauté them for 45 to 60 seconds on each side, or until they start to blacken.

Remove the tuna and refrigerate it until it is cold.

Slice the tuna into ⅛" thick pieces so that the edges of all the pieces show the blackened seasonings.

Drizzle the Teriyaki Glaze on top of the tuna slices.

serves 8

Teriyaki Glaze

1   **cup soy sauce**
1   **cup aji-mirin** *(see chef's comments on this page)*
1   **cup brown sugar**
1   **teaspoon ground ginger**
⅓   **teaspoon garlic powder**

In a medium saucepan place all the ingredients and stir them together. Cook the ingredients on low heat for 30 minutes, or until the mixture is reduced by ⅓ *(the mixture should be thick enough to coat the back of a spoon)*. Refrigerate the glaze.

makes 2 cups

"This is one of my favorite dishes. I'll eat it for lunch and then again for dinner. The chefs get mad and verbally spank me, claiming I am in a rut and should be trying other things. But it's so good and healthy and lean, that I can't resist eating just tons."

Judy Ebbinghaus
Santacafe

"The tuna has a really nice texture.....crispy and dark on the outside, and raw and red on the inside. It looks very beautiful."

Kelly Rogers
Santacafe

"Aji-mirin is a Japanese rice wine which has been fortified with sugar. It is similar to sake, but is sweeter."

Laszlo Gyermek
Santacafe

Shrimp & Corn Fritters

3½	cups flour
¾	teaspoon ground nutmeg
1	tablespoon baking powder
4	teaspoons salt
3	cups beer
3	tablespoons yellow onions, grated
3	serrano chile peppers, finely minced
¾	cup fresh chives, finely minced
1½	pounds shrimp, peeled, deveined and chopped small
3¾	cups fresh corn kernels
3	egg whites, whipped to medium stiff peaks
3	cups vegetable oil *(or as needed)*

In a large bowl place the flour, nutmeg, baking powder, and salt. Mix the ingredients together.

Slowly add the beer and stir it in.

In a small bowl place the yellow onions, serrano chile peppers, and chives. Mix the ingredients together. Add them to the batter and fold them in.

Add the shrimp and fold them in.

Add the corn and fold it in.

Add the egg whites and very gently fold them in.

In a large, heavy saucepan place the oil and heat it on medium high until it is hot. For each fritter scoop out a tablespoon of the batter. With another spoon push the batter off the tablespoon and into the hot oil. Deep-fry the fritters for 3 to 4 minutes, or until they are golden brown. Drain them on paper towels.

serves 12

Stuffed Jalapeños

12	jalapeño chile peppers, sliced in half lengthwise, seeded, rinsed and dried
8	ounces cream cheese, softened
2	eggs
2	tablespoons water
1	cup seasoned dried bread crumbs
4	cups vegetable oil *(or as needed)*
	blue cheese dressing *(your favorite, or see recipe on page 114)*

Inside each jalapeño chile pepper half place the softened cream cheese. Press the pepper halves back together.

In a small bowl place the eggs and water, and whisk them together.

Dip each stuffed pepper in the egg mixture and then dredge it in the bread crumbs so that it is well coated.

Place the coated, stuffed chile peppers on a cookie sheet and freeze them for 2 hours.

In a large saucepan place the vegetable oil and heat it on high until it is 375°. Deep-fry the chile peppers for 2 to 3 minutes, or until they are golden brown.

Serve the peppers with the blue cheese dressing on the side.

serves 6

"One time a friend of mine and I were having a party, and we put together this recipe to serve as hors d'oeuvres. They are just great.....but be warned that they are very hot! You need something on hand to quench the heat, like a cold beer or a margarita. Dipping them in the blue cheese dressing also helps."

"The reason you freeze the stuffed peppers is to keep the cream cheese from falling out when you deep-fry them."

"La Tertulia is housed in a two-hundred-year-old building that has been a brothel, convent, private home, and now a restaurant. I don't think there are any ghosts here, but if there are, they are all good ones!"

Joy Ortiz-Nashan
La Tertulia

Gambas al Ajillo

"This is a Spanish recipe that means 'shrimp in garlic sauce'. It's a favorite dish that we serve with crusty bread in the bar. People love to dip the bread in the sauce."

"I get a lot of ideas for recipes from the Mexicans who are on our kitchen staff. They know recipes that have been in their families for many generations.....things that are delicious, but that you could never find written down in a cookbook. I don't speak much Spanish, and they don't speak much English, but we still communicate quite well. We use our hands a lot."

Kit Baum
El Farol

4	cloves fresh garlic, peeled
4	tablespoons olive oil
¾	pound medium shrimp, peeled and deveined
2	tablespoons butter
1	tablespoon fresh garlic, finely chopped
1	pinch chile pequin *(hot red chile flakes)*
½	teaspoon paprika
2	tablespoons lime juice, freshly squeezed
2	tablespoons dry sherry
½	cup chicken stock *(recipe on page 311)*
	salt and black pepper *(to taste)*
2	tablespoons fresh Italian parsley, chopped

In a large sauté pan place the 4 cloves of garlic and olive oil. Heat them on medium high until the oil begins to smoke. Add the shrimp and sauté them for 30 seconds. Remove the garlic cloves and drain the oil from the pan.

Add the butter, chopped garlic, chile pequin, paprika, lime juice, sherry, chicken stock, salt, and black pepper. Stir the ingredients together.

Cook the shrimp and sauce for 3 minutes, or until the sauce is slightly reduced.

Add the Italian parsley and stir it in.

serves 6

Green Chile Apple Paté

1	tablespoon clarified butter
1	medium yellow onion, diced medium
1	large Golden Delicious apple, peeled, cored and roughly chopped
1	pound chicken livers
¼	cup mild green chile peppers, roasted, peeled, seeded and diced
¼	teaspoon ground coriander
¼	teaspoon ground allspice
¼	teaspoon ground cinnamon
⅛	teaspoon ground cardamom
⅛	teaspoon ground cloves
2	tablespoons brandy
½	pound butter, cut into chunks

In a large sauté pan place the clarified butter and heat it on medium high until it is hot. Add the yellow onions and sauté them for 5 minutes, or until they are translucent.

Add the apples and sauté them for 3 to 5 minutes, or until they begin to soften.

Add the chicken livers and sauté them for 5 minutes, or until they are just cooked *(pink in the center)*.

Add the green chile peppers, coriander, allspice, cinnamon, cardamom, cloves, and brandy. Stir the ingredients together. Remove the pan from the stove and let the ingredients sit for 15 minutes.

Place the mixture in a food processor and blend it. With the food processor constantly running, add the butter chunks one at a time.

In a lightly oiled 8" loaf pan pour the blended mixture. Cover the paté with plastic wrap and let it sit in the refrigerator overnight.

Set the pan in another shallow pan that is filled with hot water. Loosen the paté with a knife around the edges. Invert it onto a serving plate.

serves 8

"I've had paté-hating people taste this recipe, and they instantly become paté-loving converts. The blend of flavors is especially interesting. There is a subtle bite and a subtle sweetness, with a background hint of all the spices."

"When I was a little girl I hated liver, but I loved liverwurst, not realizing it was liver. I also hated fish, but loved tuna fish sandwiches, not realizing it was fish. Probably if I had tasted this dish, I would have thought it was wonderful, even though I thought I hated liver."

"I serve this with dark bread, stoneground mustard, and small gherkin pickles. People also really like it with sliced sweet red onions."

Sarah Alvord
Zia Diner

"This appetizer is from Spain, where dates are very popular as hors d'oeuvres. Americans are not used to a sweet taste before dinner, so often they are shocked when they first taste this recipe. But, after their initial surprise they realize that this particular combination of sweet and spicy is really delicious..... and, their appetites really get in gear for whatever is coming next!"

"Medjool dates are the very best in the world. They are extra large and meaty, with tender skins and an excellent flavor. They are usually sold loose by the pound in the produce section of your better markets or health food stores."

"Smoked chorizo is hard to find, unless you have access to a gourmet market that has a fairly large Mexican section. A lot of times I substitute a commercially made smoked kielbasa sausage, and that works fine. Fresh chorizo won't work because it is too greasy and it crumbles and falls apart when you cook it. Smoked chorizo is spicy, so if you do use it you might want to leave out the jalapeño."

Jonathan Horst
Adobo Catering

Deep-Fried Stuffed Dates with Chorizo & Bacon

1	5" link smoked chorizo (or kielbasa) sausage, meat removed from casing, cooked and drained
4	strips thick-sliced bacon, cut into 1" pieces, cooked and drained
3	tablespoons butter
1	jalapeño chile pepper, seeded and finely diced
1	medium yellow onion, minced
2	cloves fresh garlic, finely minced
20	large Medjool dates (see chef's comments on this page), halved and pitted
½	cup flour (or as needed)
3	eggs, well beaten
4	cups peanut oil (or as needed)

In a food processor place the chorizo and bacon, and "pulse" them until the mixture resembles a coarse paté.

In a large frying pan place the butter and heat it on medium until it is melted and hot. Add the jalapeño chile peppers, yellow onions, and garlic. Sauté the ingredients for 5 minutes, or until the onions are translucent. Add the cooked chorizo sausage and bacon mixture, and stir it in.

Remove the mixture from the pan and drain off the oil. Place the mixture in a bowl and let it cool. Stir the mixture to incorporate any extra fat that may have risen to the top.

Place ½ teaspoon of the mixture into each date half. Fold the date together lengthwise and seal the sticky ends together. Roll the stuffed dates in the flour and then dip them in the beaten eggs.

In a large, heavy pan place the peanut oil and heat it on high until it is 375°. Deep-fry the stuffed dates for 3 minutes, or until they are golden brown. Drain them on paper towels and serve them hot.

makes 40 date halves

Achiote Seared Buffalo Carpaccio with Juniper Lemon Oil

Achiote Seared Buffalo Carpaccio

2	tablespoons achiote paste *(see chef's comments on this page)*
3	dried chipotle chile peppers, seeded and crushed
1	tablespoon fresh sage, finely chopped
1	teaspoon cracked black pepper
1	5-ounce buffalo tenderloin, cleaned
1	tablespoon olive oil *(or as needed)*
2	cups wild greens
	Juniper Lemon Oil *(recipe follows)*

In a medium bowl place the achiote paste, chipotle chile peppers, sage, and cracked black pepper. Mix the ingredients together. Dredge the buffalo tenderloin in the spice mix so that it is well coated. Let it sit for 15 minutes.

In a medium skillet place the olive oil and heat it on high until it begins to smoke. Sear the tenderloin for 1 minute on each side. Set it aside so that it cools. Freeze it for 20 minutes so that it hardens slightly. Shave the meat into paper-thin slivers.

On a large serving plate place the wild greens. Arrange the meat slices on top. Dribble on the Juniper Lemon Oil.

serves 4 to 6

Juniper Lemon Oil

½	cup extra virgin olive oil
1	teaspoon juniper berries, cracked *(see chef's comments on this page)*
2	tablespoons fresh Italian parsley, finely chopped
3	lemons, juiced
¼	teaspoon cayenne pepper
¼	teaspoon salt
½	teaspoon cracked black pepper

In a small bowl place all of the ingredients and mix them together.

makes approximately 1 cup

"Buffalo is an exotic meat that can be difficult to find, although butchers can sometimes special order it for you. Buffalo meat is not gamey in flavor, although it has a subtle hint of pungency. The texture is firm and the fat content is very low, making it one of the healthiest meats there is. If desired, filet mignon can be substituted."

"Achiote (or annatto) comes either as freeze-dried seeds or in a paste. The flavor is very pungent..... hot, with a citrus taste. Although the flavor is unusual, it is not disagreeable. If you tasted it often enough, you would learn to recognize it in different dishes."

"Juniper berries can be found in the spice section of better grocery stores. Or, you can pick them off your trees here in Santa Fe. They have a wonderful lemon-cedar-pine aroma, and there is no substitute."

"This lemon oil is very intense in flavor and is excellent with the buffalo. It can be served with other items, such as shrimp, but be sure to use it sparingly, according to taste."

Pete Zimmer
Inn of the Anasazi

Southwestern Chicken Wings

2	tablespoons Chimayo red chile powder
1	tablespoon garlic powder
½	tablespoon ground thyme
½	tablespoon onion powder
½	tablespoon ground cumin
½	tablespoon black pepper *(or to taste)*
½	cup vegetable oil *(or as needed)*
15	chicken wings, cut in half

In a small bowl place the red chile powder, garlic powder, thyme, onion powder, cumin, and black pepper. Stir the ingredients together and set them aside.

In a large sauté pan place the vegetable oil and heat it on medium high until it is very hot. Add the chicken wings and sauté them for 5 minutes on each side, or until they are golden brown.

Remove the chicken wings from the pan and drain them on paper towels.

Dredge the chicken wings in the spice mixture so that they are well coated.

serves 4

"This is a great appetizer to munch on while you're watching a football game. It goes great with beer."

Dan Kelley
Peppers

"Everyone in the world sells chicken wings, but I think that these are the best I've had. What makes them unique are the spices used, and the fact that they are pan-fried in oil, so they are crispy, not soft. Usually chicken wings are baked."

Rick Helmick
Peppers

"It's hard to believe that something so easy to make could taste so good. This recipe is a perfect example of where simple is best."

Patricia Helmick
Peppers

Mex-Asian Vegetable Empanadas

1	tablespoon light sesame oil
2	teaspoons toasted sesame oil
½	head Napa cabbage, shredded
1	medium carrot, grated
4	scallions, thinly sliced
2	cloves fresh garlic, finely chopped
1	tablespoon fresh ginger root, peeled and finely chopped
2	serrano chile peppers, finely chopped
1	Szechwan red chile pepper, finely crushed
3	tablespoons fresh parsley, finely chopped
2	tablespoons fresh cilantro, finely chopped
1	teaspoon lemon grass powder
1	teaspoon anise seeds, crushed
2	teaspoons coriander seeds, crushed
4	tablespoons Thai fish sauce *(see chef's comments on page 113)*
1	tablespoon soy sauce
2	eggs, beaten
1	tablespoon water
4	sheets puff pastry, cut into 3" circles

Preheat the oven to 400°.

In a large sauté pan place the light sesame oil and toasted sesame oil, and heat them on medium high until they are hot. Add the cabbage, carrots, scallions, garlic, and ginger. Sauté the ingredients for 2 minutes, or until the cabbage begins to wilt.

Add the serrano chile peppers, crushed Szechwan chile pepper, parsley, cilantro, lemon grass, anise, and coriander. Stir the ingredients together, cover the pan with a lid, and steam them for 3 minutes *(add a splash of water if needed)*. Remove the lid.

Add the Thai fish sauce and soy sauce, and stir them in. Sauté the ingredients for 5 minutes, or until most of the moisture is evaporated.

Place the ingredients in a colander and drain them well.

In a small bowl place the eggs and water, and beat them together well.

(continued on next page)

"Empanadas are little stuffed pastries, like a turnover. They are traditionally Mexican, and are especially popular around the holidays. You can fill them with anything.....just use your imagination. They can be made ahead of time and then frozen, which makes them handy to serve at a party."

Peter Raub
Santa Fe Market

"We serve these at our catering parties, and people just gobble them up. No matter how many we make, they are always gone. Other than some prep work, they are very easy to make. The only trick is to drain off all the liquid from the mixture, because otherwise they will be soggy."

Marsha Chobol
Santa Fe Market

Cover a baking sheet with parchment paper. Place the puff pastry circles on top. In the center of each circle place a tablespoon of the vegetable mixture. Brush the egg wash around each pastry circle and fold it in half. Press a fork firmly around the edges to seal it. Brush the egg wash over the top.

Bake the empanadas for 10 minutes, or until they are golden brown.

Cool them on a wire rack for 15 minutes.

makes approximately 20 empanadas

Southwestern Pizza

2	**12" round pizza rounds** (see recipe on page 308)
2	**cups marinara sauce** (store bought, or your favorite recipe)
	Cilantro Pesto (recipe on page 112)
6	**links chorizo sausage, meat removed from casings, cooked and drained**
1	**cup green chile peppers, roasted, peeled, seeded and diced**
2	**cups Monterey Jack cheese, grated**
2	**cups mozzarella cheese, grated**
2	**tablespoons piñon nuts** (pine nuts), **toasted** (see chef's comments on page 325)
1	**tablespoon chile pequin** (hot red chile flakes)

Preheat the oven to 375°.

Place each pizza round on an oiled pizza pan.

Spread on the marinara sauce. Dribble on the Cilantro Pesto. Sprinkle on the remaining ingredients.

Bake the pizzas for 20 minutes, or until the crusts are golden brown.

serves 4

Smoked Salmon with Grilled Onion Poblano Chile Relish

3	tablespoons extra virgin olive oil
2	medium yellow onions, thickly sliced, grilled and chopped
2	medium red onions, thickly sliced, grilled and chopped
2	poblano chile peppers, roasted, peeled, seeded and chopped
2	tablespoons fresh cilantro, chopped
1	teaspoon ancho chile powder
2	limes, freshly squeezed
1	teaspoon kosher salt *(or to taste)*
2½	pounds smoked salmon, thinly sliced
¼	cup olive oil

In a large sauté pan place the 3 tablespoons of olive oil and heat it on medium high until it is hot. Add the yellow onions, red onions, and poblano chile peppers. Sauté the ingredients for 5 minutes, or until the onions are translucent.

Add the cilantro, ancho chile powder, lime juice, and kosher salt. Stir the ingredients together.

Place the relish in a bowl and cover it with plastic wrap. Chill the relish in the refrigerator.

On each of 8 individual serving plates place the smoked salmon. Dribble the olive oil on top.

Serve the chilled relish on the side.

serves 12

"When you go to the store to get the smoked salmon you probably will be asked what kind you want. There are several different types, but the best kind comes from the East Coast."

"The relish is smoky, spicy, and oniony. It's delicious with the smoked salmon. We also serve it with steak tartare."

Gina Ziluca
Geronimo

"Geronimo is in a very old, historic adobe home. I own the building, as well as the ghost (named 'Geronimo'), who lives here. When we first moved in he was cranky, and would do bad things like breaking the plumbing at crucial times. But now he seems happier, and I think he likes what we are doing here. The worst stunt he pulls now is his spitting trick. I'll be walking down the hall and a big spurt of water will hit me in the face. This happens all of the time, and there is no place where that water can come from, so I know it's him. We all feel his smiling presence."

Cliff Skoglund
Geronimo

Santacafe Shrimp with Tabasco Sauce

Santacafe Shrimp

2   tablespoons olive oil
1   cup Tabasco Sauce *(recipe follows)*
1   pound large shrimp, peeled and deveined

In a medium bowl place the olive oil, Tabasco Sauce, and shrimp. Let the shrimp marinate for 2 hours.

Grill the shrimp for 2 minutes on each side, or until they are just done. Serve the shrimp with the Tabasco Sauce in a small bowl for dipping.

serves 4

Tabasco Sauce

2   cups cayenne chile peppers *(fresh or dried)*
2   cups apple cider vinegar
2   tablespoons sugar
2   tablespoons salt

Note: This recipe should be made at least 1 week in advance.

In a food processor place the cayenne chile peppers and grind them into a powder.

Place the ground chiles, cider vinegar, sugar, and salt in a jar with a lid. Store the sauce tightly covered for 1 week.

Strain the sauce through a fine sieve.

makes approximately 2 cups

Clams in Spicy Garlic Broth

1	**cup extra virgin olive oil**
32	**Littleneck clams** *(in shells)*
6	**cloves fresh garlic, thinly sliced**
2	**tablespoons chile pequin** *(hot red chile flakes)*
2	**tablespoons fresh oregano, chopped**
¼	**cup lemon juice, freshly squeezed**
1	**cup clam juice**
	salt and black pepper *(to taste)*

In a large sauté pan place the olive oil and heat it on medium high until it is hot. Add the clams, garlic, and chile pequin. Sauté the ingredients for 5 minutes, or until the shells begin to open.

Add the oregano, lemon juice, clam juice, salt, and black pepper. Cook the ingredients for 2 minutes more, or until the clam shells are open.

In each of 4 individual bowls place the clams with the broth.

serves 4

Peppers' Ceviche

1	**pound rockfish, boned and diced medium**
¾	**pound scallops, muscles removed, and diced medium**
1	**tomato, diced medium**
1	**green bell pepper, seeded and diced medium**
1	**red bell pepper, seeded and diced medium**
¼	**medium red onion, finely chopped**
1	**jalapeño chile pepper, seeded and finely chopped**
½	**bunch scallions, finely chopped**
1	**bunch fresh cilantro, chopped**
½	**tablespoon fresh garlic, finely chopped**
½	**teaspoon ground cumin**
1½	**teaspoons salt** *(or to taste)*
½	**teaspoon black pepper** *(or to taste)*
½	**cup white vinegar**
1	**cup lime juice, freshly squeezed**

In a large bowl place all of the ingredients and stir them together. Cover the bowl with plastic wrap and let the ingredients marinate in the refrigerator for 6 hours.

serves 8

"The key to this recipe is to use the best, freshest clams possible, and don't over-cook them. They are ready when they start to open. If any of the clams stay closed, it may be because they are bad. To be safe, you probably should discard them."

"This dish is an appetizer, but you could add more clams and serve it as an entrée. Or, you could have it with pasta, for another entrée. It's very good with garlic bread because you can dip it in the broth."

Steven Lemon
Pranzo Italian Grill

"One time a couple came here to eat dinner very early.....around four o'clock. The woman ordered our ceviche as an appetizer, and ended up eating four orders of it instead of having an entrée. I didn't see her do this, so when she brought the ticket to the counter for me to ring up, I told her I thought she had been overcharged for the ceviche. She told me, no, the ticket was correct, and she had indeed eaten four orders. It turns out that she was a world traveler, and our ceviche was the best she had ever tasted..... even better than Spain, Mexico, and other countries that really know how to make it."

Patricia Helmick
Peppers

"I come from a Sicilian family, and all Sicilians love mint. When I was growing up in New York my mother always had fresh mint in our kitchen. The mint in this recipe is what gives the ceviche that subtle fresh flavor and separates it from other ceviches. Mint goes beautifully with most fish dishes."

"It's important that the tuna is very thinly sliced across the grain. Ask your fish monger if he will do this for you, because he has excellent sharp knives at his disposal. Otherwise, you can do it at home by slicing it as thin as you can, and then lightly pounding it out, as you would with veal."

"When I first moved to Santa Fe I tried to make my living as an artist. But that proved to be too difficult, so I decided to open a restaurant instead. It's been a booming success!"

Ken Calascione
La Traviata

"These are like a gourmet tostada and they make a delicious appetizer. The crab filling is the crowning touch."

Pete Zimmer
Inn of the Anasazi

Ceviche of Tuna with Mint

1	pound fresh tuna, thinly sliced
2	tablespoons red onions, finely chopped
1	teaspoon fresh garlic, finely chopped
2	tablespoons fresh Italian parsley, chopped
8	leaves fresh mint, chopped
2	dried pequin chile peppers
¼	cup olive oil
1	lime, freshly squeezed
1	tablespoon red wine vinegar
	salt *(to taste)*

In a shallow oiled pan place the tuna slices. In a small bowl place the rest of the ingredients and stir them together. Pour the mixture over the tuna. Cover the bowl with plastic wrap and marinate the tuna for 1 hour at room temperature.

serves 4

Crab Gorditas

2	tablespoons olive oil
1	pound Dungeness crab meat, cleaned
1	cup orange segments, seeds removed, and chopped
3	tomatoes, finely chopped
1	medium red onion, finely chopped
1	tablespoon dried ancho chile pepper, seeded and thinly sliced
1	teaspoon ground cumin
1	teaspoon ground coriander
	salt and black pepper *(to taste)*
2	limes, juiced
12	Gordita Shells *(recipe on page 310)*, warm

In a medium large skillet place the olive oil and heat it on medium until it is hot. Add the crab, orange pieces, tomatoes, red onions, ancho chile peppers, cumin, and coriander. Sauté the ingredients for 2 minutes, or until they are heated and well combined.

Season the mixture with the salt and black pepper. Add the lime juice and stir it in.

On each of 6 Gordita Shells place an equal amount of the mixture. Place the remaining shells on top.

serves 6

Santa Fe Ceviche

1	pound tuna, cut into ½" cubes
1	small red onion, finely diced
1	medium tomato, finely diced
½	red bell pepper, seeded and finely diced
½	yellow bell pepper, seeded and finely diced
½	green bell pepper, seeded and finely diced
½	bunch fresh cilantro, chopped
4	serrano chile peppers, seeded and finely diced
½	cup lime juice, freshly squeezed
1	tablespoon orange juice, freshly squeezed
1	tablespoon lemon juice, freshly squeezed
2	tablespoons olive oil
1	teaspoon salt
1	head Boston lettuce, leaves separated
3	limes, cut into thin wedges
6	blue corn tortillas, cut into thin strips, fried in oil until crisp and drained

In a medium bowl place all of the ingredients *(except for the lettuce, lime wedges, and fried tortilla strips)* and mix them together. Cover the bowl with plastic wrap and let the ceviche sit for 30 minutes at room temperature.

In the center of each lettuce leaf place a spoonful of the ceviche *(make sure to include a piece of the tuna)*. Serve each portion with a lime wedge and some of the tortilla strips.

serves 6

"This is a great spicy, tart ceviche recipe. The tuna works well and the presentation is nice. You can roll each lettuce leaf up and eat it that way, or you can fold the lettuce over in half and eat it like a little taco."

Don Fortel
On Water

"When you pick out your tuna you want it to be a reddish mauve color. If it is too dark or has some purple in it, then it might not be as fresh or tender."

"I used to be only a chef, now I am both a chef and an owner of a restaurant.....and there is all the difference in the world. If I make a mistake I have nobody to answer to, and the responsibility is all mine. There is a lot more work, but the satisfaction is greater."

Rocky Packard
On Water

"This recipe comes from a friend of mine who was in the Peace Corps in Turkey. He used to enjoy eating a little salad that the sheep-herders made out of tomatoes, peppers, onions, feta cheese, lemon juice, and cilantro. I really became fond of that recipe and used to make it frequently. One day I had some left over, and decided to roll it up in a tortilla. It was really tasty, and I immediately realized that it would make an excellent appetizer. I added some jalapeños to make it a spicy dish, but you can leave them out with no problem. This is a fresh, light dish that takes only moments to put together."

"When I was a child my parents opened the original 'Shed', which was an actual shed in Burro Alley. Our family renovated it and turned it into a restaurant. I remember sitting in the kitchen as a child, absorbing the aromas and activity of cooking. I believe that these experiences gave me a strong sense of how to put different ingredients together in a way that people enjoy."

Courtney Carswell
The Shed

Blue Corn Feta Taquitos

1	ounce feta cheese, crumbled
2	medium tomatoes, diced medium
1	green bell pepper, seeded and diced medium
1	jalapeño chile pepper, seeded and finely chopped
½	cup yellow onions, diced medium
¼	cup fresh cilantro, chopped
1	lemon, freshly juiced
¼	cup vegetable oil
6	blue corn tortillas
4	cups vegetable oil

In a medium bowl place the feta cheese, tomatoes, green bell peppers, jalapeño chile peppers, yellow onions, cilantro, and lemon juice. Mix the ingredients together and then set them aside.

In a medium sauté pan place the ¼ cup of vegetable oil and heat it on medium high until it is hot. Fry each tortilla for 15 seconds, or until it softens. Drain the tortillas on paper towels.

In a large, heavy pan place the 4 cups of vegetable oil and heat it on high until it is very hot. Loosely roll each tortilla and deep-fry it for 1 to 2 minutes, or until it is crisp. Drain the tortillas on paper towels.

Stuff the vegetable mixture inside each tortilla. Cut the taquitos in half, crosswise.

serves 6

LP CALDWELL

Soups

Smoky Ancho Chile Black Bean Soup

3	cups dried black beans, washed
9	cups water *(or as needed)*
3	dried ancho chile peppers, soaked in hot water for 2 hours, drained, stems and seeds removed
½	can chipotle chile peppers *(in adobo sauce)*
3	cloves fresh garlic, coarsely chopped
2	tablespoons paprika
1	tablespoon ground cumin
1	tablespoon dried oregano
4	stalks celery, chopped medium
2	yellow onions, chopped medium
2	green bell peppers, seeded and chopped medium
1	tablespoon salt *(or to taste)*
½	cup sour cream
4	scallions, minced

In a large, heavy stockpot place the black beans and water. Bring the ingredients to a boil on high heat. Reduce the heat to low and simmer the ingredients for 1 hour *(skim off any foam that rises to the top)*.

In a food processor place the ancho and chipotle chile peppers, garlic, paprika, cumin, and oregano. Purée the ingredients so that a paste is formed.

Add the chile paste to the beans and stir it in. Cook the ingredients for 30 to 45 minutes, or until the beans begin to get tender.

Add the celery, yellow onions, and green bell peppers. Cook the ingredients for 30 more minutes, or until the beans and vegetables are tender *(add more water if needed)*.

Season the soup with the salt.

In each of eight individual serving bowls place the soup. Garnish each serving with a dollop of sour cream and a sprinkling of scallions.

serves 8

"We used to serve a really traditional black bean soup which was full of ham and bacon. I wanted to develop a recipe that was meatless, but still had that wonderful smoky flavor..... and, here it is. The chipotle chile peppers in adobo sauce are the key to the great taste. Not only do they add smokiness, but they also add heat. This is the most popular soup that we sell in the restaurant."

Isaac Modivah
Ore House

"In the restaurant we joke a lot about what we call our 'fear of food customers'. They are usually tourists and they are truly afraid of trying any food that contains chiles. If they do have the nerve to order a dish with green chile or whatever, they ask for it on the side. Other people, however, are very adventurous in their eating habits and want to taste everything that is indigenous to Northern New Mexico. They drink our margaritas, eat our hot chile, and have a great time! My recommendation to people who are nervous about what kind of food a restaurant serves is to first call and speak to someone there who can give them information on what the dishes are and what ingredients are in them."

Daniella Croce Carr
Ore House

Santa Fe Chicken Soup

¼	**pound butter, melted**
1	**medium yellow onion, finely diced**
¾	**cup flour**
1½	**quarts chicken stock** *(recipe on page 311)*
2	**cups cooked chicken, diced**
1	**cup hot green chile peppers, roasted, peeled, seeded and diced**
1	**cup cream**
	salt *(to taste)*

In a large stockpot place the butter and heat it on medium high until it is hot. Add the yellow onions and sauté them for 5 minutes, or until they are translucent. Add the flour and stir it for 2 minutes, or until the roux is smooth. Add the chicken stock. While constantly stirring, simmer the mixture for 5 minutes, or until it thickens. Add the chicken, green chile peppers, cream, and salt.

serves 6 to 8

Sopa Verde

4	**cups chicken stock** *(recipe on page 311)*
1	**bunch fresh spinach, stems removed, washed and coarsely chopped**
½	**cup green chile peppers, roasted, peeled, seeded and diced medium**
½	**green bell pepper, seeded and finely diced**
½	**cup zucchini, peeled and diced medium**
¼	**cup celery, finely diced**
¼	**cup yellow onions, finely diced**
1	**tablespoon fresh basil, chopped**
½	**tablespoon dried tarragon**
½	**tablespoon dried sage**
	salt *(to taste)*
1	**avocado, peeled, pitted and finely diced**

In a large stockpot place the chicken stock and bring it to a boil on high heat. Add the rest of the ingredients *(except the avocados)*. Reduce the heat to low and simmer the soup for 1 hour.

Garnish each serving with the avocados.

serves 8

Chipotle Clam & Posole Chowder

4	tablespoons olive oil
1	medium yellow onion, coarsely chopped
3	stalks celery, coarsely chopped
3	cloves fresh garlic, finely chopped
2	tablespoons flour
1	cup posole, cooked and drained
½	cup red bell pepper, diced medium
3	chipotle chile peppers *(in adobo sauce),* **finely chopped**
¼	cup fresh basil, chopped
½	cup heavy cream
6	cups clam juice
¼	cup white wine
	salt and white pepper *(to taste)*
1½	cups cooked clams, chopped

In a large saucepan place the olive oil and heat it on medium high until it is hot. Add the yellow onions, celery, and garlic. Sauté the ingredients for 5 minutes, or until the onions are translucent.

While stirring constantly, sprinkle in the flour so that the vegetables are well coated.

Add the posole, red bell peppers, chipotle chile peppers, basil, heavy cream, clam juice, white wine, salt, and white pepper. Stir the ingredients together and simmer them for 15 minutes.

Add the clams and stir them in.

serves 6

"I developed this recipe because I love clam chowder and I was looking for a way to turn it into a Southwestern version. Be careful when you add the chipotle chiles. Add one at first and then taste the soup before adding more."

"To me, posole is tasteless, and I'm always looking for ways to prepare it so that it is palatable. Usually it is just boiled with some red chile. But once I had some at Tesuque Pueblo, where there was everything but the kitchen sink thrown in, and it was great! The posole was just a small part of the soup, as it is in this recipe also. I think that's the key to cooking posole.....don't serve it by itself, but use it as an ingredient in something else."

Kit Baum
El Farol

Sopa de Lima

2	tablespoons olive oil
1	medium yellow onion, finely diced
3	cloves fresh garlic, finely chopped
2	poblano chile peppers, roasted, peeled, seeded and finely diced
2	tomatoes, seeded and finely diced
½	teaspoon ground oregano
½	teaspoon ground thyme
1	teaspoon salt *(or to taste)*
½	teaspoon black pepper *(or to taste)*
2	quarts chicken stock *(recipe on page 311)*
1	pound boneless chicken breasts, skin removed, poached and shredded
¼	cup lime juice, freshly squeezed
1	avocado, peeled, pitted and sliced
1	serrano chile pepper, finely diced
8	corn tortillas, cut into thin strips, deep-fried and drained on paper towels
1	lime, cut into wheels
½	bunch fresh cilantro, chopped

In a large sauté pan place the olive oil and heat it on medium high until it is hot. Add the yellow onions and garlic. Sauté them for 5 minutes, or until the onions are translucent.

Add the poblano chile peppers, tomatoes, oregano, thyme, salt, black pepper, and chicken stock. Stir the ingredients together and simmer them for 15 minutes.

Add the shredded chicken and lime juice, and simmer the soup for 10 minutes.

Garnish each serving of soup with the avocado slices, serrano chile peppers, tortilla strips, lime wheels, and cilantro.

serves 8

Coyote Cafe Pinto Bean Soup with Green Tortillas & Crema

Coyote Cafe Pinto Bean Soup

½	cup olive oil
1	medium white onion, chopped medium
4	cloves fresh garlic, finely chopped
6	Roma tomatoes, halved and roasted
4	strips bacon, diced, cooked and drained
2	tablespoons chipotle chile peppers *(in adobo sauce)*, **puréed**
1	pound dried pinto beans, rinsed, cooked al dente and drained
8	cups water
2	tablespoons fresh marjoram, chopped
	salt *(to taste)*
	Green Tortillas *(recipe follows)*
	Crema *(recipe on next page)*

In a large saucepan place the olive oil and heat it on medium until it is hot. Add the white onions and garlic. Sauté them for 5 minutes, or until the onions are translucent.

Add the Roma tomatoes, bacon, puréed chipotle chile peppers, pinto beans, and water. Cook the ingredients for 30 minutes, or until the beans are tender. Stir in the marjoram and salt.

Serve the beans with the Green Tortilla wedges and the Crema.

serves 8

Green Tortillas

1	tablespoon jalapeño chile peppers, seeded and finely chopped
1	tablespoon fresh basil, chopped
1	tablespoon fresh cilantro, chopped
1	tablespoon fresh parsley, chopped
½	cup olive oil
½	cup water
6	flour tortillas

Preheat the oven to 350°.

In a small bowl place the jalapeño chile peppers, basil, cilantro, parsley, olive oil, and water. Stir the ingredients together.

(continued on next page)

"Roast the tomatoes in a 350° oven for thirty minutes."

"Elizabeth Berry is an organic produce grower from Abiquiu, about an hour north of Santa Fe. She grows a lot of different kinds of beans and gets the local chefs to come up with recipes for them. This dish was created for her pinto beans. It's very down-to-earth and has a wonderful flavor."

"To be a chef is difficult in that the hours are very long, and the work is physically demanding. But it also is a rewarding profession in that you get immediate feedback about the success or failure of your creations. American chefs are getting better all the time. Now some of them are elevated to celebrity status."

"In this part of the country a lot of people like tortillas with their soup instead of bread. We came up with this recipe as a snappy alternative to a plain flour tortilla. Basically, you are making a pesto that you spread on top, and then baking it."

Mark Kiffin
Coyote Cafe

On a baking sheet place the tortillas. Thinly spread the herb mixture over each one. Bake the tortillas for 15 minutes, or until they are crisp. Cut each tortilla into 6 wedges.

serves 8

Crema

1   **cup sour cream**
1   **tablespoon lime juice, freshly squeezed**

In a small bowl place the sour cream and the lime juice, and stir them together. Cover the bowl with plastic wrap and keep it refrigerated until it is served.

makes 1 cup

"When you buy creama down in Mexico, it is a cultured product like crème fraîche, and has a tang to it. This recipe is a close duplicate to the flavor, although the texture is thicker."

Mark Kiffin
Coyote Cafe

"I know that the idea of bananas in a curry lentil soup may sound a little strange, but all of the flavors blend really well together. This is an excellent recipe that I hope you will try."

Jeff Moses
Staab House

"When I was growing up my sister did a lot of the cooking. Frequently she would make country fried steak with milk gravy, and the gravy was always lumpy. One day when I was about ten years old I offered to make the gravy for her. So I did, and it came out creamy smooth, with no lumps at all. Boy, was she ever mad! It took her years to get over it. I think I must have been a chef in another life."

Rustin Newton
Staab House

Banana Curry Lentil Soup

2   **tablespoons olive oil**
1   **small yellow onion, finely diced**
1   **banana, peeled, sliced and mashed**
1½   **cups dried lentils, soaked in water overnight and drained**
1   **cube chicken bouillon**
5   **cups water**
1   **tablespoon curry powder**
½   **teaspoon cayenne pepper** *(or to taste)*
     salt and white pepper *(to taste)*
1   **cup apples, peeled, cored and diced**

In a large stockpot place the olive oil and heat it on medium high until it is hot. Add the yellow onions and sauté them for 5 minutes, or until they are translucent.

Add the banana, lentils, chicken bouillon, and water. Bring the ingredients to a boil on high heat. Reduce the heat to medium low and simmer them for 1½ hours.

Add the curry powder and stir it in. Simmer the soup for 30 minutes, or until the lentils are soft.

Place the soup in a blender and purée it. Add the cayenne pepper, salt, and white pepper.

Garnish each serving with the apples.

serves 4 to 6

Watermelon Chile Gazpacho

1	large watermelon, rind and seeds removed, and cut into 1" cubes
1	large honeydew melon, rind and seeds removed, and cut into 1" cubes
2	medium red onions, diced medium
12	cloves fresh garlic, finely chopped
3	poblano chile peppers, roasted, peeled, seeded and diced medium
3	jalapeño chile peppers, seeded and finely diced
1	dried habanero chile pepper, seeded and finely diced
3	tablespoons dried bread crumbs
2	tablespoons raspberry vinegar
	salt and white pepper *(to taste)*
1½	cups walnut oil

In a food processor place the watermelon and honeydew melons, and coarsely purée them. Strain the purée through a sieve and set it aside.

In the food processor place the red onions, garlic, poblano, jalapeño, and habanero chile peppers, bread crumbs, raspberry vinegar, salt, and white pepper. Purée the ingredients together.

With the food processor constantly running, slowly dribble in the walnut oil.

Add the puréed onion-pepper mixture to the puréed melons, and stir them together.

serves 8

"One day I was shopping at Farmer's Market here in Santa Fe, and I found some of the best watermelons I'd ever seen, so I bought them all. Then I was left with the problem of what to do with them. My food processor started talking to me, and said 'Hey, Dakota, let's make some watermelon gazpacho with those things.' (I get a lot of my ideas by communicating with my various kitchen appliances.) It came out just delicious and was very easy to put together. The same recipe can be used with other kinds of melons as well, such as honeydews or cantaloupes."

Dakota
Piñon Grill

Green Chile Chicken Soup

½	**pound butter**
1	**large white onion, diced medium**
¼	**celery stalk, diced medium**
2	**cups flour**
8	**cups milk**
2	**cups cooked chicken, skin and bones removed, and diced medium**
2½	**cups green chile peppers, roasted, peeled, seeded and chopped medium**
1	**cup heavy cream**
2	**tablespoons fresh garlic, finely chopped**
2	**tablespoons ground cumin**
1	**teaspoon black pepper** *(or to taste)*
	salt *(to taste)*
4	**cups water**

In a large stockpot place the butter and heat it on medium high until it is melted and hot. Add the white onions and celery. Sauté them for 10 minutes, or until the onions are translucent.

While stirring constantly, add the flour and cook it for 2 minutes.

While continuing to stir, slowly add the milk. Stir the ingredients for 5 minutes, or until the sauce thickens.

Add the chicken, green chile peppers, heavy cream, garlic, cumin, black pepper, salt, and water. Stir the ingredients together.

Simmer the soup on low heat for 30 minutes *(do not boil)*.

makes approximately 3 quarts

Santa Fe Corn Chowder

3	tablespoons vegetable oil
1	medium red onion, finely chopped
7	cloves fresh garlic, finely chopped
3	poblano chile peppers, roasted, peeled, seeded and diced medium
1	jalapeño chile pepper, seeded and finely chopped
4	cups fresh corn kernels
2	tablespoons fresh sage, chopped
1	teaspoon ground mace
1	cup dry vermouth
2	cups vegetable stock *(see chef's comments on this page)*
1	quart heavy cream
	salt and white pepper *(to taste)*
1	red bell pepper, seeded and finely diced
1	bunch fresh cilantro, chopped

In a large stockpot place the vegetable oil and heat it on medium high until it is hot. Add the red onions, garlic, poblano chile peppers and jalapeño chile peppers. Sauté the ingredients for 5 minutes, or until the onions are translucent.

Add the corn, sage, and mace. Sauté the ingredients for 3 minutes.

Add the dry vermouth and deglaze the pan.

Add the vegetable stock. Simmer the ingredients for 30 minutes.

Add the heavy cream and simmer the ingredients for 30 minutes more.

Season the soup with the salt and white pepper.

Place ⅓ of the soup in a food processor and coarsely purée it. Return the purée to the stockpot and stir it in.

In each of 8 individual serving bowls place the chowder.

Garnish each serving with the red bell peppers and cilantro.

serves 8

"I have a New England background and so I have always loved chowders. When I got to Santa Fe where corn and chiles are staples, I started adding them to a basic chowder stock. Then I added sage and cilantro to give the soup a real Southwestern flavor. It's a rich, hearty soup, and all people love it. Unfortunately you can't substitute milk for the heavy cream, so save up your cholesterol points for when you eat it."

"Food has to look appealing, but it doesn't have to be a contrived painting. Personally, I like to scatter. I put the entrée in the center of the plate, put down the veggies, and scatter some potatoes around, along with some salsa and chopped parsley."

"A simple vegetable stock can be made by melting two tablespoons of butter in a large pot. Add two cups chopped onions, one cup celery, one cup carrots, some parsley, dill, bay leaves, black peppercorns, one tablespoon of salt, and three ounces white vinegar. Cook everything covered with a lid for ten minutes. Add five quarts of water and lightly simmer the ingredients for one hour. Strain out the stock."

Dakota
Piñon Grill

Chicken Gumbo Soup

3	cups chicken stock *(recipe on page 311)*
1	cup yellow onions, diced medium
½	cup celery, diced medium
½	cup green bell pepper, seeded and diced medium
½	cup red bell pepper, seeded and diced medium
2	tablespoons all-purpose flour
2	teaspoons tomato paste
2	cups chicken stock
8	ounces boneless chicken breast, skin removed, cooked and diced medium
1	cup fresh tomatoes, diced medium
½	cup fresh okra, diced medium
1	teaspoon cajun spice *(or to taste)*
1	teaspoon cayenne pepper *(or to taste)*

"This soup has always been a favorite here at the restaurant. Sometimes we make it with shrimp and fish, and then pour it over cooked white rice. If the soup doesn't seem to be thick enough, add a couple of tablespoons of rice and let it simmer for a while longer."

Robbie Day
San Francisco St. Bar & Grill

Preheat the oven to 300°.

In a large stockpot place the 3 cups of chicken stock and bring it to a boil.

Add the yellow onions, celery, and green and red bell peppers. Reduce the heat to low and simmer the ingredients for 20 to 30 minutes, or until the vegetables are tender.

On a small baking sheet place the flour and spread it out over the pan. Bake the flour for 3 to 4 minutes, or until it is browned.

Add the baked flour and tomato paste to the soup, and stir them in well.

While stirring constantly, gradually add the 2 cups of chicken stock. Reduce the heat to low and simmer the ingredients for 15 minutes.

Add the chicken, tomatoes, and okra. Stir the ingredients together and simmer them for 5 minutes.

Season the soup with the cajun spice and cayenne pepper.

serves 6

Casa Sena Black Bean Soup

1	**pound dried black beans, rinsed and drained**
2	**quarts water**
2	**stalks celery, thinly sliced**
2	**large carrots, thinly sliced**
2	**medium yellow onions, diced medium**
2	**chipotle chile peppers** *(in adobo sauce),* **finely chopped**
1	**pinch ground nutmeg**
1	**pinch cayenne pepper**
1	**teaspoon yellow mustard**
1	**tablespoon Worcestershire sauce**
1	**cup dry sherry**
	salt *(to taste)*
8	**lemon slices**

In a large stockpot place the black beans and water, and bring them to a boil. Remove the pan from the heat and let the beans sit for 1 hour.

Add the celery, carrots, yellow onions, chipotle chile peppers, nutmeg, cayenne pepper, yellow mustard, and Worcestershire sauce. Bring the ingredients to a boil on high heat. Reduce the heat to low and simmer the ingredients for 3 hours, or until the beans are tender. Remove the pan from the heat and let the ingredients sit for 30 minutes.

In a food processor place the ingredients and coarsely purée them.

Return the puréed soup to the stockpot.

Add the sherry and salt, and stir them in.

Reheat the soup.

Garnish each serving of soup with a lemon slice.

serves 8

"This soup has been on our menu since day one. We serve it in a 'galleta', which is a little round loaf of bread with the middle scooped out so that a bowl is made. We also serve it with a tiny flask of sherry on the side, which the customers can add to their taste. If you like, you can add bacon, ham, or salt pork."

Gordon Heiss
Casa Sena

"Gordon (Heiss) certainly has my respect because no one knows the restaurant business like he does. He seems to have a lot of trust in me and gives me freedom in the kitchen. But if I ever need to discuss a problem with him he is always available. I feel fortunate to be here."

"Northern New Mexican cuisine is a lot different from what I grew up with in Sweden. We don't have green chile over there, and we don't eat spicy foods. We use more sour flavors than hot."

Ambjorn Lindskog
Casa Sena

Spicy Roasted Tomato Soup

"This is one of my favorite soups. I like it so much that I make it at home for myself, in smaller quantities. Roasting the tomatoes is such a simple thing to do, and yet it adds so much extra flavor to the soup. Vine ripened tomatoes are best, but if it's the wrong time of year you can use a combination of fresh and canned."

"We use an excellent applewood smoked bacon at the restaurant. It has a slightly sweet flavor. You should use the best quality bacon that you can find."

Jane Stacey
Pranzo Italian Grill

"I make a lot of soups, and this is one of my best recipes. A lot of home cooks claim they are never able to make a soup that tastes as good as what you eat at a fine restaurant. The secret is that all of the ingredients must be of the highest quality, and the stock must be excellent. The flavors should be balanced and rounded out, which takes some practice and experimentation. Always keep tasting the soup as you are making it."

Marta Mueller
Pranzo Italian Grill

¼	cup olive oil
3	strips bacon, diced, cooked and drained
1	large potato, peeled, diced, boiled until almost tender and drained
4	pounds Roma tomatoes, quartered
1	red bell pepper, seeded and diced medium
1	large carrot, grated
1	small yellow onion, diced medium
3	cloves fresh garlic, finely chopped
½	teaspoon chile pequin *(hot red chile flakes)*
1	tablespoon red chile powder
1	tablespoon ground cumin
1	teaspoon salt *(or to taste)*
½	teaspoon black pepper *(or to taste)*
6	cups chicken stock *(recipe on page 311)*
1	cup heavy cream
2	teaspoons honey
2	tablespoons balsamic vinegar

Preheat the oven to 350°.

In a large roasting pan place the olive oil, bacon, potatoes, Roma tomatoes, red bell peppers, carrots, yellow onions, garlic, chile pequin, red chile powder, ground cumin, salt, and black pepper. Mix the ingredients together. Roast the ingredients *(uncovered)* for 30 minutes, or until everything is tender.

In a food processor place the roasted ingredients and purée them so that they are smooth. Strain the mixture through a fine sieve into a large saucepan.

Add the chicken stock, heavy cream, honey, and balsamic vinegar. Stir the ingredients together.

Simmer the soup on low heat for 15 minutes.

serves 6

Garlic Soup

½	**cup fresh garlic, peeled, roasted** *(see chef's comments on this page)* **and finely minced**
½	**small yellow onion, chopped**
½	**large carrot, chopped**
1	**pasilla chile pepper, roasted, peeled, seeded and chopped**
¾	**cup tomato juice**
2	**quarts chicken stock** *(recipe on page 311),* **heated**
	salt and black pepper *(to taste)*
1¼	**cups dried bread crumbs**

In a large stockpot place the roasted garlic, yellow onions, carrots, pasilla chile peppers, tomato juice, and chicken stock. Stir the ingredients together and simmer them for 30 minutes, or until the vegetables are tender. Season the soup with the salt and black pepper. Place the soup in a food processor and purée it so that it is smooth.

Garnish each serving of soup with the bread crumbs.

serves 8

"By roasting the garlic you make it taste smoky and sweet. The garlic flavor comes through nicely, but you won't feel like you have just walked out of an Italian restaurant."

"Roast the garlic by putting it on a flat sheet under the broiler. It should turn a nice, dark brown. Don't let it burn!"

Margueritte Meier
Old Mexico Grill

Spicy Apple Soup

6	**Granny Smith apples, cored, peeled and coarsely chopped**
½	**cup sugar**
2	**teaspoons Hungarian paprika**
½	**teaspoon cayenne pepper** *(or to taste)*
1	**pinch ground cloves**
1	**pinch ground cinnamon**
1	**pinch ground nutmeg**
2½	**cups chicken stock** *(recipe on page 311)*
½	**cup sour cream**
½	**teaspoon Hungarian paprika**

In a large saucepan place the apples, sugar, the 2 teaspoons of Hungarian paprika, cayenne pepper, cloves, cinnamon, nutmeg, and chicken stock. Cook the ingredients on medium heat for 15 minutes, or until the apples are tender. In a food processor place the mixture and purée it so that it is smooth.

Garnish each serving of soup with a dollop of sour cream and a pinch of paprika.

serves 6

"This soup tastes very elegant, and it is the easiest thing in the world to make. I like a chicken-based stock with fruit and herbs. Granny Smith apples are available all year-round, so you can make the soup in any season. Serve it cold in the summer and hot in the winter."

"When I was growing up I was never allowed in the kitchen. My mother despised cooking and she was an obsessively neat person who hated messes. I guess I don't take after her because I absolutely love to cook, and I always make big messes in the kitchen!"

Sylvia Johnson
Celebrations

Mex-Asian Green Chile Coconut Chicken Soup

2	tablespoons vegetable oil
4	scallions, chopped medium
3	cloves fresh garlic, finely chopped
3	stalks lemon grass, cut into 2" pieces
2	green chile peppers, roasted, peeled, seeded and chopped medium
6	kaffir lime leaves *(see chef's comments on page 233)*
1	quarter-size piece galangal *(see chef's comments on this page)*
1	tablespoon Thai red curry paste *(see chef's comments on this page)*
2	tablespoons black pepper *(or to taste)*
2½	cups chicken stock *(recipe on page 311)*
4	whole chicken breasts, skin and bones removed, and thinly sliced
3	tablespoons cornstarch
½	pound mushrooms, thinly sliced
1	can coconut milk *(see chef's comments on page 113)*
¼	cup Thai fish sauce *(see chef's comments on page 113)*
¼	cup lime juice, freshly squeezed
½	cup fresh cilantro, chopped

In a large saucepan place the vegetable oil and heat it on medium high until it is hot. Add the scallions, garlic, lemon grass, green chile peppers, kaffir lime leaves, galangal, Thai red curry paste, and black pepper. Sauté the ingredients for 3 minutes.

Add the chicken stock and bring it to a boil.

In a medium bowl place the chicken pieces and cornstarch. Toss them together so that the chicken is well coated.

Add the chicken to the soup. While stirring constantly, simmer it for 5 minutes.

Add the mushrooms, coconut milk, Thai fish sauce, and lime juice. Stir the ingredients together and simmer them for 5 minutes.

Remove the lemon grass and galangal. Garnish the soup with the cilantro.

serves 4 to 6

"This recipe is a combination of different Thai flavors that I personally love. The only Southwestern ingredients are the green chile and cilantro. It's a rich, filling soup that would be excellent as a first course for an elegant dinner party. Or, it would be perfect for a light meal if accompanied by a green salad."

Marsha Chobol
Santa Fe Market

"Galangal is a root, similar to ginger, and is very common in Thai cooking. It has a unique flavor, and can be found in Oriental specialty stores."

"Thai red curry paste is deadly hot, with a strong curry flavor. Look for it in the Oriental section of a large supermarket."

Peter Raub
Santa Fe Market

Cream of Green Chile Chicken Soup

1	whole chicken, innards removed, washed and dried
1	medium yellow onion, peeled
1	bay leaf
2	cups green chile peppers, roasted, peeled, seeded and diced
2	stalks celery, chopped medium
1	zucchini, thinly sliced
1	carrot, peeled and thinly sliced
1	clove fresh garlic, finely chopped
1	cup milk
2	tablespoons flour
1	cup water
	salt and white pepper *(to taste)*

In a large saucepan place the chicken, yellow onion, and bay leaf. Cover the ingredients with water. Bring them to a boil and then simmer them for 1 hour.

Remove the chicken from the water and let it cool. Remove the skin and bones, and discard them. Cut the chicken meat into bite-size pieces. Return the chicken to the same pan with the broth.

Add the green chile peppers, celery, zucchini, carrots, garlic, and milk. Stir the ingredients together, and then simmer them for 15 minutes. Remove the bay leaf.

In a small bowl place the flour and water, and whisk them together.

Add the flour mixture to the soup and stir it in well.

Season the soup with the salt and white pepper. Simmer it for 5 minutes.

serves 8

"Here is my version of a classic green chile chicken soup. It's something that everyone loves, and it is very easy to make. I use milk in this recipe to keep it healthier, but you can use cream if you prefer. It will make the soup taste much richer. As with any cream soup, it's important not to overcook or scald the milk or cream."

"When I was in college I shared an apartment with some big time jocks. In exchange for their doing all of the cleaning, including dishes, I did the cooking. They hated to clean, and I loved to cook, so I think I got a pretty good deal!"

Courtney Carswell
The Shed

Avocado Tomatillo Soup

5	**medium Haas avocados, peeled, pitted and coarsely chopped**
3	**tomatillos, blanched and skins removed** *(see chef's comments on this page)*
2	**serrano chile peppers, coarsely chopped**
2	**oranges, zested** *(outer orange part grated off)* **and juiced**
1½	**limes, zested and juiced**
½	**lemon, zested and juiced**
1	**tablespoon sherry** *(or to taste)*
½	**teaspoon ground cumin** *(or to taste)*
1	**teaspoon salt** *(or to taste)*
1½	**cups buttermilk**
1	**quart heavy cream**
1	**lime, very thinly sliced**

In a food processor place the avocados, tomatillos, serrano chile peppers, the zest and juice of the oranges, limes and lemon, the sherry, cumin, salt, and a small amount of the buttermilk. Purée the ingredients together so that they are smooth.

Strain the purée through a fine sieve into a medium large bowl. Add the rest of the buttermilk and heavy cream, and stir them in. Adjust the seasonings if necessary.

Serve the soup cold with the lime slices on top.

serves 6

Tecolote Tomato Clam Soup

2	tablespoons olive oil
1	medium yellow onion, diced
1	teaspoon fresh garlic, chopped
1½	tablespoon fresh oregano, chopped
½	teaspoon black pepper
6	cups canned *(or fresh)* tomatoes
3	cups tomato juice
1	cup clam juice
1½	tablespoons clam base
1½	pounds cooked clams, chopped
1	teaspoon tabasco sauce *(or to taste)*
	salt *(to taste)*

In a large, heavy stockpot place the olive oil and heat it on medium high until it is hot. Add the yellow onions and sauté them for 5 minutes, or until they are translucent.

Add the garlic, oregano, and black pepper. Sauté the ingredients for 2 minutes.

Add the tomatoes, tomato juice, clam juice, and clam base. Simmer the ingredients for 20 minutes.

Add the clams and tabasco sauce. Return the soup to a simmer.

Season the soup with the salt.

makes 6 cups

"Years ago there was a restaurant on Canyon Road called the 'Three Cities of Spain'. They served a delicious tomato clam soup which I've always remembered. That's what this recipe is based on, although I added a few more ingredients. Clam base is needed because the clam juice doesn't have enough punch by itself. You should be able to find it in a good market or seafood shop. If you want the soup to be heartier, add some diced potatoes."

"Eating out at other restaurants is one of my greatest pleasures. To have someone else serve me a nice meal with a good bottle of wine.....that's heaven!"

Bill Jennison
Tecolote Cafe

Chicken & Baby Greens Salad with Spicy Asian Vinaigrette

Chicken & Baby Greens Salad

2	tablespoons light sesame oil
1½	pounds chicken breast, skin and bones removed, and cut into thin strips.
1	pound mixed baby greens
6	Roma tomatoes, thinly sliced
1	bunch scallions, thinly sliced
	Spicy Asian Vinaigrette *(recipe follows)*
1	tablespoon sesame seeds, toasted *(see chef's comments on this page)*

In a large sauté pan place the sesame oil and heat it on medium high until it is very hot. Add the chicken strips and sauté them for 3 to 4 minutes, or until they are just cooked. Remove the pan from the heat and let the chicken cool.

On each of 6 individual serving plates place the baby greens. Arrange the chicken, tomatoes, and scallions on top of the greens. Dribble on the Spicy Asian Vinaigrette. Sprinkle on the toasted sesame seeds.

serves 6

Spicy Asian Vinaigrette

1	teaspoon sugar
1	tablespoon soy sauce
2	tablespoons lemon juice, freshly squeezed
¼	cup rice wine vinegar
2	tablespoons chile oil
3	tablespoons toasted sesame oil
½	cup peanut oil

In a medium bowl place the sugar, soy sauce, lemon juice, and rice wine vinegar. While whisking constantly, slowly dribble in the three oils.

makes approximately 1 cup

"This is a light, easy-to-assemble salad that would be perfect for a brunch or lunch dish. You could easily substitute grilled shrimp for the chicken."

"I recommend buying unbleached sesame seeds in the bulk section of a health food store. You can toast them under the broiler, or in a dry pan on top of the stove. Just let them get lightly brown."

"This vinaigrette is one of those wonderful American mish-mash recipes that borrows from Asian flavors. It's one of our most popular dressings at the restaurant."

Sarah Alvord
Zia Diner

Adobo Pasta Salad with Chipotle Sundried Tomato Dressing

Adobo Pasta Salad

2	pounds penne pasta *(see chef's comments on page 156)*, **cooked al dente, rinsed in cold water and drained**
2	small yellow squash, sliced into long strips, grilled and diced
2	small zucchini, sliced into long strips, grilled and diced
1	small red onion, finely chopped
1	red bell pepper, seeded and finely chopped
½	cup sundried tomatoes, reconstituted and thinly sliced
3	Roma tomatoes, chopped small
1	16-ounce can corn, drained
1	cup Chipotle Sundried Tomato Dressing *(recipe follows)*
½	cup asiago cheese, freshly grated

In a large bowl place all of the ingredients *(except for the asiago cheese)* and toss them together. Sprinkle the cheese on top of each serving.

serves 8

Chipotle Sundried Tomato Dressing

½	teaspoon ground coriander
½	teaspoon ground cumin
½	teaspoon ground cinnamon
½	teaspoon ground anise
½	cup sundried tomatoes, reconstituted and chopped
1	chipotle chile pepper *(in adobo sauce)*, **puréed**
½	cup tomato juice
2	tablespoons molasses
3	tablespoons sherry vinegar
¼	teaspoon liquid smoke
½	tablespoon salt
2	cups olive oil

Heat a small, non-stick sauté pan on high until it is hot. Add the coriander, cumin, cinnamon, and anise. Roll the spices around until their perfume reaches your nose.

(continued on next page)

"I love to eat out at other restaurants. I think I'm a great customer, because I'm very understanding, tip well, and often send my compliments to the chef. Of course, if the food or service is bad, I'll let the restaurant people know that as well."

Rocky Durham
Zia Diner

"I love chipotle peppers in adobo sauce and use them in a lot of my recipes. This particular dressing is the result of one of my many experimentations in the kitchen."

"I did not like to cook until I started cooking in restaurants. It's wonderful, because everything is right there at your fingertips..... all the different food products, pots and pans, and exotic utensils. There is no need to go grocery shopping, which I hate!"

Kristy Rawson
Zia Diner

In a food processor place the toasted spices, puréed chipotle chile pepper, tomato juice, molasses, sherry vinegar, liquid smoke, and salt. Purée the ingredients together.

With the food processor constantly running, slowly drizzle in the olive oil.

makes 3 cups

Curried Chicken Salad

1	**cup mayonnaise**
¼	**cup lemon juice, freshly squeezed**
¼	**cup Curry Oil** *(recipe on page 305)*
4	**boneless chicken breasts, skin removed, cooked and cut into 1" cubes**
3	**celery stalks, sliced medium**
1	**bunch scallions, thinly sliced**
½	**cup seedless grapes**
¼	**cup fresh Italian parsley, chopped**
1	**tablespoon paprika**
1	**teaspoon cayenne pepper** *(or to taste)*
	salt and white pepper *(to taste)*
1	**head red leaf lettuce, leaves separated, washed and dried**

In a medium bowl place the mayonnaise, lemon juice, and Curry Oil. Stir the ingredients together.

In another medium bowl place the chicken, celery, scallions, grapes, Italian parsley, paprika, cayenne pepper, salt, and white pepper. Toss the ingredients together.

Add the curried mayonnaise mixture *(see chef's comments on this page)* and mix it in well.

Cover the salad with plastic wrap and refrigerate it for 2 hours.

On each of 4 individual serving plates place several leaves of the red leaf lettuce. Place the Curried Chicken Salad on top.

serves 4

"This dish has been served at El Farol since its beginning, and probably is the most popular thing we offer. People are constantly asking us for the recipe, and we find it difficult to explain verbally because of the curry oil, which is made separately several days in advance. I'm looking forward to the publication of this book so that I can refer our future customers to it."

"When you make this dish it is safest to add only part of the curried mayonnaise at first, and then taste it. The color of the salad should not be too neon or bright, and the curry flavor should not be overwhelming. Keep tasting and adding more mayonnaise until it seems to be right. Also, remember that the heat will increase after the salad sits for several hours."

Kit Baum
El Farol

Warm Spinach Salad with Charred Tomato Chile Vinaigrette

Warm Spinach Salad

2	bunches spinach, stems and veins removed, washed and dried
1	cup shiitake mushrooms, sliced
	Charred Tomato Chile Vinaigrette *(recipe follows)*, **heated**
¼	cup Reggiano cheese *(parmesan)*, **freshly grated**
	cracked black pepper *(to taste)*

On each of 6 individual serving plates place the spinach. Arrange the shiitake mushroom slices on top.

Pour the Charred Tomato Chile Vinaigrette on top. Sprinkle on the Reggiano cheese and cracked black pepper.

serves 6

Charred Tomato Chile Vinaigrette

4	large tomatoes, grilled and finely chopped
2	medium red onions, grilled and minced
2	dried chipotle chile peppers, minced
1	tablespoon fresh basil, chopped
½	tablespoon fresh Italian parsley, chopped
2	limes, juiced
1	tablespoon balsamic vinegar
¼	teaspoon cayenne pepper
½	teaspoon salt
¼	teaspoon black pepper

In a jar with a tight lid place all of the ingredients. Shake them together so they are well blended.

makes approximately 2 cups

"This is a very simple, light salad that has a delicious flavor. Once the vinaigrette is made, it takes only minutes to put together. The only thing I recommend is to buy the loose spinach leaves that are bound, instead of the kind that are packaged in cellophane. The leaves will be much more tender. It's a mystery to me why people buy the pre-packaged spinach, because they still have to wash it and remove the stems and veins."

"I love this vinaigrette. Not only does it have a fantastic flavor, it is easy to make and is extremely versatile. It's excellent as a sauce for grilled chicken, shrimp, or fish. And, if you add it to a pasta along with some mozzarella cheese and Italian sausage, you will have a gourmet entrée!"

Pete Zimmer
Inn of the Anasazi

Spicy Fried Chicken Salad

"This is an old, classic recipe from the South. Thanks to our new President, Mr. Clinton, I believe that there is going to be a revival of southern cooking. This makes me happy, because I'm from Louisiana, and I have always loved the cooking from that part of the country."

4	**whole chicken breasts, skin and bones removed, and cut into 1" strips**
1	**cup buttermilk**
2	**cups flour**
2	**teaspoons cayenne pepper**
1	**teaspoon salt** *(or to taste)*
1	**teaspoon black pepper** *(or to taste)*
3	**cups vegetable oil**
4	**cups baby greens, washed and dried**
	Blue Cheese Dressing *(recipe on page 114)*
½	**cup cooked beets, sliced into thin strips**

"The chicken is very spicy, but its heat is cooled down with the Blue Cheese Dressing. I love the different tastes and textures in this salad, with the crispiness of the chicken and baby greens, and the rich creaminess of the dressing."

In a large bowl place the chicken breasts and buttermilk. Cover the bowl with plastic wrap and marinate the chicken at room temperature for 1 hour.

In a medium bowl place the flour, cayenne pepper, salt, and black pepper. Mix the ingredients together.

Remove the chicken from the buttermilk *(let a small amount of the buttermilk drain off the pieces)*.

Dredge the chicken strips in the flour mixture so that they are well coated.

"When you wash your baby greens be sure that they get completely dried before you serve them. Otherwise, the dressing will just run off."

In a large, heavy sauté pan place the vegetable oil and heat it on medium high until it is hot. Place the coated chicken strips in the hot oil and fry them for 4 minutes on each side, or until they are golden brown and just done.

On each of 8 individual serving plates place the baby greens. Arrange the chicken strips around each plate in a spoke-like pattern. Place the Blue Cheese Dressing in the center. Place the sliced beets on top.

serves 8

"I am not a chef. I am just a very good cook who likes to eat."

Sylvia Johnson
Celebrations

Nopalito Walnut Salad with Jalapeño Raspberry Vinaigrette

Nopalito Walnut Salad

6	heads baby romaine lettuce, washed and dried
2	heads Boston bibb lettuce, washed and dried
2	tangerines, peeled, segmented and seeds removed
½	cup walnuts, toasted
12	mushrooms, cleaned
12	black olives, pitted
4	ounces Nopalito cactus *(see chef's comments on this page)*, **cut into thin strips**
1	small jicama, peeled and cut into matchsticks that are ¼" thick and 2" long
1	pint fresh raspberries
	Jalapeño Raspberry Vinaigrette *(recipe follows)*

On each of 6 individual salad plates place the romaine lettuce. Place the bibb lettuce on top. Artfully arrange the tangerines, walnuts, mushrooms, olives, Nopalito strips, jicama, and raspberries on top. Dribble on the Jalapeño Raspberry Vinaigrette.

serves 6

Jalapeño Raspberry Vinaigrette

1	jalapeño chile pepper, seeded and finely chopped
1½	cups walnut oil
½	cup raspberry vinegar
½	teaspoon lemon juice, freshly squeezed
1	tablespoon sugar
1	bay leaf

In a medium bowl place the jalapeño chile pepper, walnut oil, raspberry vinegar, lemon juice, and sugar. Whisk the ingredients together.

Add the bay leaf to the vinaigrette.

Cover the bowl with plastic wrap and refrigerate the vinaigrette overnight. Remove the bay leaf. Mix the vinaigrette well before serving.

makes 2 cups

"Nopalitos are cactus leaves. They come in jars and you can find them in the gourmet section of your grocery store. You can eat them raw, sauté them, or bake them. The flavor is hard to describe. It's kind of a surprise taste. You have to experience it directly in order to know what it's like."

Lela Cross
La Plazuela

"This is a very interesting salad that we serve during raspberry season. It's especially popular with people who are health conscious and who love fruit. If the idea of the Nopalito cactus is too strange for you, leave it out."

Tomas Cross
La Plazuela

Thai Carrot Salad

3	cloves fresh garlic, finely chopped
1	teaspoon Thai pepper flakes *(see chef's comments on this page)*
1	tablespoon light sesame seeds
1	tablespoon dark sesame seeds
3	tablespoons Thai fish sauce *(see chef's comments on page 113)*
¼	cup rice wine vinegar
¼	cup peanut oil
2	cups carrots, peeled and shredded

In a medium bowl place the garlic, pepper flakes, light and dark sesame seeds, Thai fish sauce, rice wine vinegar, and peanut oil. Whisk the ingredients together.

Add the carrots and toss them in.

serves 8

Thai Cucumber Salad

2	cucumbers, peeled, seeded and thinly sliced
½	small red onion, finely diced
1	ounce tree ear mushrooms, softened in warm water and sliced *(see chef's comments on this page)*
1	tablespoon jalapeño chile pepper, seeded and finely chopped
1½	tablespoons Thai fish sauce *(see chef's comments on page 113)*
1	tablespoon toasted sesame oil
1½	tablespoons lime juice, freshly squeezed

In a medium bowl place all of the ingredients and toss them together.

serves 8

Grilled Shrimp Salad with Mixed Greens & Spicy Tomatillo Salsa

Grilled Shrimp Salad with Mixed Greens

4	tablespoons olive oil
2	tablespoons balsamic vinegar
	salt and black pepper *(to taste)*
4	cups mixed baby greens, cleaned and dried
12	jumbo shrimp, peeled and deveined *(leave tails intact)*
	Spicy Tomatillo Salsa *(recipe on next page)*

In a small bowl place the olive oil, balsamic vinegar, salt, and black pepper. Whisk the ingredients so that they are well blended.

In a salad bowl place the baby greens and toss them with the vinaigrette.

Grill the shrimp for 1 to 2 minutes on each side, or until they are opaque.

In the center of each of 4 individual serving plates place the dressed greens. Place the shrimp on top of the greens. Spoon the Spicy Tomatillo Salsa on top of the shrimp.

serves 4

"We feature this on our menu and it is well loved by our guests, especially in the summertime. It's light, healthy, and simple to make."

"I would say that I do about eighty percent of the cooking at home. When we first got married my wife wouldn't cook at all, because she didn't like the competition from me, a professional chef. But now she is gradually cooking more, and I really do appreciate it."

Jim Makinson
Bishop's Lodge

Spicy Tomatillo Salsa

2   **limes**
6   **tomatillos, husks removed, blanched, skins removed** (see chef's comments of this page), **and diced medium**
3   **serrano chile peppers, seeded and finely diced**
¼   **cup red onions, finely diced**
¼   **bunch fresh cilantro, chopped**
¼   **cup extra virgin olive oil**

Remove the zest of the limes by carefully grating off the outer green skin. Blanch the zest in boiling water for 30 seconds and then place it in ice water. Chop the zest finely.

Separate the lime into sections and remove the seeds. Dice the lime meat into ¼" pieces.

In a medium bowl place the lime zest, diced limes, and the rest of the ingredients. Mix everything together well.

makes approximately 1 cup

Spicy Black Bean Salad

1   **pound dried black beans, cooked** (see chef's comments on this page)
4   **Roma tomatoes, seeded and diced**
1   **small red onion, diced**
1   **green bell pepper, seeded and diced**
1   **red bell pepper, seeded and diced**
½   **cup fresh cilantro, chopped**
3   **hot fresh chile peppers** (jalapeño, habanero or serrano), **seeded and finely diced**
½   **cup lime juice, freshly squeezed**
½   **cup olive oil**
½   **teaspoon salt** (or to taste)

In a large bowl place all of the ingredients and stir them together. Serve the salad at room temperature.

serves 8

"We used to serve this salsa with our fish entrées, and then decided to try it with our cold shrimp salad. It's excellent both ways."

"Most people don't blanch and skin their tomatillos, but I find the skin to be fairly tough. Score the tomatillos in several places, place them in boiling water for ten seconds, or until the skin starts to loosen, and then plunge them into ice water."

Jim Makinson
Bishop's Lodge

"To cook the beans you should put them in a large pot, add about eight cups of water, bring them to a boil, cover the pot, remove the pot from the heat, and let them soak overnight. This process helps to eliminate the gas in the beans, which eventually will end up in your system. It also cuts their cooking time in half. Another trick to speed up the cooking time is to add ½ teaspoon of baking soda. After the beans are cooked, add salt to taste."

"This recipe can easily be converted to a salsa dish for chips. Purée about two cups of the salad with a little water, and then add it back to the salad and stir it in. Your guests will love it!"

Jonathan Horst
Adobo Catering

Sauces, Dips & Condiments

Southwestern Barbecue Sauce

1   **chipotle chile pepper** *(in adobo sauce)*
3   **pickled jalapeño chile peppers**
1   **clove fresh garlic, finely chopped**
1½   **cups barbecue sauce** *(your favorite)*
1   **cup red chile powder**
2   **tablespoons sugar**
2   **tablespoons cider vinegar**
      salt and black pepper *(to taste)*

In a food processor place all the ingredients and purée them so that they are smooth.

makes approximately 3 cups

"We made this recipe up at the restaurant. It's based on a Texas-style barbecue sauce and then embellished with some red chile powder and smoky chipotle chiles. It is more of a hot sauce, rather than a sweet sauce, and it's delicious on anything you can imagine."

Harry Shapiro
Harry's Road House

Apple Green Chile Chutney

1   **tablespoon peanut oil**
¼   **medium yellow onion, diced medium**
2   **teaspoons dried oregano**
2   **green chile peppers, roasted, peeled, seeded and diced small**
2   **tablespoons dried pasado chile peppers, coarsely ground**
2   **red jalapeño chile peppers, seeded and finely chopped**
2   **tablespoons sugar**
1½   **cups apple cider** *(unfiltered)*
¼   **cup cider vinegar**
3   **Granny Smith apples, peeled, cored and diced medium**

In a large saucepan place the peanut oil and heat it on medium high until it is hot. Add the yellow onions and sauté them for 5 minutes, or until they are translucent. Add the oregano and cook the ingredients for 2 minutes.

Add the green, pasado and jalapeño chile peppers, sugar, apple cider, and cider vinegar. Stir everything together well. Simmer the ingredients for 10 minutes, or until the liquid is reduced by ½.

Add the apples and simmer them for 5 minutes, or until they are tender.

makes approximately 2 cups

"We developed this recipe as something really nice to serve with our wild game, such as quail and rabbit. Kids love it and eat it like applesauce. It's also delicious with quesadillas."

"I really admire the way Europeans sit around the dinner table for hours. A meal is a real family event. You can laugh, cry, yell, or whatever, but you are there at the table interacting with everyone else. The cohesiveness of the family culminates around food. In our country people are so busy, with both parents usually working, that most meals are rushed, with the different members often eating at different times."

Mark Kiffin
Coyote Cafe

"This is a wonderful salsa that is excellent with fish or chicken. It's spicy and lightly smoky, with a subtle sweet flavor. The morita chile peppers may be hard to find. If so, you can substitute a chipotle chile pepper."

Margueritte Meier
Old Mexico Grill

"You have to purée the ingredients for quite a while to get them smooth. They will never get completely smooth, but you don't want any big chunks in the salsa. Season it lightly with the salt and then taste it before adding more."

Marc Greene
Old Mexico Grill

Almond Smoked Morita Salsa

2	tablespoons butter
½	pound blanched almonds
⅛	ounce dried morita chile peppers
1½	ounces sundried tomatoes
½	bunch fresh cilantro, chopped
3	cups canned pineapple juice
6	ounces clam juice
2	cups water
	salt *(to taste)*

In a large sauté pan place the butter and heat it on medium high until it is melted and hot. Add the almonds and sauté the ingredients for 5 minutes, or until they are golden brown.

Add the morita chile peppers, sundried tomatoes, cilantro, pineapple juice, clam juice, water, and salt. Cook the ingredients on medium heat for 30 minutes.

Place all of the ingredients in a food processor and purée them so that they are as smooth as possible.

Season the salsa with the salt.

makes approximately 1 quart

Salsa Tropical

1	medium mango, peeled, meat removed from the core and diced medium
1	banana, peeled and diced medium
1	cup fresh pineapple, peeled, cored and diced medium
½	small red onion, finely diced
1	clove fresh garlic, finely chopped
1	jalapeño chile pepper, seeded and finely chopped
1	tablespoon fresh cilantro, chopped
1	teaspoon lemon juice, freshly squeezed
1	teaspoon salt *(or to taste)*

"We serve this salsa with halibut, salmon, swordfish, and mahi-mahi. It is very flavorful and makes a great summer item."

Robbie Day
San Francisco St. Bar & Grill

In a medium bowl place all of the ingredients and toss them together.

makes approximately 3 cups

Pasqual's Red Chile Sauce

¾ pound dried New Mexico red chile peppers, rinsed, stemmed, seeded, covered with hot water and soaked for 30 minutes *(reserve the water)*
1 medium white onion, coarsely chopped
8 cloves fresh garlic
2 teaspoons dried Mexican oregano
1 teaspoon ground cumin
2 teaspoons kosher salt *(or to taste)*

In a large stockpot place the rehydrated red chile peppers, reserved water, white onions, garlic, Mexican oregano, and cumin. Bring the ingredients to a boil over high heat.

Reduce the heat to low and simmer the ingredients for 20 minutes.

Drain off the liquid and reserve it.

In a blender place batches of the chile pepper mixture with a small amount of the reserved water. Purée all of the ingredients so that a thick, ketchup-like consistency is achieved. Strain the sauce through a fine mesh sieve.

Season the sauce with the salt.

makes approximately 1 quart

"I really believe in using chile pods versus powdered chile, because they have a much stronger, fruitier flavor. When you rehydrate the peppers you should weight them down with a plate so that they don't float to the top of the water. The fumes are released during this process and might give you some difficulty in breathing, so fling open the windows and the kitchen door!"

"Making this sauce can be a messy process, but it is definitely worth the effort. It freezes perfectly well, so you could double the recipe and save part of it for future dishes. Also, be forewarned that the sauce stains. Don't wear white when you make it, and if you spill any be sure to wipe it up immediately."

Katharine Kagel
Cafe Pasqual's

Paul's Red Chile Sauce

16 ounces canned tomatoes *(whole or crushed)*
1 small yellow onion, chopped
¼ cup hot red chile powder
½ cup water
1 teaspoon salt
½ teaspoon black pepper

In a medium saucepan place all of the ingredients. Simmer them for 10 minutes, or until the flavors are blended.

Place the sauce in a food processor and purée it.

makes 3 cups

"This is a basic red chile sauce. Make it as hot or mild as you prefer. We make it medium at our restaurant because a lot of our customers are what I would respectfully call 'wimpy', and don't want their food too spicy."

Paul Hunsicker
Paul's Restaurant

Guajillo Salsa

8	**dried guajillo chile peppers, seeded, stemmed and dry toasted** *(see chef's comments on this page)*
4	**large tomatoes, broiled** *(see chef's comments on this page)*
1	**medium red onion, chopped**
1	**clove fresh garlic, chopped**
1	**cup chicken stock** *(recipe on page 311)*
3	**tablespoons olive oil**
1	**teaspoon salt** *(or to taste)*

In a food processor place the toasted guajillo chile peppers, broiled tomatoes, red onions, garlic, and chicken stock. Purée the ingredients so that they are almost smooth.

In a medium saucepan place the olive oil and heat it on high until it just starts to smoke. Add the puréed mixture *(be careful because the oil will spatter)* and reduce the heat to low. Simmer the sauce for 5 minutes, or until it thickens. Season the salsa with the salt.

makes approximately 2 cups

"This is a delicious Mexican salsa that is excellent with grilled meats. Another idea is to sauté some mushrooms, add them to the salsa, cook them together, and then serve them as a side dish."

"To dry toast the guajillo chile peppers you put them in a sauté pan and constantly move and toss them on a medium heat. They are ready when they are lightly toasted and their fragrance is released. Don't burn them or else they will be bitter."

"When you broil the tomatoes you should put them in a shallow baking dish and broil them on all sides so that they are blackened and blistered. This makes the tomatoes very sweet and adds an important dimension to the sauce, as does the toasting of the chile pods."

Don Fortel
On Water

Jalapeño Tartar Sauce

2	**cups mayonnaise**
1	**dill pickle, finely chopped**
1	**jalapeño chile pepper, seeded and finely chopped**
1	**pickled jalapeño chile pepper, seeded and finely chopped**
2	**tablespoons hot sauce**
1	**teaspoon cayenne pepper**
1	**teaspoon red chile powder**
1	**teaspoon ground thyme**
1	**lemon, freshly squeezed**
1	**teaspoon salt** *(or to taste)*
1	**teaspoon black pepper** *(or to taste)*

In a medium bowl place all the ingredients and mix them together well.

makes approximately 3 cups

"I've tasted a lot of different tartar sauces, and this is the one I like best. It's very spicy and crunchy, with a wonderful robust flavor."

Harry Shapiro
Harry's Road House

Cilantro Pesto

½   **cup piñon nuts** *(pine nuts)*
½   **cup parmesan cheese, freshly grated**
2   **tablespoons fresh garlic, finely chopped**
2   **bunches fresh cilantro, chopped**
1   **bunch fresh parsley, chopped**
1¼ **cups olive oil**
1   **tablespoon salt** *(or to taste)*
1   **tablespoon black pepper** *(or to taste)*

In a food processor place all of the ingredients. Purée them so that they are smooth.

makes approximately 3 cups

Roasted Tomatillo Chipotle Poblano Sauce

12 **tomatillos, husks removed, roasted** *(see chef's comments on page 72),* **and coarsely chopped**
6   **poblano chile peppers, roasted, peeled, seeded and coarsely chopped**
1   **7-ounce can chipotle chile peppers** *(in adobo sauce)*
2   **cups chicken stock** *(recipe on page 311)*
    salt *(to taste)*

In a food processor place the tomatillos, poblano and chipotle chile peppers, and chicken stock. Purée the ingredients so that they are smooth.

Season the sauce with the salt.

makes approximately 1 quart

"This is a great, super easy pesto recipe. Just throw everything in a blender and pulse it. You can keep a jar of pesto in the refrigerator and use it as a flavoring for soups, stews, and pastas. You also can freeze it in small plastic containers and then scoop it out as you need it. It will have the consistency of ice cream."

"Piñon nuts are very expensive, so feel free to substitute either almonds or walnuts. Pecans would be too strong."

"Cilantro has a very distinct and strong flavor, and does not necessarily appeal to everyone who first tastes it. For some people it is an acquired taste."

James Lamoureux
The Evergreen

"Of all the sauces I make, this is one of my favorites. It has a good chile kick to it, and is very simple to prepare. Serve it with raw vegetables as a dipping sauce."

Rustin Newton
Staab House

"The lovely thing about this sauce is that you can add your own ingredients. It's a wonderful foil for your favorite foods..... stewed vegetables, shrimp, scallops, chicken, or meat."

"We buy coconut milk in cans. Gourmet markets carry it, and sometimes you can find it in the liquor section of grocery stores, with the mixes."

Katharine Kagel
Cafe Pasqual's

"Thai shrimp paste can be difficult to find, but if you have access to an Oriental store, you're set. It's made out of fermented shrimp that is ground down to a paste. Like anchovy paste, you only need to use a tiny bit, but it provides that special flavor you can't get from anything else."

"Thai fish sauce is Thailand's answer to soy sauce. It's very salty, and is not that hard to find."

Laura Taylor
Cafe Pasqual's

"Serve this sauce with grilled meats, such as a chicken breast, pork tenderloin, or with a heartier fish steak."

Robbie Day
San Francisco St. Bar & Grill

Green Curry Sauce

2	**Thai chile peppers** *(see chef's comments on page 233)*, **stems removed**
6	**cups fresh cilantro, coarsely chopped**
4	**tablespoons fresh ginger root, peeled and coarsely chopped**
8	**kaffir lime leaves** *(see chef's comments on page 233)*
18	**cloves fresh garlic**
1	**tablespoon Thai shrimp paste** *(see chef's comments on this page)*
2	**tablespoons coriander seeds**
⅓	**cup Thai fish sauce** *(see chef's comments on this page)*
1⅔	**cups unsweetened coconut milk** *(see chef's comments on this page)*
	water *(as necessary)*

In a blender place all the ingredients and purée them. Add water if it is needed to liquify the sauce so that it is a thin consistency.

Strain the sauce through a fine sieve.

makes approximately 3 cups

Romanesca Sauce

3	**cups tomatoes, diced**
1	**clove fresh garlic, finely chopped**
¼	**cup fresh basil, chopped**
2	**teaspoons chile pequin** *(hot red chile flakes)*
¾	**cup balsamic vinegar**
1	**teaspoon salt** *(or to taste)*

In a food processor place all of the ingredients. Purée them so that they are smooth.

makes approximately 1 quart

Romesco Sauce

¾ cup sliced almonds, toasted
10 cloves fresh garlic
1 ounce dried hot red chile peppers
½ cup olive oil
¼ cup red wine vinegar
¼ teaspoon salt *(or to taste)*
2 cups red bell peppers, roasted, peeled, seeded and coarsely chopped

In a food processor place all the ingredients *(except the red bell peppers)* and purée them.

Add the red bell peppers. Purée them so that the sauce is smooth.

makes approximately 3 cups

Chile Pequin

4 cups tomatoes, peeled and diced medium
¼ cup yellow onion, diced medium
1½ cloves fresh garlic, finely chopped
5 whole pequin chile peppers, crushed
1 tablespoon fresh cilantro, chopped
½ teaspoon salt *(or to taste)*

In a food processor place all of the ingredients and purée them so that they are smooth.

makes approximately 4 cups

Blue Cheese Dressing

1 cup blue cheese, crumbled
1 pint sour cream
¼ cup white wine
salt and black pepper *(to taste)*

In a small bowl place all the ingredients and stir them together. Cover the bowl with plastic wrap and refrigerate it.

makes approximately 3 cups

"Use this sauce as a spread on sandwiches, with scrambled eggs, or as a dipping sauce for marinated raw vegetables. The consistency can be varied by adding more or less of the red bell peppers at the end."

"The name 'El Farol' means 'The Lantern'. Our restaurant serves Spanish tapas, which are little appetizer dishes. People can order two or three different things and have a meal that is unique. It's also fun for them to share their food with everyone else at their table, so they really get to experience a lot of different items."

Kit Baum
El Farol

"Chile Pequin is spicy, like Pico de Gallo, only it has a smoother texture because it is puréed. It's good with grilled meats and chicken."

Robbie Day
San Francisco St. Bar & Grill

"I love this dressing on baked potatoes. It is so good that I eat it almost every day."

"Cooking is as satisfying to me as running a big corporation is satisfying to a business executive. I especially love to feed large groups of people."

Sylvia Johnson
Celebrations

Green Chile Vinaigrette

1	cup green chile peppers, roasted, peeled, seeded and diced medium
2	cloves fresh garlic, finely chopped
¼	cup fresh cilantro, chopped
1	tablespoon fresh oregano, chopped
2	tablespoons yellow mustard
2½	teaspoons sugar
1½	cups olive oil
½	teaspoon salt *(or to taste)*
1½	teaspoons black pepper *(or to taste)*

Place the green chile peppers, garlic, cilantro, oregano, yellow mustard, and sugar in a food processor. Coarsely purée the ingredients. With the food processor constantly running, slowly dribble in the olive oil.

Season the vinaigrette with the salt and black pepper.

makes approximately 2 cups

Bêchamel Sauce

4	tablespoons butter
4	tablespoons flour
2	cups milk
4	whole cloves
1	small white onion, peeled
1	small bay leaf
	salt and white pepper *(to taste)*

In a medium saucepan place the butter and heat it on low until it is melted and hot. Add the flour and stir it in well. Cook the mixture for 3 to 5 minutes.

While constantly stirring, slowly add the milk.

Insert the cloves into the onion. Place the onion and bay leaf in the saucepan. Continue to cook the sauce for 10 to 15 minutes, or until it thickens.

Remove the onion and bay leaf.

Season the sauce with the salt and white pepper.

makes 2 cups

Green Chile Sauce

¼	cup flour
1	cup water
2	tablespoons butter
½	medium yellow onion, chopped
3	cloves fresh garlic, finely chopped
1	pound green chile peppers, roasted, peeled, seeded and diced
½	teaspoon dried Mexican oregano
1½	teaspoons salt
2	cups water

In a blender place the flour and the 1 cup of water, and blend them so that they form a smooth roux. Pour the roux through a fine sieve to remove any lumps, and set it aside.

In a medium saucepan place the butter and heat it on medium high until it is melted and hot. Add the yellow onions and garlic. Sauté them for 5 minutes, or until the onions are translucent.

Add the green chile peppers, Mexican oregano, salt, and the 2 cups of water. Stir the ingredients together. Bring them to a boil and then simmer them for 30 minutes.

Return the heat to a boil. While stirring constantly, slowly pour in the roux. When the sauce begins to thicken, turn off the heat.

makes approximately 1 quart

Jalapeño Citrus Relish

1	jicama, peeled and diced small
⅓	fresh pineapple, peeled, cored and diced small
½	green bell pepper, seeded and diced small
4	oranges, peeled, seeded, segmented and diced small
6	red jalapeño chile peppers, seeded and diced small
½	bunch scallions, thinly sliced
⅛	cup fresh parsley, chopped
¼	cup fresh cilantro, chopped
2	tablespoons sugar
¼	cup rice wine vinegar
¼	cup apple cider vinegar

In a large bowl place all the ingredients and toss them together.

makes approximately 1 quart

"I think there's a magical, addictive power to green chile. Even though I can't handle it anymore because of digestive problems, every now and then I can't resist having some.....especially when it's fresh. Just the smell of it makes me want to go grab a tortilla and put a whole roasted green chile pepper in it with a little salt, and eat it like that."

"My mother and grandmother lived next door to each other when I was growing up, and both of them were fantastic cooks. My brothers and sisters and I would go from one house to the other, to check out what each one was making for dinner, so we could eat at the house with the best meal. Sometimes we would eat twice because they both were so good."

Ivan Macias
Tortilla Flats

"This is a spicy relish. I like to use the red jalapeños instead of the green, because they have a little more flavor and they add a nice color. If you can't find them use the green, but add a little red bell pepper."

Rustin Newton
Staab House

Tequila Dill Lime Butter

1	pound butter, softened
⅛	cup fresh dill, finely chopped
1	lime, zested (outer green part grated off), **zest finely minced and lime freshly squeezed**
1½	shots Cuervo Especial tequila

In a medium mixing bowl place all the ingredients and mix them together well.

Form the butter into a log and wrap it in plastic wrap. Freeze the butter and cut off slices as they are needed.

makes 1 pound

"I developed this recipe years ago when I was in Albuquerque, and brought it with me to this restaurant in Santa Fe. At the time I had the only tequila butter around, but by the next summer it seemed that everyone had it. This tastes best with fish."

Tony Trujillo
Inn at Loretto

Roasted Corn & Black Bean Salsa

1	tablespoon peanut oil
4	Roma tomatoes, seeded and finely diced
1	small yellow onion, finely diced
1	clove fresh garlic, finely chopped
¾	cup cooked black beans
2	ears corn, roasted (see chef's comments on this page) **and kernels removed**
1	jalapeño chile pepper, finely chopped
3	tablespoons fresh cilantro, chopped
⅛	teaspoon cumin seeds, toasted (see chef's comments on page 68) **and ground**
2	tablespoons honey
1	tablespoon olive oil
1	lime, freshly juiced
	salt (to taste)

In a medium sauté pan place the peanut oil and heat it on medium high until it is hot. Add the tomatoes, yellow onions, and garlic. Sauté the ingredients for 5 minutes, or until the onions are translucent.

In a medium bowl place the tomato mixture and the rest of the ingredients. Stir them together. Cover the bowl with plastic wrap and let the salsa sit for 2 hours at room temperature.

makes approximately 3 cups

"I serve this salsa warm with grilled fish or chicken, or cold with chips. It has such a wonderful taste that you could use it with almost anything, and it looks gorgeous because of all the different colors. Just be sure that you don't overcook the black beans.....they should be a bit al dente."

Peter Raub
Santa Fe Market

"We roast the corn with the husks removed, so the kernels get a bit browned. The sweetness of the corn really comes out this way, and gives the salsa a delicious flavor."

Marsha Chobol
Santa Fe Market

Cranberry Chipotle Compote

1	tablespoon vegetable oil
3	medium apples, peeled, cored and diced medium
2	medium pears, peeled, cored and diced medium
⅓	cup raisins
¼	cup Grand Marnier
1	pound fresh cranberries, rinsed and drained
4	ounces chipotle chile peppers *(in adobo sauce)*, **finely chopped**
2	teaspoons ground cinnamon
1	cup sugar
½	orange, zested *(outer orange part grated off)* **and finely chopped**
½	cup orange juice, freshly squeezed
½	teaspoon nutmeg
¼	cup Grand Marnier

In a large saucepan place the vegetable oil and heat it on medium high until it is hot. Add the apples, pears, and raisins. Sauté the ingredients for 3 to 5 minutes, or until they soften.

Add the first ¼ cup of Grand Marnier and deglaze the pan. Add the cranberries, chipotle chile peppers, cinnamon, sugar, orange zest, and orange juice. Stir the ingredients together and simmer them for 40 to 50 minutes, or until they begin to thicken. Add the nutmeg and the second ¼ cup of Grand Marnier, and stir them in.

Place the compote in an airtight container and refrigerate it.

makes approximately 1 quart

Salsa Molcajete

5	medium tomatoes, roasted *(see chef's comments on page 72)* and peeled
15	jalapeño chile peppers, roasted and peeled
1	teaspoon granulated garlic
1	teaspoon salt
6	sprigs fresh cilantro, chopped

In a food processor place the tomatoes, jalapeño chile peppers, garlic, and salt. Process the ingredients for 3 to 4 seconds, or until the salsa is slightly chunky.

Add the cilantro and stir it in.

makes approximately 2 cups

Sauces, Dips, and Condiments

"I've never been a big cranberry relish fan, but this recipe is one that I love. The chipotle chile peppers together with all of the fruits make a delicious combination of sweet and hot. Serve this at your Thanksgiving dinner for a delightful Southwestern change."

"Long ago I learned a theory about food, which basically is this: If you have two flavors, they should both be detectable, but they also should combine to create a third new taste. This way there is an explosion of flavors."

Rustin Newton
Staab House

"To really appreciate this salsa you have to be a true fiery foods lover, because it is really hot! I like to eat it with chips or scrambled eggs. This is the kind of thing, like tabasco, that you would use to give other foods a kick."

"I got this recipe from Nicho Nuñez, a Mexican chef. 'Molcajete' refers to the mortar and pestle the Mexicans use to grind the ingredients."

Darrell Hedgecoke
Mañana

Green Chile Cheese Sauce

8	tablespoons butter *(unsalted)*
6	tablespoons all purpose flour
3	cups milk
¼	cup green chile peppers, roasted, peeled, seeded and diced
½	teaspoon paprika
¼	teaspoon ground nutmeg
	salt and white pepper *(to taste)*
¼	cup cheddar cheese, grated

In a medium saucepan place the butter and heat it on medium until it is melted. Add the flour and whisk it in for 3 minutes.

While whisking constantly, slowly add the milk. Cook the sauce for 5 minutes, or until it thickens. Add the green chile peppers, paprika, nutmeg, salt, and white pepper. Stir the ingredients together. While whisking constantly, slowly add the cheddar cheese. Simmer the sauce for 3 minutes, or until the cheese is melted and it is thick and smooth.

makes approximately 3 cups

Ginger Jalapeño Lime Vinaigrette

1	2" piece fresh ginger root, peeled and finely chopped
3	jalapeño chile peppers, seeded and finely chopped
1½	teaspoons fresh garlic, finely chopped
2	teaspoons chile pequin *(hot red chile flakes)*
1	teaspoon ground ginger
⅓	cup sugar
½	cup lime juice, freshly squeezed
⅛	cup white vinegar
2	cups olive oil
¼	cup red bell peppers, diced small
¼	cup fresh parsley, chopped
	salt and white pepper *(to taste)*

In a food processor place the ginger root, jalapeño chile peppers, garlic, chile pequin, ground ginger, sugar, lime juice, and white vinegar. Purée the ingredients for 45 seconds. Let the purée sit for 10 minutes. With the food processor constantly running, slowly dribble in the olive oil. Add the red bell peppers, parsley, salt, and white pepper.

makes approximately 3 cups

"This is a basic cheese sauce with a little spice from the green chiles. It's very good with macaroni or as a topping for vegetables, such as cauliflower."

"I enjoy cooking at home because it's a nice diversion from doing huge quantities. It's fun to listen to good music when I cook and have people over for dinner."

Peter Raub
Santa Fe Market

"One reason why I like to cook is that I like to eat what I make. Both of my grandmothers were chefs and I grew up eating really wonderful, unusual, exotic food."

Marsha Chobol
Santa Fe Market

"I developed this recipe because of America's growing interest in Asian cuisines. The ginger goes very well with the hot chiles, garlic, and lime. It's a snappy vinaigrette, full of character and flavor. Serve it as a dipping sauce for crab or bay shrimp, or as a dressing for a seafood salad."

Rustin Newton
Staab House

Eggs, Cheese & Vegetarian

Baked Potato & Cheese Enchiladas with Zucchini Avocado Sauce

Baked Potato & Cheese Enchiladas

½	cup olive oil
3	large baking potatoes, peeled and diced into ¼" pieces
1	medium red onion, finely minced
2	green bell peppers, seeded and finely diced
½	cup fresh cilantro, chopped
½	teaspoon epazote *(see chef's comments on next page)*
	salt and black pepper *(to taste)*
¼	cup olive oil *(or as needed)*
12	corn tortillas
3	cups raw milk Monterey Jack cheese, grated
	Zucchini Avocado Sauce *(recipe on next page)*

Preheat the oven to 375°.

In a large skillet place the ½ cup of olive oil and heat it on medium high until it is hot. Add the potatoes, red onions, green bell peppers, cilantro, and epazote. Sauté the ingredients for 10 minutes, or until the potatoes begin to brown.

Add the salt and black pepper. Remove the skillet from the heat and let the mixture cool.

In another large skillet place the ¼ cup of olive oil and heat it on medium until it is hot. Place each tortilla in the hot oil for a few seconds so that it softens. Remove it and drain it on a paper towel.

In the center of each tortilla place several tablespoons of the potato mixture. Sprinkle on some of the grated cheese. Roll the tortilla up and place it in a long, oiled baking dish with the seam side down. Repeat this process for the rest of the tortillas. Pour the Zucchini Avocado Sauce on top. Sprinkle on any remaining cheese.

Bake the enchiladas *(uncovered)* for 35 to 40 minutes, or until everything is hot and bubbly.

serves 6

"People are often shocked when they hear of potato enchiladas. This sounds like it would be an incredibly heavy dish, but it's not heavy at all. It's rich, filling, but not over-powering.....it's perfect!"

"The traditional way to soften tortillas is to quickly sauté them in lard. I call for olive oil in this dish because I wanted to keep it truly vegetarian."

"I try to use raw milk Monterey Jack cheese instead of pasteurized, because this adds another dimension of flavor to the dish. I first tasted raw milk cheese when I worked in New York at a large specialty food store, Dean & Deluca. I was amazed at its incredible flavor. If you can't find it, then just use the pasteurized kind."

Jonathan Horst
Adobo Catering

Zucchini Avocado Sauce

¼	cup olive oil
1	habanero chile pepper, finely minced
3	small zucchini, diced into ¼" pieces
1	large yellow onion, diced small
2	cloves fresh garlic, finely chopped
¼	cup fresh cilantro, chopped
3	large avocados, peeled, pits removed, mashed and puréed
	water *(as needed)*
	salt *(to taste)*

In a large skillet place the olive oil and heat it on medium high until it is hot. Add the habanero chile pepper, zucchini, yellow onions, garlic, and cilantro. Sauté the ingredients for 5 minutes, or until they are barely tender.

Add the mashed avocados and stir them in. Add and stir in enough water so that a thick sauce is achieved.

Season the sauce with the salt.

makes approximately 4 cups

"Most vegetarians find this sauce to be outrageously good. The avocados are cooked, which gives them a unique flavor.....slightly nutty and squash-like. And, the diced zucchini adds a nice texture. Use this sauce on any kind of enchiladas.....especially chicken or cheese. It's great!"

Jonathan Horst
Adobo Catering

Chipotle Chile Black Beans

1	cup dried black beans, washed and drained
2	quarts cold water
1	small yellow onion, finely diced
1	clove fresh garlic, finely chopped
1	dried chipotle chile pepper
1	tablespoon epazote *(see chef's comments on this page)*
1	teaspoon dried sage, crushed
1	teaspoon ground Mexican oregano
2	bay leaves
	salt *(to taste)*

In a large saucepan place all of the ingredients *(except for the salt)*. Bring the ingredients to a boil.

Reduce the heat and simmer the beans for 3 hours, or until they are tender. Add the salt.

Remove the chipotle chile pepper and the bay leaves before serving the beans.

serves 4 to 6

"When I cook beans, I like to use a lot of water. The beans keep a better texture and they will be easier to digest."

"If you can't find a dried chipotle chile pepper you can use one that is canned in adobo sauce."

"Epazote is an herb that has a very distinctive, earthy flavor. To me it is an essential ingredient for the success of this black bean recipe. It's kind of like an anchovy in that it gives a vague, background flavor that you don't really focus on."

Peter Raub
Santa Fe Market

Tortilla Stew

¼	cup vegetable oil
¼	cup olive oil
12	corn tortillas, cut into 8 wedges each
2	large yellow onions, quartered and then sliced
6	poblano chile peppers, seeds and ribs removed, and chopped
2	cups tomatoes, peeled, seeded and chopped
2	cloves fresh garlic, finely chopped
1	teaspoon epazote *(see chef's comments on page 123)*
6	cups chicken stock *(see chef's comments on this page)*
1	cup heavy cream
½	cup fresh cilantro, chopped
½	cup Reggiano *(parmesan)* cheese, freshly grated
	salt and black pepper *(to taste)*

In a small bowl place the vegetable and olive oils, and stir them together.

In a large frying pan place half of the oil mixture and heat it on medium high until it is hot. Add the tortilla wedges and fry them for 1 to 2 minutes on each side, or until they are crisp. Drain them on paper towels and set them aside.

In a medium stockpot place the rest of the oil mixture and heat it on medium until it is hot. Add the yellow onions and poblano chile peppers. Sauté them for 5 minutes or until the onions are translucent. Add the tomatoes, garlic, and epazote. Cook the ingredients for 2 minutes. Add the chicken stock and simmer everything for 10 minutes. Turn off the heat.

Add the fried tortilla chips, heavy cream, cilantro, and cheese. Let the stew sit for several minutes so that the tortilla chips soak up the broth.

Add the salt and black pepper. Serve the stew immediately.

serves 8

"Tortilla soup is from Mexico and there are a million different recipes for it. I call this one a stew because it is very thick, with hardly any broth. It is really rich and delicious. Serve just a small amount at the beginning of a meal, followed by a simple entrée, such as a grilled meat with a steamed vegetable."

"Be careful not to overcook the tortillas or they will be bitter. Don't brown them.....just let them get crisp."

"It's important that the chicken stock is homemade and not canned. For a simple stock just poach a whole chicken (or pieces) in about two quarts of water with a teaspoon of salt. You don't need to add any vegetables to the broth because it should have a pure chicken taste. Then, according to the recipe you are making, you add the other flavors."

Jonathan Horst
Adobo Catering

Spicy Migas

"What makes this dish good is the contrast of textures, with the crisp tortillas and soft eggs, and all of the wonderful different flavors..... especially when you get a little bit of the hot jalapeño to really wake you up!"

"I've had training in a lot of different fields, from economics to city planning to teaching to counseling in a psychiatric hospital. Although I enjoyed the mental exercise of my other professions, I really do love the feeling of working with my hands and creating something for people to enjoy. Also, because I am basically an impatient person, I find the immediate feedback from people to be wonderful."

Harry Shapiro
Harry's Road House

4	tablespoons butter
½	medium yellow onion, diced medium
½	green bell pepper, seeded and diced medium
2	pickled jalapeño chile peppers, finely chopped
½	tomato, seeded and diced medium
8	eggs, well beaten
4	corn tortillas, cut into thin strips and deep-fried
1	cup cheddar cheese, grated
1	cup salsa *(your favorite)*
4	flour tortillas, warmed
1	cup refried beans *(recipe on page 294)*

In a large sauté pan place the butter and heat it on medium high until it is melted and hot. Add the yellow onions and green bell peppers. Sauté them for 5 minutes, or until the onions are translucent.

Add the pickled jalapeño chile peppers, tomatoes, and eggs. Scramble the ingredients until the eggs begin to set. Add the tortilla strips and stir them in.

On each of 4 individual serving plates place the migas. Top them with the grated cheese. Serve the salsa, flour tortilla, and refried beans on the side.

serves 4

Stuffed Pumpkin Bread with Red Chile Sauce, Queso Blanco & Caramelized Apples

Stuffed Pumpkin Bread

1	tablespoon olive oil
¼	cup hot green chile peppers, roasted, peeled, seeded and diced
¼	cup yellow squash, diced
1	cup corn kernels
1	small yellow onion, chopped
¼	cup piñon nuts *(pine nuts)*, toasted *(see chef's comments on page 325)*
1	24-ounce can pumpkin purée
2	eggs
¼	cup molasses
¼	cup honey
¼	cup vegetable oil
3	cups flour
¼	teaspoon ground cinnamon
¼	teaspoon ground nutmeg
1½	teaspoons baking powder
1½	tablespoons baking soda
	Paul's Red Chile Sauce *(recipe on page 110)*
	Queso Blanco *(recipe on next page)*
	Caramelized Apples *(recipe on next page)*

Preheat the oven to 400°.

In a large sauté pan place the olive oil and heat it on medium high until it is hot. Add the green chile peppers, squash, corn, yellow onions, and piñon nuts. Sauté the ingredients for 5 minutes. Set the mixture aside.

In a medium bowl place the pumpkin purée, eggs, molasses, honey, and vegetable oil. Mix the ingredients together and set them aside.

In a medium large bowl sift together the flour, cinnamon, nutmeg, baking powder, and baking soda. Add the pumpkin mixture and fold it in *(do not over mix)*.

(continued on next page)

"A vegetarian ex-girlfriend of mine came up with this recipe. I liked it so much that I decided to put it on our menu, where it has remained since the day we opened. It is one of the most interesting vegetarian dishes that I have ever come across."

"The flavors of the Red Chile, Queso Blanco, and Caramelized Apples do a wonderful job together. And the presentation is really neat, with the deep red sauce on the brown pumpkin bread, and the clean white color of the cheese sauce."

Paul Hunsicker
Paul's Restaurant

"I've never done anything else but cook. My first job was in a kitchen at the age of sixteen. I didn't really start to appreciate cooking, however, until I was allowed to experiment and be creative. What I love most about being a chef is that the reward is instantaneous. You know immediately if the food you have prepared is good or bad. Also, the positive feedback from the customers is a definite rush."

"Queso blanco means a white cheese sauce. Here we use feta and Swiss cheese with cream. The combination is simple, but exquisite. Be sure to use Greek feta that is packed in brine, and not goat cheese. This sauce is wonderful with casseroles, pastas, and vegetables."

"These caramelized apples are heavenly on vanilla ice cream. Or you can purée them for an applesauce, or use them in a pie."

Paul Hunsicker
Paul's Restaurant

Lightly oil 2 loaf pans and dust them with flour. Divide the dough into 4 equal amounts. In the bottom of each pan place ¼ of the dough and pat it down. Place the sautéed vegetable mixture on top. Pat out another ¼ of the dough and place it on top.

Bake the bread for 45 minutes, or until a toothpick inserted in the center comes out clean.

Slice each loaf into 4 sections *(about 3" wide)*.

In the center of each of 8 individual serving plates pour Paul's Red Chile Sauce. Place a bread slice on top. Pour on the Queso Blanco. Garnish the dish with the Caramelized Apples.

serves 8

Queso Blanco

¼   **cup feta cheese, crumbled**
¼   **cup Swiss cheese, grated**
½   **cup heavy cream**

In a small saucepan place the feta cheese, Swiss cheese, and heavy cream. While whisking constantly, simmer the ingredients for 5 to 10 minutes, or until the cheeses are melted and a smooth sauce is formed.

makes 1 cup

Caramelized Apples

¼   **pound butter**
4   **Granny Smith apples, peeled, cored and sliced**
¼   **cup sugar**
1   **dash cinnamon**

In a medium saucepan place the butter and heat it on high until the butter is melted and hot. Add the apples, sugar, and cinnamon. Sauté the ingredients for 10 minutes, or until the apples are tender and the sugar is caramelized.

makes approximately 2 cups

Black Bean Flautas

½   **cup vegetable oil** *(or as needed)*
12   **blue corn tortillas**
¼   **cup red onion, finely chopped**
2   **dried red chile peppers, crushed**
2   **tablespoons fresh cilantro, chopped**
2   **cloves fresh garlic, finely chopped**
½   **teaspoon white pepper** *(or to taste)*
¼   **cup dry sherry**
1   **cup dried black beans, washed, cooked, drained and**
     coarsely puréed
3½   **cups vegetable oil**
½   **pound smoked gouda cheese, grated**
1   **small red bell pepper, seeded and thinly sliced**
1   **small green bell pepper, seeded and thinly sliced**
1   **small yellow bell pepper, seeded and thinly sliced**
     Guacamole *(recipe on page 245)*
1   **cup sour cream**

Preheat the oven to 350°.

In a medium sauté pan place the ½ cup of vegetable oil and heat it on medium high until it is hot. One at a time, place each tortilla in the hot oil and fry it for 10 seconds, or until it is softened. Drain the tortillas on paper towels and set them aside.

Remove all but 3 tablespoons of the oil from the pan *(add more oil if needed)* and heat it on medium high until it is hot. Add the red onions, crushed red chile peppers, cilantro, garlic, and white pepper. Cook the ingredients for 3 minutes.

Add the sherry and stir it in. Cook the ingredients for 2 minutes.

Transfer the mixture to a large bowl. Add the black bean purée and fold it in.

Spread the mixture on each tortilla *(leave 1" of the tortilla bare around the edges)*. Roll the tortilla up and insert a toothpick through each end to keep it closed.

In a large saucepan place the 3½ cups of vegetable oil and heat it on medium high until it is very hot. Place each flauta in the oil and deep-fry it for 2 minutes, or until it is crisp.

Drain the flautas on paper towels and remove the toothpicks.

(continued on next page)

"We have a seasonal restaurant on top of La Fonda, called La Terraza, which is open during the summer. This recipe was developed as one of our vegetarian dishes for its menu. We took our black bean soup recipe and altered it to make a filling for the flautas.....and it came out wonderful. The combination of the different flavors of the beans, cheese, and bell peppers is delicious."

Lela Cross
La Plazuela

"In Mexico, flautas are flat and grilled. But this is New Mexico, and here we have re-defined what a flauta is. To us, they are rolled up and deep-fried. You can make flautas with just about anything.....cheeses, vegetables, seafood, beef, or chicken."

"I like to deep-fry the flautas just a little bit, to give the tortilla a crunch. They are still cool in the middle, so that's why I finish them off in the oven."

Tomas Cross
La Plazuela

Chicken & Baby Greens Salad with Spicy Asian Vinaigrette

Chicken & Baby Greens Salad

"This is a light, easy-to-assemble salad that would be perfect for a brunch or lunch dish. You could easily substitute grilled shrimp for the chicken."

2	tablespoons light sesame oil
1½	pounds chicken breast, skin and bones removed, and cut into thin strips.
1	pound mixed baby greens
6	Roma tomatoes, thinly sliced
1	bunch scallions, thinly sliced
	Spicy Asian Vinaigrette *(recipe follows)*
1	tablespoon sesame seeds, toasted *(see chef's comments on this page)*

In a large sauté pan place the sesame oil and heat it on medium high until it is very hot. Add the chicken strips and sauté them for 3 to 4 minutes, or until they are just cooked. Remove the pan from the heat and let the chicken cool.

"I recommend buying unbleached sesame seeds in the bulk section of a health food store. You can toast them under the broiler, or in a dry pan on top of the stove. Just let them get lightly brown."

On each of 6 individual serving plates place the baby greens. Arrange the chicken, tomatoes, and scallions on top of the greens. Dribble on the Spicy Asian Vinaigrette. Sprinkle on the toasted sesame seeds.

serves 6

Spicy Asian Vinaigrette

"This vinaigrette is one of those wonderful American mish-mash recipes that borrows from Asian flavors. It's one of our most popular dressings at the restaurant."

Sarah Alvord
Zia Diner

1	teaspoon sugar
1	tablespoon soy sauce
2	tablespoons lemon juice, freshly squeezed
¼	cup rice wine vinegar
2	tablespoons chile oil
3	tablespoons toasted sesame oil
½	cup peanut oil

In a medium bowl place the sugar, soy sauce, lemon juice, and rice wine vinegar. While whisking constantly, slowly dribble in the three oils.

makes approximately 1 cup

Adobo Pasta Salad with Chipotle Sundried Tomato Dressing

Adobo Pasta Salad

2	pounds penne pasta *(see chef's comments on page 156)*, **cooked al dente, rinsed in cold water and drained**
2	small yellow squash, sliced into long strips, grilled and diced
2	small zucchini, sliced into long strips, grilled and diced
1	small red onion, finely chopped
1	red bell pepper, seeded and finely chopped
½	cup sundried tomatoes, reconstituted and thinly sliced
3	Roma tomatoes, chopped small
1	16-ounce can corn, drained
1	cup Chipotle Sundried Tomato Dressing *(recipe follows)*
½	cup asiago cheese, freshly grated

In a large bowl place all of the ingredients *(except for the asiago cheese)* and toss them together. Sprinkle the cheese on top of each serving.

serves 8

"I love to eat out at other restaurants. I think I'm a great customer, because I'm very understanding, tip well, and often send my compliments to the chef. Of course, if the food or service is bad, I'll let the restaurant people know that as well."

Rocky Durham
Zia Diner

Chipotle Sundried Tomato Dressing

½	teaspoon ground coriander
½	teaspoon ground cumin
½	teaspoon ground cinnamon
½	teaspoon ground anise
½	cup sundried tomatoes, reconstituted and chopped
1	chipotle chile pepper *(in adobo sauce)*, **puréed**
½	cup tomato juice
2	tablespoons molasses
3	tablespoons sherry vinegar
¼	teaspoon liquid smoke
½	tablespoon salt
2	cups olive oil

Heat a small, non-stick sauté pan on high until it is hot. Add the coriander, cumin, cinnamon, and anise. Roll the spices around until their perfume reaches your nose.

(continued on next page)

"I love chipotle peppers in adobo sauce and use them in a lot of my recipes. This particular dressing is the result of one of my many experimentations in the kitchen."

"I did not like to cook until I started cooking in restaurants. It's wonderful, because everything is right there at your fingertips..... all the different food products, pots and pans, and exotic utensils. There is no need to go grocery shopping, which I hate!"

Kristy Rawson
Zia Diner

In a food processor place the toasted spices, puréed chipotle chile pepper, tomato juice, molasses, sherry vinegar, liquid smoke, and salt. Purée the ingredients together.

With the food processor constantly running, slowly drizzle in the olive oil.

makes 3 cups

Curried Chicken Salad

"This dish has been served at El Farol since its beginning, and probably is the most popular thing we offer. People are constantly asking us for the recipe, and we find it difficult to explain verbally because of the curry oil, which is made separately several days in advance. I'm looking forward to the publication of this book so that I can refer our future customers to it."

"When you make this dish it is safest to add only part of the curried mayonnaise at first, and then taste it. The color of the salad should not be too neon or bright, and the curry flavor should not be overwhelming. Keep tasting and adding more mayonnaise until it seems to be right. Also, remember that the heat will increase after the salad sits for several hours."

Kit Baum
El Farol

1	cup mayonnaise
¼	cup lemon juice, freshly squeezed
¼	cup Curry Oil *(recipe on page 305)*
4	boneless chicken breasts, skin removed, cooked and cut into 1" cubes
3	celery stalks, sliced medium
1	bunch scallions, thinly sliced
½	cup seedless grapes
¼	cup fresh Italian parsley, chopped
1	tablespoon paprika
1	teaspoon cayenne pepper *(or to taste)*
	salt and white pepper *(to taste)*
1	head red leaf lettuce, leaves separated, washed and dried

In a medium bowl place the mayonnaise, lemon juice, and Curry Oil. Stir the ingredients together.

In another medium bowl place the chicken, celery, scallions, grapes, Italian parsley, paprika, cayenne pepper, salt, and white pepper. Toss the ingredients together.

Add the curried mayonnaise mixture *(see chef's comments on this page)* and mix it in well.

Cover the salad with plastic wrap and refrigerate it for 2 hours.

On each of 4 individual serving plates place several leaves of the red leaf lettuce. Place the Curried Chicken Salad on top.

serves 4

Warm Spinach Salad with Charred Tomato Chile Vinaigrette

Warm Spinach Salad

2   **bunches spinach, stems and veins removed, washed and dried**
1   **cup shiitake mushrooms, sliced**
     Charred Tomato Chile Vinaigrette *(recipe follows)*, **heated**
¼   **cup Reggiano cheese** *(parmesan)*, **freshly grated**
     cracked black pepper *(to taste)*

On each of 6 individual serving plates place the spinach. Arrange the shiitake mushroom slices on top.

Pour the Charred Tomato Chile Vinaigrette on top. Sprinkle on the Reggiano cheese and cracked black pepper.

serves 6

Charred Tomato Chile Vinaigrette

4   **large tomatoes, grilled and finely chopped**
2   **medium red onions, grilled and minced**
2   **dried chipotle chile peppers, minced**
1   **tablespoon fresh basil, chopped**
½   **tablespoon fresh Italian parsley, chopped**
2   **limes, juiced**
1   **tablespoon balsamic vinegar**
¼   **teaspoon cayenne pepper**
½   **teaspoon salt**
¼   **teaspoon black pepper**

In a jar with a tight lid place all of the ingredients. Shake them together so they are well blended.

makes approximately 2 cups

"This is a very simple, light salad that has a delicious flavor. Once the vinaigrette is made, it takes only minutes to put together. The only thing I recommend is to buy the loose spinach leaves that are bound, instead of the kind that are packaged in cellophane. The leaves will be much more tender. It's a mystery to me why people buy the pre-packaged spinach, because they still have to wash it and remove the stems and veins."

"I love this vinaigrette. Not only does it have a fantastic flavor, it is easy to make and is extremely versatile. It's excellent as a sauce for grilled chicken, shrimp, or fish. And, if you add it to a pasta along with some mozzarella cheese and Italian sausage, you will have a gourmet entrée!"

Pete Zimmer
Inn of the Anasazi

Spicy Fried Chicken Salad

4	whole chicken breasts, skin and bones removed, and cut into 1" strips
1	cup buttermilk
2	cups flour
2	teaspoons cayenne pepper
1	teaspoon salt *(or to taste)*
1	teaspoon black pepper *(or to taste)*
3	cups vegetable oil
4	cups baby greens, washed and dried
	Blue Cheese Dressing *(recipe on page 114)*
½	cup cooked beets, sliced into thin strips

In a large bowl place the chicken breasts and buttermilk. Cover the bowl with plastic wrap and marinate the chicken at room temperature for 1 hour.

In a medium bowl place the flour, cayenne pepper, salt, and black pepper. Mix the ingredients together.

Remove the chicken from the buttermilk *(let a small amount of the buttermilk drain off the pieces)*.

Dredge the chicken strips in the flour mixture so that they are well coated.

In a large, heavy sauté pan place the vegetable oil and heat it on medium high until it is hot. Place the coated chicken strips in the hot oil and fry them for 4 minutes on each side, or until they are golden brown and just done.

On each of 8 individual serving plates place the baby greens. Arrange the chicken strips around each plate in a spoke-like pattern. Place the Blue Cheese Dressing in the center. Place the sliced beets on top.

serves 8

"This is an old, classic recipe from the South. Thanks to our new President, Mr. Clinton, I believe that there is going to be a revival of southern cooking. This makes me happy, because I'm from Louisiana, and I have always loved the cooking from that part of the country."

"The chicken is very spicy, but its heat is cooled down with the Blue Cheese Dressing. I love the different tastes and textures in this salad, with the crispiness of the chicken and baby greens, and the rich creaminess of the dressing."

"When you wash your baby greens be sure that they get completely dried before you serve them. Otherwise, the dressing will just run off."

"I am not a chef. I am just a very good cook who likes to eat."

Sylvia Johnson
Celebrations

Nopalito Walnut Salad with Jalapeño Raspberry Vinaigrette

Nopalito Walnut Salad

6	heads baby romaine lettuce, washed and dried
2	heads Boston bibb lettuce, washed and dried
2	tangerines, peeled, segmented and seeds removed
½	cup walnuts, toasted
12	mushrooms, cleaned
12	black olives, pitted
4	ounces Nopalito cactus *(see chef's comments on this page)*, **cut into thin strips**
1	small jicama, peeled and cut into matchsticks that are ¼" thick and 2" long
1	pint fresh raspberries
	Jalapeño Raspberry Vinaigrette *(recipe follows)*

On each of 6 individual salad plates place the romaine lettuce. Place the bibb lettuce on top. Artfully arrange the tangerines, walnuts, mushrooms, olives, Nopalito strips, jicama, and raspberries on top. Dribble on the Jalapeño Raspberry Vinaigrette.

serves 6

Jalapeño Raspberry Vinaigrette

1	jalapeño chile pepper, seeded and finely chopped
1½	cups walnut oil
½	cup raspberry vinegar
½	teaspoon lemon juice, freshly squeezed
1	tablespoon sugar
1	bay leaf

In a medium bowl place the jalapeño chile pepper, walnut oil, raspberry vinegar, lemon juice, and sugar. Whisk the ingredients together.

Add the bay leaf to the vinaigrette.

Cover the bowl with plastic wrap and refrigerate the vinaigrette overnight. Remove the bay leaf. Mix the vinaigrette well before serving.

makes 2 cups

"Nopalitos are cactus leaves. They come in jars and you can find them in the gourmet section of your grocery store. You can eat them raw, sauté them, or bake them. The flavor is hard to describe. It's kind of a surprise taste. You have to experience it directly in order to know what it's like."

Lela Cross
La Plazuela

"This is a very interesting salad that we serve during raspberry season. It's especially popular with people who are health conscious and who love fruit. If the idea of the Nopalito cactus is too strange for you, leave it out."

Tomas Cross
La Plazuela

"This carrot salad is very popular in Thailand. It is served with other dishes and is used as a cleansing item for the palate, with small bites taken between bites of other foods that are spicy. The Thai pepper flakes have a distinct flavor; they can be found in Oriental stores. Otherwise, use chile pequin."

"We serve what is called high style Thai cuisine, which is what used to be royal Thai cuisine. It incorporates the French methods of cooking techniques with far Eastern ingredients. It's usually spicy, although not always, and is very rich in flavor, even though no dairy products are typically used. It is marvelous food because it is both healthy and wonderfully flavorful."

Ron Messick
Restaurant Thao

"Tree ear mushrooms are a common Asian ingredient. They are purported to have powerful healing qualities. They are easy to find in this country and are very easy to cook with. All you have to do is reconstitute them in water."

Patrick Lambert
Restaurant Thao

Thai Carrot Salad

3	cloves fresh garlic, finely chopped
1	teaspoon Thai pepper flakes *(see chef's comments on this page)*
1	tablespoon light sesame seeds
1	tablespoon dark sesame seeds
3	tablespoons Thai fish sauce *(see chef's comments on page 113)*
¼	cup rice wine vinegar
¼	cup peanut oil
2	cups carrots, peeled and shredded

In a medium bowl place the garlic, pepper flakes, light and dark sesame seeds, Thai fish sauce, rice wine vinegar, and peanut oil. Whisk the ingredients together.

Add the carrots and toss them in.

serves 8

Thai Cucumber Salad

2	cucumbers, peeled, seeded and thinly sliced
½	small red onion, finely diced
1	ounce tree ear mushrooms, softened in warm water and sliced *(see chef's comments on this page)*
1	tablespoon jalapeño chile pepper, seeded and finely chopped
1½	tablespoons Thai fish sauce *(see chef's comments on page 113)*
1	tablespoon toasted sesame oil
1½	tablespoons lime juice, freshly squeezed

In a medium bowl place all of the ingredients and toss them together.

serves 8

Grilled Shrimp Salad with Mixed Greens & Spicy Tomatillo Salsa

Grilled Shrimp Salad with Mixed Greens

4   tablespoons olive oil
2   tablespoons balsamic vinegar
     salt and black pepper *(to taste)*
4   cups mixed baby greens, cleaned and dried
12   jumbo shrimp, peeled and deveined *(leave tails intact)*
     Spicy Tomatillo Salsa *(recipe on next page)*

In a small bowl place the olive oil, balsamic vinegar, salt, and black pepper. Whisk the ingredients so that they are well blended.

In a salad bowl place the baby greens and toss them with the vinaigrette.

Grill the shrimp for 1 to 2 minutes on each side, or until they are opaque.

In the center of each of 4 individual serving plates place the dressed greens. Place the shrimp on top of the greens. Spoon the Spicy Tomatillo Salsa on top of the shrimp.

serves 4

"We feature this on our menu and it is well loved by our guests, especially in the summertime. It's light, healthy, and simple to make."

"I would say that I do about eighty percent of the cooking at home. When we first got married my wife wouldn't cook at all, because she didn't like the competition from me, a professional chef. But now she is gradually cooking more, and I really do appreciate it."

Jim Makinson
Bishop's Lodge

Spicy Tomatillo Salsa

2	**limes**
6	**tomatillos, husks removed, blanched, skins removed** *(see chef's comments of this page)*, **and diced medium**
3	**serrano chile peppers, seeded and finely diced**
¼	**cup red onions, finely diced**
¼	**bunch fresh cilantro, chopped**
¼	**cup extra virgin olive oil**

Remove the zest of the limes by carefully grating off the outer green skin. Blanch the zest in boiling water for 30 seconds and then place it in ice water. Chop the zest finely.

Separate the lime into sections and remove the seeds. Dice the lime meat into ¼" pieces.

In a medium bowl place the lime zest, diced limes, and the rest of the ingredients. Mix everything together well.

makes approximately 1 cup

Spicy Black Bean Salad

1	**pound dried black beans, cooked** *(see chef's comments on this page)*
4	**Roma tomatoes, seeded and diced**
1	**small red onion, diced**
1	**green bell pepper, seeded and diced**
1	**red bell pepper, seeded and diced**
½	**cup fresh cilantro, chopped**
3	**hot fresh chile peppers** *(jalapeño, habanero or serrano)*, **seeded and finely diced**
½	**cup lime juice, freshly squeezed**
½	**cup olive oil**
½	**teaspoon salt** *(or to taste)*

In a large bowl place all of the ingredients and stir them together. Serve the salad at room temperature.

serves 8

Sauces, Dips & Condiments

Southwestern Barbecue Sauce

1   chipotle chile pepper *(in adobo sauce)*
3   pickled jalapeño chile peppers
1   clove fresh garlic, finely chopped
1½   cups barbecue sauce *(your favorite)*
1   cup red chile powder
2   tablespoons sugar
2   tablespoons cider vinegar
     salt and black pepper *(to taste)*

In a food processor place all the ingredients and purée them so that they are smooth.

makes approximately 3 cups

> "We made this recipe up at the restaurant. It's based on a Texas-style barbecue sauce and then embellished with some red chile powder and smoky chipotle chiles. It is more of a hot sauce, rather than a sweet sauce, and it's delicious on anything you can imagine."
>
> Harry Shapiro
> Harry's Road House

Apple Green Chile Chutney

1   tablespoon peanut oil
¼   medium yellow onion, diced medium
2   teaspoons dried oregano
2   green chile peppers, roasted, peeled, seeded and diced small
2   tablespoons dried pasado chile peppers, coarsely ground
2   red jalapeño chile peppers, seeded and finely chopped
2   tablespoons sugar
1½   cups apple cider *(unfiltered)*
¼   cup cider vinegar
3   Granny Smith apples, peeled, cored and diced medium

In a large saucepan place the peanut oil and heat it on medium high until it is hot. Add the yellow onions and sauté them for 5 minutes, or until they are translucent. Add the oregano and cook the ingredients for 2 minutes.

Add the green, pasado and jalapeño chile peppers, sugar, apple cider, and cider vinegar. Stir everything together well. Simmer the ingredients for 10 minutes, or until the liquid is reduced by ½.

Add the apples and simmer them for 5 minutes, or until they are tender.

makes approximately 2 cups

> "We developed this recipe as something really nice to serve with our wild game, such as quail and rabbit. Kids love it and eat it like applesauce. It's also delicious with quesadillas."
>
> "I really admire the way Europeans sit around the dinner table for hours. A meal is a real family event. You can laugh, cry, yell, or whatever, but you are there at the table interacting with everyone else. The cohesiveness of the family culminates around food. In our country people are so busy, with both parents usually working, that most meals are rushed, with the different members often eating at different times."
>
> Mark Kiffin
> Coyote Cafe

Almond Smoked Morita Salsa

2	tablespoons butter
½	pound blanched almonds
⅛	ounce dried morita chile peppers
1½	ounces sundried tomatoes
½	bunch fresh cilantro, chopped
3	cups canned pineapple juice
6	ounces clam juice
2	cups water
	salt *(to taste)*

In a large sauté pan place the butter and heat it on medium high until it is melted and hot. Add the almonds and sauté the ingredients for 5 minutes, or until they are golden brown.

Add the morita chile peppers, sundried tomatoes, cilantro, pineapple juice, clam juice, water, and salt. Cook the ingredients on medium heat for 30 minutes.

Place all of the ingredients in a food processor and purée them so that they are as smooth as possible.

Season the salsa with the salt.

makes approximately 1 quart

Salsa Tropical

1	medium mango, peeled, meat removed from the core and diced medium
1	banana, peeled and diced medium
1	cup fresh pineapple, peeled, cored and diced medium
½	small red onion, finely diced
1	clove fresh garlic, finely chopped
1	jalapeño chile pepper, seeded and finely chopped
1	tablespoon fresh cilantro, chopped
1	teaspoon lemon juice, freshly squeezed
1	teaspoon salt *(or to taste)*

In a medium bowl place all of the ingredients and toss them together.

makes approximately 3 cups

Pasqual's Red Chile Sauce

¾   **pound dried New Mexico red chile peppers, rinsed, stemmed, seeded, covered with hot water and soaked for 30 minutes** *(reserve the water)*
1   **medium white onion, coarsely chopped**
8   **cloves fresh garlic**
2   **teaspoons dried Mexican oregano**
1   **teaspoon ground cumin**
2   **teaspoons kosher salt** *(or to taste)*

In a large stockpot place the rehydrated red chile peppers, reserved water, white onions, garlic, Mexican oregano, and cumin. Bring the ingredients to a boil over high heat.

Reduce the heat to low and simmer the ingredients for 20 minutes.

Drain off the liquid and reserve it.

In a blender place batches of the chile pepper mixture with a small amount of the reserved water. Purée all of the ingredients so that a thick, ketchup-like consistency is achieved. Strain the sauce through a fine mesh sieve.

Season the sauce with the salt.

makes approximately 1 quart

> *"I really believe in using chile pods versus powdered chile, because they have a much stronger, fruitier flavor. When you rehydrate the peppers you should weight them down with a plate so that they don't float to the top of the water. The fumes are released during this process and might give you some difficulty in breathing, so fling open the windows and the kitchen door!"*
>
> *"Making this sauce can be a messy process, but it is definitely worth the effort. It freezes perfectly well, so you could double the recipe and save part of it for future dishes. Also, be forewarned that the sauce stains. Don't wear white when you make it, and if you spill any be sure to wipe it up immediately."*
>
> Katharine Kagel
> Cafe Pasqual's

Paul's Red Chile Sauce

16   **ounces canned tomatoes** *(whole or crushed)*
1   **small yellow onion, chopped**
¼   **cup hot red chile powder**
½   **cup water**
1   **teaspoon salt**
½   **teaspoon black pepper**

In a medium saucepan place all of the ingredients. Simmer them for 10 minutes, or until the flavors are blended.

Place the sauce in a food processor and purée it.

makes 3 cups

> *"This is a basic red chile sauce. Make it as hot or mild as you prefer. We make it medium at our restaurant because a lot of our customers are what I would respectfully call 'wimpy', and don't want their food too spicy."*
>
> Paul Hunsicker
> Paul's Restaurant

Guajillo Salsa

8	dried guajillo chile peppers, seeded, stemmed and dry toasted *(see chef's comments on this page)*
4	large tomatoes, broiled *(see chef's comments on this page)*
1	medium red onion, chopped
1	clove fresh garlic, chopped
1	cup chicken stock *(recipe on page 311)*
3	tablespoons olive oil
1	teaspoon salt *(or to taste)*

In a food processor place the toasted guajillo chile peppers, broiled tomatoes, red onions, garlic, and chicken stock. Purée the ingredients so that they are almost smooth.

In a medium saucepan place the olive oil and heat it on high until it just starts to smoke. Add the puréed mixture *(be careful because the oil will spatter)* and reduce the heat to low. Simmer the sauce for 5 minutes, or until it thickens. Season the salsa with the salt.

makes approximately 2 cups

Jalapeño Tartar Sauce

2	cups mayonnaise
1	dill pickle, finely chopped
1	jalapeño chile pepper, seeded and finely chopped
1	pickled jalapeño chile pepper, seeded and finely chopped
2	tablespoons hot sauce
1	teaspoon cayenne pepper
1	teaspoon red chile powder
1	teaspoon ground thyme
1	lemon, freshly squeezed
1	teaspoon salt *(or to taste)*
1	teaspoon black pepper *(or to taste)*

In a medium bowl place all the ingredients and mix them together well.

makes approximately 3 cups

"This is a delicious Mexican salsa that is excellent with grilled meats. Another idea is to sauté some mushrooms, add them to the salsa, cook them together, and then serve them as a side dish."

"To dry toast the guajillo chile peppers you put them in a sauté pan and constantly move and toss them on a medium heat. They are ready when they are lightly toasted and their fragrance is released. Don't burn them or else they will be bitter."

"When you broil the tomatoes you should put them in a shallow baking dish and broil them on all sides so that they are blackened and blistered. This makes the tomatoes very sweet and adds an important dimension to the sauce, as does the toasting of the chile pods."

Don Fortel
On Water

"I've tasted a lot of different tartar sauces, and this is the one I like best. It's very spicy and crunchy, with a wonderful robust flavor."

Harry Shapiro
Harry's Road House

Cilantro Pesto

½   **cup piñon nuts** *(pine nuts)*
½   **cup parmesan cheese, freshly grated**
2   **tablespoons fresh garlic, finely chopped**
2   **bunches fresh cilantro, chopped**
1   **bunch fresh parsley, chopped**
1¼   **cups olive oil**
1   **tablespoon salt** *(or to taste)*
1   **tablespoon black pepper** *(or to taste)*

In a food processor place all of the ingredients. Purée them so that they are smooth.

makes approximately 3 cups

"This is a great, super easy pesto recipe. Just throw everything in a blender and pulse it. You can keep a jar of pesto in the refrigerator and use it as a flavoring for soups, stews, and pastas. You also can freeze it in small plastic containers and then scoop it out as you need it. It will have the consistency of ice cream."

"Piñon nuts are very expensive, so feel free to substitute either almonds or walnuts. Pecans would be too strong."

"Cilantro has a very distinct and strong flavor, and does not necessarily appeal to everyone who first tastes it. For some people it is an acquired taste."

James Lamoureux
The Evergreen

Roasted Tomatillo Chipotle Poblano Sauce

12   **tomatillos, husks removed, roasted** *(see chef's comments on page 72),* **and coarsely chopped**
6   **poblano chile peppers, roasted, peeled, seeded and coarsely chopped**
1   **7-ounce can chipotle chile peppers** *(in adobo sauce)*
2   **cups chicken stock** *(recipe on page 311)*
     salt *(to taste)*

In a food processor place the tomatillos, poblano and chipotle chile peppers, and chicken stock. Purée the ingredients so that they are smooth.

Season the sauce with the salt.

makes approximately 1 quart

"Of all the sauces I make, this is one of my favorites. It has a good chile kick to it, and is very simple to prepare. Serve it with raw vegetables as a dipping sauce."

Rustin Newton
Staab House

Green Curry Sauce

2 **Thai chile peppers** *(see chef's comments on page 233),* **stems removed**
6 **cups fresh cilantro, coarsely chopped**
4 **tablespoons fresh ginger root, peeled and coarsely chopped**
8 **kaffir lime leaves** *(see chef's comments on page 233)*
18 **cloves fresh garlic**
1 **tablespoon Thai shrimp paste** *(see chef's comments on this page)*
2 **tablespoons coriander seeds**
⅓ **cup Thai fish sauce** *(see chef's comments on this page)*
1⅔ **cups unsweetened coconut milk** *(see chef's comments on this page)*
water *(as necessary)*

In a blender place all the ingredients and purée them. Add water if it is needed to liquify the sauce so that it is a thin consistency.

Strain the sauce through a fine sieve.

makes approximately 3 cups

Romanesca Sauce

3 **cups tomatoes, diced**
1 **clove fresh garlic, finely chopped**
¼ **cup fresh basil, chopped**
2 **teaspoons chile pequin** *(hot red chile flakes)*
¾ **cup balsamic vinegar**
1 **teaspoon salt** *(or to taste)*

In a food processor place all of the ingredients. Purée them so that they are smooth.

makes approximately 1 quart

Romesco Sauce

¾   cup sliced almonds, toasted
10   cloves fresh garlic
1   ounce dried hot red chile peppers
½   cup olive oil
¼   cup red wine vinegar
¼   teaspoon salt *(or to taste)*
2   cups red bell peppers, roasted, peeled, seeded and coarsely
     chopped

In a food processor place all the ingredients *(except the red bell peppers)* and purée them.

Add the red bell peppers. Purée them so that the sauce is smooth.

makes approximately 3 cups

Chile Pequin

4   cups tomatoes, peeled and diced medium
¼   cup yellow onion, diced medium
1½   cloves fresh garlic, finely chopped
5   whole pequin chile peppers, crushed
1   tablespoon fresh cilantro, chopped
½   teaspoon salt *(or to taste)*

In a food processor place all of the ingredients and purée them so that they are smooth.

makes approximately 4 cups

Blue Cheese Dressing

1   cup blue cheese, crumbled
1   pint sour cream
¼   cup white wine
      salt and black pepper *(to taste)*

In a small bowl place all the ingredients and stir them together. Cover the bowl with plastic wrap and refrigerate it.

makes approximately 3 cups

"Use this sauce as a spread on sandwiches, with scrambled eggs, or as a dipping sauce for marinated raw vegetables. The consistency can be varied by adding more or less of the red bell peppers at the end."

"The name 'El Farol' means 'The Lantern'. Our restaurant serves Spanish tapas, which are little appetizer dishes. People can order two or three different things and have a meal that is unique. It's also fun for them to share their food with everyone else at their table, so they really get to experience a lot of different items."

Kit Baum
El Farol

"Chile Pequin is spicy, like Pico de Gallo, only it has a smoother texture because it is puréed. It's good with grilled meats and chicken."

Robbie Day
San Francisco St. Bar & Grill

"I love this dressing on baked potatoes. It is so good that I eat it almost every day."

"Cooking is as satisfying to me as running a big corporation is satisfying to a business executive. I especially love to feed large groups of people."

Sylvia Johnson
Celebrations

Green Chile Vinaigrette

1	cup green chile peppers, roasted, peeled, seeded and diced medium
2	cloves fresh garlic, finely chopped
¼	cup fresh cilantro, chopped
1	tablespoon fresh oregano, chopped
2	tablespoons yellow mustard
2½	teaspoons sugar
1½	cups olive oil
½	teaspoon salt *(or to taste)*
1½	teaspoons black pepper *(or to taste)*

Place the green chile peppers, garlic, cilantro, oregano, yellow mustard, and sugar in a food processor. Coarsely purée the ingredients. With the food processor constantly running, slowly dribble in the olive oil.

Season the vinaigrette with the salt and black pepper.

makes approximately 2 cups

"This vinaigrette makes a wonderful salad dressing or dipping sauce. It's not really that hot. Rather, it is mildly spicy with a sour flavor at the same time."

"I come up with my recipe ideas by first seeing what ingredients I have available. In one sense it is easier to be creative in a restaurant kitchen as opposed to a home kitchen, because there is such a plethora of ingredients available right at your fingertips, with no shopping to be done. On the other hand, it is more difficult, because there is a lot of pressure to come up with something excellent in a very short period of time."

Scott Shampine
El Nido

"I like simple dishes, even though they may take some time to prepare. Take polenta, for example. Although it is a very basic dish, at least forty-five minutes are required to make it properly."

Robbie Day
San Francisco St. Bar & Grill

Bêchamel Sauce

4	tablespoons butter
4	tablespoons flour
2	cups milk
4	whole cloves
1	small white onion, peeled
1	small bay leaf
	salt and white pepper *(to taste)*

In a medium saucepan place the butter and heat it on low until it is melted and hot. Add the flour and stir it in well. Cook the mixture for 3 to 5 minutes.

While constantly stirring, slowly add the milk.

Insert the cloves into the onion. Place the onion and bay leaf in the saucepan. Continue to cook the sauce for 10 to 15 minutes, or until it thickens.

Remove the onion and bay leaf.

Season the sauce with the salt and white pepper.

makes 2 cups

Green Chile Sauce

¼	cup flour
1	cup water
2	tablespoons butter
½	medium yellow onion, chopped
3	cloves fresh garlic, finely chopped
1	pound green chile peppers, roasted, peeled, seeded and diced
½	teaspoon dried Mexican oregano
1½	teaspoons salt
2	cups water

In a blender place the flour and the 1 cup of water, and blend them so that they form a smooth roux. Pour the roux through a fine sieve to remove any lumps, and set it aside.

In a medium saucepan place the butter and heat it on medium high until it is melted and hot. Add the yellow onions and garlic. Sauté them for 5 minutes, or until the onions are translucent.

Add the green chile peppers, Mexican oregano, salt, and the 2 cups of water. Stir the ingredients together. Bring them to a boil and then simmer them for 30 minutes.

Return the heat to a boil. While stirring constantly, slowly pour in the roux. When the sauce begins to thicken, turn off the heat.

makes approximately 1 quart

Jalapeño Citrus Relish

1	jicama, peeled and diced small
⅓	fresh pineapple, peeled, cored and diced small
½	green bell pepper, seeded and diced small
4	oranges, peeled, seeded, segmented and diced small
6	red jalapeño chile peppers, seeded and diced small
½	bunch scallions, thinly sliced
⅛	cup fresh parsley, chopped
¼	cup fresh cilantro, chopped
2	tablespoons sugar
¼	cup rice wine vinegar
¼	cup apple cider vinegar

In a large bowl place all the ingredients and toss them together.

makes approximately 1 quart

"I think there's a magical, addictive power to green chile. Even though I can't handle it anymore because of digestive problems, every now and then I can't resist having some.....especially when it's fresh. Just the smell of it makes me want to go grab a tortilla and put a whole roasted green chile pepper in it with a little salt, and eat it like that."

"My mother and grandmother lived next door to each other when I was growing up, and both of them were fantastic cooks. My brothers and sisters and I would go from one house to the other, to check out what each one was making for dinner, so we could eat at the house with the best meal. Sometimes we would eat twice because they both were so good."

Ivan Macias
Tortilla Flats

"This is a spicy relish. I like to use the red jalapeños instead of the green, because they have a little more flavor and they add a nice color. If you can't find them use the green, but add a little red bell pepper."

Rustin Newton
Staab House

Tequila Dill Lime Butter

"I developed this recipe years ago when I was in Albuquerque, and brought it with me to this restaurant in Santa Fe. At the time I had the only tequila butter around, but by the next summer it seemed that everyone had it. This tastes best with fish."

Tony Trujillo
Inn at Loretto

1	pound butter, softened
⅛	cup fresh dill, finely chopped
1	lime, zested *(outer green part grated off)*, zest finely minced and lime freshly squeezed
1½	shots Cuervo Especial tequila

In a medium mixing bowl place all the ingredients and mix them together well.

Form the butter into a log and wrap it in plastic wrap. Freeze the butter and cut off slices as they are needed.

makes 1 pound

Roasted Corn & Black Bean Salsa

"I serve this salsa warm with grilled fish or chicken, or cold with chips. It has such a wonderful taste that you could use it with almost anything, and it looks gorgeous because of all the different colors. Just be sure that you don't overcook the black beans.....they should be a bit al dente."

Peter Raub
Santa Fe Market

"We roast the corn with the husks removed, so the kernels get a bit browned. The sweetness of the corn really comes out this way, and gives the salsa a delicious flavor."

Marsha Chobol
Santa Fe Market

1	tablespoon peanut oil
4	Roma tomatoes, seeded and finely diced
1	small yellow onion, finely diced
1	clove fresh garlic, finely chopped
¾	cup cooked black beans
2	ears corn, roasted *(see chef's comments on this page)* and kernels removed
1	jalapeño chile pepper, finely chopped
3	tablespoons fresh cilantro, chopped
⅛	teaspoon cumin seeds, toasted *(see chef's comments on page 68)* and ground
2	tablespoons honey
1	tablespoon olive oil
1	lime, freshly juiced
	salt *(to taste)*

In a medium sauté pan place the peanut oil and heat it on medium high until it is hot. Add the tomatoes, yellow onions, and garlic. Sauté the ingredients for 5 minutes, or until the onions are translucent.

In a medium bowl place the tomato mixture and the rest of the ingredients. Stir them together. Cover the bowl with plastic wrap and let the salsa sit for 2 hours at room temperature.

makes approximately 3 cups

Cranberry Chipotle Compote

1	tablespoon vegetable oil
3	medium apples, peeled, cored and diced medium
2	medium pears, peeled, cored and diced medium
⅓	cup raisins
¼	cup Grand Marnier
1	pound fresh cranberries, rinsed and drained
4	ounces chipotle chile peppers *(in adobo sauce)*, finely chopped
2	teaspoons ground cinnamon
1	cup sugar
½	orange, zested *(outer orange part grated off)* and finely chopped
½	cup orange juice, freshly squeezed
½	teaspoon nutmeg
¼	cup Grand Marnier

In a large saucepan place the vegetable oil and heat it on medium high until it is hot. Add the apples, pears, and raisins. Sauté the ingredients for 3 to 5 minutes, or until they soften.

Add the first ¼ cup of Grand Marnier and deglaze the pan. Add the cranberries, chipotle chile peppers, cinnamon, sugar, orange zest, and orange juice. Stir the ingredients together and simmer them for 40 to 50 minutes, or until they begin to thicken. Add the nutmeg and the second ¼ cup of Grand Marnier, and stir them in.

Place the compote in an airtight container and refrigerate it.

makes approximately 1 quart

Salsa Molcajete

5	medium tomatoes, roasted *(see chef's comments on page 72)* and peeled
15	jalapeño chile peppers, roasted and peeled
1	teaspoon granulated garlic
1	teaspoon salt
6	sprigs fresh cilantro, chopped

In a food processor place the tomatoes, jalapeño chile peppers, garlic, and salt. Process the ingredients for 3 to 4 seconds, or until the salsa is slightly chunky.

Add the cilantro and stir it in.

makes approximately 2 cups

"I've never been a big cranberry relish fan, but this recipe is one that I love. The chipotle chile peppers together with all of the fruits make a delicious combination of sweet and hot. Serve this at your Thanksgiving dinner for a delightful Southwestern change."

"Long ago I learned a theory about food, which basically is this: If you have two flavors, they should both be detectable, but they also should combine to create a third new taste. This way there is an explosion of flavors."

Rustin Newton
Staab House

"To really appreciate this salsa you have to be a true fiery foods lover, because it is really hot! I like to eat it with chips or scrambled eggs. This is the kind of thing, like tabasco, that you would use to give other foods a kick."

"I got this recipe from Nicho Nuñez, a Mexican chef. 'Molcajete' refers to the mortar and pestle the Mexicans use to grind the ingredients."

Darrell Hedgecoke
Mañana

Green Chile Cheese Sauce

8	**tablespoons butter** *(unsalted)*
6	**tablespoons all purpose flour**
3	**cups milk**
¼	**cup green chile peppers, roasted, peeled, seeded and diced**
½	**teaspoon paprika**
¼	**teaspoon ground nutmeg**
	salt and white pepper *(to taste)*
¼	**cup cheddar cheese, grated**

In a medium saucepan place the butter and heat it on medium until it is melted. Add the flour and whisk it in for 3 minutes.

While whisking constantly, slowly add the milk. Cook the sauce for 5 minutes, or until it thickens. Add the green chile peppers, paprika, nutmeg, salt, and white pepper. Stir the ingredients together. While whisking constantly, slowly add the cheddar cheese. Simmer the sauce for 3 minutes, or until the cheese is melted and it is thick and smooth.

makes approximately 3 cups

Ginger Jalapeño Lime Vinaigrette

1	**2" piece fresh ginger root, peeled and finely chopped**
3	**jalapeño chile peppers, seeded and finely chopped**
1½	**teaspoons fresh garlic, finely chopped**
2	**teaspoons chile pequin** *(hot red chile flakes)*
1	**teaspoon ground ginger**
⅓	**cup sugar**
½	**cup lime juice, freshly squeezed**
⅛	**cup white vinegar**
2	**cups olive oil**
¼	**cup red bell peppers, diced small**
¼	**cup fresh parsley, chopped**
	salt and white pepper *(to taste)*

In a food processor place the ginger root, jalapeño chile peppers, garlic, chile pequin, ground ginger, sugar, lime juice, and white vinegar. Purée the ingredients for 45 seconds. Let the purée sit for 10 minutes. With the food processor constantly running, slowly dribble in the olive oil. Add the red bell peppers, parsley, salt, and white pepper.

makes approximately 3 cups

"This is a basic cheese sauce with a little spice from the green chiles. It's very good with macaroni or as a topping for vegetables, such as cauliflower."

"I enjoy cooking at home because it's a nice diversion from doing huge quantities. It's fun to listen to good music when I cook and have people over for dinner."

Peter Raub
Santa Fe Market

"One reason why I like to cook is that I like to eat what I make. Both of my grandmothers were chefs and I grew up eating really wonderful, unusual, exotic food."

Marsha Chobol
Santa Fe Market

"I developed this recipe because of America's growing interest in Asian cuisines. The ginger goes very well with the hot chiles, garlic, and lime. It's a snappy vinaigrette, full of character and flavor. Serve it as a dipping sauce for crab or bay shrimp, or as a dressing for a seafood salad."

Rustin Newton
Staab House

Eggs, Cheese & Vegetarian

Baked Potato & Cheese Enchiladas with Zucchini Avocado Sauce

Baked Potato & Cheese Enchiladas

½	cup olive oil
3	large baking potatoes, peeled and diced into ¼" pieces
1	medium red onion, finely minced
2	green bell peppers, seeded and finely diced
½	cup fresh cilantro, chopped
½	teaspoon epazote *(see chef's comments on next page)*
	salt and black pepper *(to taste)*
¼	cup olive oil *(or as needed)*
12	corn tortillas
3	cups raw milk Monterey Jack cheese, grated
	Zucchini Avocado Sauce *(recipe on next page)*

Preheat the oven to 375°.

In a large skillet place the ½ cup of olive oil and heat it on medium high until it is hot. Add the potatoes, red onions, green bell peppers, cilantro, and epazote. Sauté the ingredients for 10 minutes, or until the potatoes begin to brown.

Add the salt and black pepper. Remove the skillet from the heat and let the mixture cool.

In another large skillet place the ¼ cup of olive oil and heat it on medium until it is hot. Place each tortilla in the hot oil for a few seconds so that it softens. Remove it and drain it on a paper towel.

In the center of each tortilla place several tablespoons of the potato mixture. Sprinkle on some of the grated cheese. Roll the tortilla up and place it in a long, oiled baking dish with the seam side down. Repeat this process for the rest of the tortillas. Pour the Zucchini Avocado Sauce on top. Sprinkle on any remaining cheese.

Bake the enchiladas *(uncovered)* for 35 to 40 minutes, or until everything is hot and bubbly.

serves 6

"People are often shocked when they hear of potato enchiladas. This sounds like it would be an incredibly heavy dish, but it's not heavy at all. It's rich, filling, but not over-powering.....it's perfect!"

"The traditional way to soften tortillas is to quickly sauté them in lard. I call for olive oil in this dish because I wanted to keep it truly vegetarian."

"I try to use raw milk Monterey Jack cheese instead of pasteurized, because this adds another dimension of flavor to the dish. I first tasted raw milk cheese when I worked in New York at a large specialty food store, Dean & Deluca. I was amazed at its incredible flavor. If you can't find it, then just use the pasteurized kind."

Jonathan Horst
Adobo Catering

Zucchini Avocado Sauce

¼	cup olive oil
1	habanero chile pepper, finely minced
3	small zucchini, diced into ¼" pieces
1	large yellow onion, diced small
2	cloves fresh garlic, finely chopped
¼	cup fresh cilantro, chopped
3	large avocados, peeled, pits removed, mashed and puréed
	water *(as needed)*
	salt *(to taste)*

In a large skillet place the olive oil and heat it on medium high until it is hot. Add the habanero chile pepper, zucchini, yellow onions, garlic, and cilantro. Sauté the ingredients for 5 minutes, or until they are barely tender.

Add the mashed avocados and stir them in. Add and stir in enough water so that a thick sauce is achieved.

Season the sauce with the salt.

makes approximately 4 cups

"Most vegetarians find this sauce to be outrageously good. The avocados are cooked, which gives them a unique flavor.....slightly nutty and squash-like. And, the diced zucchini adds a nice texture. Use this sauce on any kind of enchiladas.....especially chicken or cheese. It's great!"

Jonathan Horst
Adobo Catering

Chipotle Chile Black Beans

1	cup dried black beans, washed and drained
2	quarts cold water
1	small yellow onion, finely diced
1	clove fresh garlic, finely chopped
1	dried chipotle chile pepper
1	tablespoon epazote *(see chef's comments on this page)*
1	teaspoon dried sage, crushed
1	teaspoon ground Mexican oregano
2	bay leaves
	salt *(to taste)*

In a large saucepan place all of the ingredients *(except for the salt)*. Bring the ingredients to a boil.

Reduce the heat and simmer the beans for 3 hours, or until they are tender. Add the salt.

Remove the chipotle chile pepper and the bay leaves before serving the beans.

serves 4 to 6

"When I cook beans, I like to use a lot of water. The beans keep a better texture and they will be easier to digest."

"If you can't find a dried chipotle chile pepper you can use one that is canned in adobo sauce."

"Epazote is an herb that has a very distinctive, earthy flavor. To me it is an essential ingredient for the success of this black bean recipe. It's kind of like an anchovy in that it gives a vague, background flavor that you don't really focus on."

Peter Raub
Santa Fe Market

Tortilla Stew

¼	**cup vegetable oil**
¼	**cup olive oil**
12	**corn tortillas, cut into 8 wedges each**
2	**large yellow onions, quartered and then sliced**
6	**poblano chile peppers, seeds and ribs removed, and chopped**
2	**cups tomatoes, peeled, seeded and chopped**
2	**cloves fresh garlic, finely chopped**
1	**teaspoon epazote** *(see chef's comments on page 123)*
6	**cups chicken stock** *(see chef's comments on this page)*
1	**cup heavy cream**
½	**cup fresh cilantro, chopped**
½	**cup Reggiano** *(parmesan)* **cheese, freshly grated**
	salt and black pepper *(to taste)*

In a small bowl place the vegetable and olive oils, and stir them together.

In a large frying pan place half of the oil mixture and heat it on medium high until it is hot. Add the tortilla wedges and fry them for 1 to 2 minutes on each side, or until they are crisp. Drain them on paper towels and set them aside.

In a medium stockpot place the rest of the oil mixture and heat it on medium until it is hot. Add the yellow onions and poblano chile peppers. Sauté them for 5 minutes or until the onions are translucent. Add the tomatoes, garlic, and epazote. Cook the ingredients for 2 minutes. Add the chicken stock and simmer everything for 10 minutes. Turn off the heat.

Add the fried tortilla chips, heavy cream, cilantro, and cheese. Let the stew sit for several minutes so that the tortilla chips soak up the broth.

Add the salt and black pepper. Serve the stew immediately.

serves 8

"Tortilla soup is from Mexico and there are a million different recipes for it. I call this one a stew because it is very thick, with hardly any broth. It is really rich and delicious. Serve just a small amount at the beginning of a meal, followed by a simple entrée, such as a grilled meat with a steamed vegetable."

"Be careful not to overcook the tortillas or they will be bitter. Don't brown them.....just let them get crisp."

"It's important that the chicken stock is homemade and not canned. For a simple stock just poach a whole chicken (or pieces) in about two quarts of water with a teaspoon of salt. You don't need to add any vegetables to the broth because it should have a pure chicken taste. Then, according to the recipe you are making, you add the other flavors."

Jonathan Horst
Adobo Catering

Spicy Migas

4	**tablespoons butter**
½	**medium yellow onion, diced medium**
½	**green bell pepper, seeded and diced medium**
2	**pickled jalapeño chile peppers, finely chopped**
½	**tomato, seeded and diced medium**
8	**eggs, well beaten**
4	**corn tortillas, cut into thin strips and deep-fried**
1	**cup cheddar cheese, grated**
1	**cup salsa** *(your favorite)*
4	**flour tortillas, warmed**
1	**cup refried beans** *(recipe on page 294)*

In a large sauté pan place the butter and heat it on medium high until it is melted and hot. Add the yellow onions and green bell peppers. Sauté them for 5 minutes, or until the onions are translucent.

Add the pickled jalapeño chile peppers, tomatoes, and eggs. Scramble the ingredients until the eggs begin to set. Add the tortilla strips and stir them in.

On each of 4 individual serving plates place the migas. Top them with the grated cheese. Serve the salsa, flour tortilla, and refried beans on the side.

serves 4

Stuffed Pumpkin Bread with Red Chile Sauce, Queso Blanco & Caramelized Apples

Stuffed Pumpkin Bread

1	tablespoon olive oil
¼	cup hot green chile peppers, roasted, peeled, seeded and diced
¼	cup yellow squash, diced
1	cup corn kernels
1	small yellow onion, chopped
¼	cup piñon nuts *(pine nuts),* toasted *(see chef's comments on page 325)*
1	24-ounce can pumpkin purée
2	eggs
¼	cup molasses
¼	cup honey
¼	cup vegetable oil
3	cups flour
¼	teaspoon ground cinnamon
¼	teaspoon ground nutmeg
1½	teaspoons baking powder
1½	tablespoons baking soda
	Paul's Red Chile Sauce *(recipe on page 110)*
	Queso Blanco *(recipe on next page)*
	Caramelized Apples *(recipe on next page)*

Preheat the oven to 400°.

In a large sauté pan place the olive oil and heat it on medium high until it is hot. Add the green chile peppers, squash, corn, yellow onions, and piñon nuts. Sauté the ingredients for 5 minutes. Set the mixture aside.

In a medium bowl place the pumpkin purée, eggs, molasses, honey, and vegetable oil. Mix the ingredients together and set them aside.

In a medium large bowl sift together the flour, cinnamon, nutmeg, baking powder, and baking soda. Add the pumpkin mixture and fold it in *(do not over mix)*.

(continued on next page)

"A vegetarian ex-girlfriend of mine came up with this recipe. I liked it so much that I decided to put it on our menu, where it has remained since the day we opened. It is one of the most interesting vegetarian dishes that I have ever come across."

"The flavors of the Red Chile, Queso Blanco, and Caramelized Apples do a wonderful job together. And the presentation is really neat, with the deep red sauce on the brown pumpkin bread, and the clean white color of the cheese sauce."

Paul Hunsicker
Paul's Restaurant

"I've never done anything else but cook. My first job was in a kitchen at the age of sixteen. I didn't really start to appreciate cooking, however, until I was allowed to experiment and be creative. What I love most about being a chef is that the reward is instantaneous. You know immediately if the food you have prepared is good or bad. Also, the positive feedback from the customers is a definite rush."

"Queso blanco means a white cheese sauce. Here we use feta and Swiss cheese with cream. The combination is simple, but exquisite. Be sure to use Greek feta that is packed in brine, and not goat cheese. This sauce is wonderful with casseroles, pastas, and vegetables."

"These caramelized apples are heavenly on vanilla ice cream. Or you can purée them for an applesauce, or use them in a pie."

Paul Hunsicker
Paul's Restaurant

Lightly oil 2 loaf pans and dust them with flour. Divide the dough into 4 equal amounts. In the bottom of each pan place ¼ of the dough and pat it down. Place the sautéed vegetable mixture on top. Pat out another ¼ of the dough and place it on top.

Bake the bread for 45 minutes, or until a toothpick inserted in the center comes out clean.

Slice each loaf into 4 sections *(about 3" wide)*.

In the center of each of 8 individual serving plates pour Paul's Red Chile Sauce. Place a bread slice on top. Pour on the Queso Blanco. Garnish the dish with the Caramelized Apples.

serves 8

Queso Blanco

¼	**cup feta cheese, crumbled**
¼	**cup Swiss cheese, grated**
½	**cup heavy cream**

In a small saucepan place the feta cheese, Swiss cheese, and heavy cream. While whisking constantly, simmer the ingredients for 5 to 10 minutes, or until the cheeses are melted and a smooth sauce is formed.

makes 1 cup

Caramelized Apples

¼	**pound butter**
4	**Granny Smith apples, peeled, cored and sliced**
¼	**cup sugar**
1	**dash cinnamon**

In a medium saucepan place the butter and heat it on high until the butter is melted and hot. Add the apples, sugar, and cinnamon. Sauté the ingredients for 10 minutes, or until the apples are tender and the sugar is caramelized.

makes approximately 2 cups

Black Bean Flautas

½   **cup vegetable oil** *(or as needed)*
12   **blue corn tortillas**
¼   **cup red onion, finely chopped**
2   **dried red chile peppers, crushed**
2   **tablespoons fresh cilantro, chopped**
2   **cloves fresh garlic, finely chopped**
½   **teaspoon white pepper** *(or to taste)*
¼   **cup dry sherry**
1   **cup dried black beans, washed, cooked, drained and coarsely puréed**
3½   **cups vegetable oil**
½   **pound smoked gouda cheese, grated**
1   **small red bell pepper, seeded and thinly sliced**
1   **small green bell pepper, seeded and thinly sliced**
1   **small yellow bell pepper, seeded and thinly sliced**
       Guacamole *(recipe on page 245)*
1   **cup sour cream**

Preheat the oven to 350°.

In a medium sauté pan place the ½ cup of vegetable oil and heat it on medium high until it is hot. One at a time, place each tortilla in the hot oil and fry it for 10 seconds, or until it is softened. Drain the tortillas on paper towels and set them aside.

Remove all but 3 tablespoons of the oil from the pan *(add more oil if needed)* and heat it on medium high until it is hot. Add the red onions, crushed red chile peppers, cilantro, garlic, and white pepper. Cook the ingredients for 3 minutes.

Add the sherry and stir it in. Cook the ingredients for 2 minutes.

Transfer the mixture to a large bowl. Add the black bean purée and fold it in.

Spread the mixture on each tortilla *(leave 1" of the tortilla bare around the edges)*. Roll the tortilla up and insert a toothpick through each end to keep it closed.

In a large saucepan place the 3½ cups of vegetable oil and heat it on medium high until it is very hot. Place each flauta in the oil and deep-fry it for 2 minutes, or until it is crisp.

Drain the flautas on paper towels and remove the toothpicks.

(continued on next page)

"We have a seasonal restaurant on top of La Fonda, called La Terraza, which is open during the summer. This recipe was developed as one of our vegetarian dishes for its menu. We took our black bean soup recipe and altered it to make a filling for the flautas.....and it came out wonderful. The combination of the different flavors of the beans, cheese, and bell peppers is delicious."

Lela Cross
La Plazuela

"In Mexico, flautas are flat and grilled. But this is New Mexico, and here we have re-defined what a flauta is. To us, they are rolled up and deep-fried. You can make flautas with just about anything.....cheeses, vegetables, seafood, beef, or chicken."

"I like to deep-fry the flautas just a little bit, to give the tortilla a crunch. They are still cool in the middle, so that's why I finish them off in the oven."

Tomas Cross
La Plazuela

Place the flautas in a large baking dish and sprinkle on the gouda cheese. Bake them in the oven for 10 minutes, or until the cheese is melted.

On each of 6 individual serving plates place 2 of the flautas. Garnish them with the red, green, and yellow bell peppers, Guacamole, and sour cream.

serves 6

Grilled Eggplant Burrito

1	**large eggplant, cut into ½" slices**
¼	**cup olive oil**
¼	**cup vegetable oil**
5	**ounces tempeh, diced small**
2	**tablespoons water**
4	**flour tortillas, warmed**
2	**cups cooked black beans**
2	**cups Southwestern Barbecue Sauce** *(recipe on page 108)*
1	**cup Asadero cheese, grated**

Preheat the oven to 350°.

Brush the eggplant slices on both sides with the olive oil. Grill them for 3 minutes on each side, or until they are tender. Dice them into ¼" pieces.

In a medium sauté pan place the vegetable oil and heat it on medium high until it is hot. Add the tempeh and sauté it for 5 minutes, or until it is brown on all sides. Add the water, cover the pan with a lid, and steam the tempeh on low heat for 5 minutes.

In the center of each warmed tortilla place ¼ of the eggplant pieces, tempeh, and black beans. Roll up the tortilla and place it on a baking sheet. Top the burritos with the Southwestern Barbecue Sauce and the grated Asadero cheese.

Bake the burritos for 10 minutes, or until the cheese is hot and melted.

serves 4

Sheepherder's Breakfast

4	**tablespoons butter** *(or as needed)*
4	**cups small red potatoes, cooked and cubed medium**
4	**tablespoons jalapeño chile peppers, chopped**
1	**cup yellow onions, minced**
2	**cups Green Chile Sauce** *(recipe on page 116),* **heated**
1	**cup Monterey Jack cheese, grated**
4	**eggs, fried**

Preheat the oven to 400°.

In a large sauté pan place the butter and heat it on medium high until it is melted and hot. Add the potatoes, jalapeño chile peppers, and yellow onions. Sauté the ingredients for 6 to 8 minutes, or until the potatoes are browned.

In each of 4 individual baking dishes *(or one medium baking dish)* place the potato mixture. Spoon the Green Chile Sauce on top. Sprinkle on the cheese.

Place the dishes in the oven for 3 to 4 minutes, or until the cheese is melted. Top each serving with a fried egg.

serves 4

"Northern New Mexico used to be one of the largest sheep producing areas in the country, and the Basque people came here to be the sheepherders. A typical meal for them would be potatoes, onions, and green chiles."

"If I eat a meal out and have a bad experience, I am usually forgiving, because no one understands better than I do how things can go wrong. However, if I eat at a new place that I consider to be pretentious and they don't get anything right....then I go off the wall!"

"I like working with food. It's creative, without being overly so. I even enjoy the routine of cooking. It's a day-to-day thing, but at the same time it is always different."

Bill Jennison
Tecolote Cafe

Vegetarian Gringo Chili

2	tablespoons vegetable oil
2	medium yellow onions, chopped medium
4	cloves fresh garlic, finely chopped
¼	cup red chile powder
2	tablespoons ground cumin
1	teaspoon ground Mexican oregano
4	cups puréed tomatoes
1	cup raw bulgur
2	cups cooked red kidney beans
	salt and black pepper *(to taste)*
½	cup Monterey Jack cheese, grated
½	cup sour cream
¼	cup red onions, chopped medium
4	tablespoons fresh cilantro, chopped

"I am the chef at the Santa Fe Opera, and we feed as many as five hundred people a day during opera season. This dish was developed because so many of the people are vegetarians. But the great thing about it is that it satisfies the meat eaters as well. The bulgur has a consistency similar to that of ground beef, and so people do not really know that it is meatless. Because most of the opera people are from out-of-town and are not used to Santa Fe chile, I make it only mildly spicy. This is why I call it 'Gringo' chili."

Marsha Chobol
Santa Fe Market

In a large saucepan place the vegetable oil and heat it on medium high until it is hot. Add the yellow onions, garlic, red chile powder, cumin, and oregano. Sauté the ingredients for 5 to 7 minutes, or until the onions are translucent.

Add the puréed tomatoes and cook the ingredients for 5 minutes.

Add the bulgur. Cook the mixture for 15 minutes, or until the bulgur is soft.

Add the kidney beans and cook the chile for 15 minutes. Season it with the salt and black pepper.

Serve the chili garnished with the Monterey Jack cheese, sour cream, red onions, and cilantro on top.

serves 4 to 6

Roasted Corn Omelette with Goat Cheese & Wild Mushrooms

2	tablespoons butter
½	pound wild mushrooms, sliced
4	shallots, finely chopped
2	jalapeño chile peppers, finely chopped
1	ear corn, husked, roasted and kernels removed
½	pound goat cheese
4	tablespoons butter
12	eggs, well beaten

In a medium sauté pan place the 2 tablespoons of butter and heat it on medium high until it is melted and hot. Add the wild mushrooms, shallots, and jalapeño chile peppers. Sauté the ingredients for 2 to 3 minutes, or until the shallots are translucent.

Add the roasted corn and goat cheese, and stir them in. Set the ingredients aside and keep them warm.

For each omelette place 1 of the 4 tablespoons of butter in a medium sauté pan *(or omelette pan)* and heat it on medium until it is melted and hot. Add ¼ of the eggs and cook them until they are done *(see chef's comments on this page)*.

Place ¼ of the sautéed ingredients in the center of each omelette and fold it over. Slip the omelette onto a warm plate.

serves 4

"*Almost everyone knows how NOT to make an omelette, but just a few know how to make one correctly. First, make sure that the pan is hot enough so that the butter is sizzling. Then add the eggs and stir them until the top of the omelette is fairly well jelled. Then you stop and let it sit for a minute more, or until the eggs are done. A lot of people scrape the uncooked eggs from the center of the omelette out to the sides and pull them underneath, but this is not the correct way. To make a good omelette requires some skill.*"

"*I like to eat out at other restaurants, but I can't resist being analytical. It's a disease of the trade.*"

Gordon Heiss
Casa Sena

"*Before I came to Santa Fe I was working at a restaurant in the Bay Area in California. Living expenses were very high, it was overcrowded, and there were earthquakes. When I was invited to work at Casa Sena I flew out to Santa Fe and liked the town right away. I love the different cultures, the art, and the architecture.*"

Ambjorn Lindskog
Casa Sena

Chile Rellenos

8   **large green chile peppers, roasted and peeled** (leave the stems on)
1   **pound Monterey Jack cheese, sliced into thin strips**
1   **large egg, well beaten**
1   **cup flour**
2   **teaspoons baking powder**
½   **teaspoon salt** (or to taste)
1½   **cups water**
6   **cups vegetable oil** (or as needed)

Make a 2-inch slit lengthwise in each green chile pepper. Very carefully remove the seeds.

Place ⅛ of the cheese strips inside each pepper.

In a large bowl place the egg, flour, baking powder, salt, and water. Whisk the ingredients together so that the batter has a thick consistency.

In a large heavy pan place the vegetable oil and heat it on high until it is hot.

Dip the stuffed green chile peppers in the batter. Cook the chile peppers in the hot oil for 3 to 4 minutes, or until they are golden brown. Drain the rellenos on paper towels.

serves 4

Green Chile Migas
with Guadalupe Salsa

Green Chile Migas

4	tablespoons butter
8	eggs, well beaten
4	tablespoons scallions, chopped
4	tablespoons longhorn cheese, grated
4	tablespoons Monterey Jack cheese, grated
4	tablespoons green chile pepper, roasted, peeled, seeded and chopped
2	handfuls tortilla chips, crumbled
1	cup Guadalupe Salsa *(recipe follows)*

In a small sauté pan place the butter and melt it on medium heat. Add the eggs, scallions, the longhorn and Monterey Jack cheeses, and the green chile peppers. Scramble the ingredients together until they are cooked.

Add the tortilla chips and mix them in.

Serve the migas with the Guadalupe Salsa on the side.

serves 4

Guadalupe Salsa

6	medium tomatoes, diced medium
1	red bell pepper, seeded and diced medium
1	green bell pepper, seeded and diced medium
1	small yellow onion, finely diced
3	jalapeño chile peppers, seeded and finely diced
½	bunch fresh cilantro, chopped
1	tablespoon chile pequin *(hot red chile flakes)*
½	teaspoon ground cumin
1	teaspoon garlic salt

In a large bowl place all the ingredients and mix them together well.

makes approximately 1 quart

"Migas is a Tex-Mex dish that we have had on the menu for eighteen years. It came from a Texan girl who used to come to work decked out in full make-up and high heels. She didn't last here more than four days, but she did leave us a dynamite recipe!"

"I think the tortilla chips are what make these eggs so good. If you want them spicier, mix in the Guadalupe Salsa."

"Santa Fe is great, but its green chile is even greater. That's why I moved here.....for the chile experience!"

Rubin Rodriquez
Guadalupe Cafe

"Everything is fresh in this salsa. It's chunky, and it definitely is hot. We serve it with chips, and on the side with some of our dishes like soft tacos, burritos, or egg dishes."

Isabelle Koomoa
Guadalupe Cafe

Potato Strudel

4	**russet potatoes, baked and meat scooped out**
1	**teaspoon chile pequin** *(hot red pepper flakes)*
	salt and black pepper *(to taste)*
6	**sheets filo dough, thawed** *(keep them covered with a slightly damp cloth)*
1	**cube butter** *(or as needed)*, **melted**
1	**cup fresh bread crumbs**

Preheat the oven to 375°.

In a medium bowl place the meat from the potatoes, chile pequin, salt, and black pepper. Mix the ingredients together well. Form them into a log shape that is approximately 2" shorter than the length of the filo dough.

Place a sheet of filo dough on a clean surface. Brush the top of the filo with the melted butter. Sprinkle on ⅕ of the bread crumbs. *(Work quickly!)* Lay another sheet of filo on top of the first. Repeat this process until all the filo has been used.

Place the potato log, lengthwise, on the top layer of the filo dough, along the edge that is closest to you. While constantly brushing it with butter, roll the potato log up in the filo dough. Brush the top layer of filo with a generous portion of the melted butter. Tuck the ends of the filo in.

On a baking sheet place the potato strudel with the seam side down. Slash the filo every 2", crosswise, along the top of the strudel.

Bake the strudel for 15 minutes, or until it is golden brown.

Slice the strudel along the slash marks.

serves 4

"Don't be intimidated by filo dough. It is easy to work with, and you can make incredible, impressive dishes with it. The secret is to work really fast when you are assembling the strudel. Keep the unused pieces covered with a damp cloth so they don't dry out. And if your melted butter cools, reheat it. Filo dough will keep in the refrigerator for up to a week. You can take the basic concept of this recipe and use any kind of filling that sounds good, from pie cherries to creamed chicken."

"I love my restaurant. It has been open for five years, and many of the same people come in every single day. We get movie stars and other famous people. The waitstaff are always running back to the kitchen in excitement saying, 'Guess who's in the dining room!' We get a lot of soap opera actors, but I don't know who they are because I never watch television during the day.....I am always at the restaurant."

Sylvia Johnson
Celebrations

Spicy Spaghetti Squash Pancakes

4	tablespoons olive oil
1	tablespoon fresh garlic, minced
⅓	cup yellow onions, diced small
1	cup red bell pepper, seeded and diced small
1	cup spaghetti squash, steamed until tender, seeded, flesh scooped out and broken into small pieces
1	tablespoon red chile powder
1	teaspoon ground cumin
1	teaspoon salt
¾	cup blue cornmeal
¾	cup flour
2	tablespoons baking powder
3	eggs
¾	cup milk
¼	cup vegetable oil (or as needed)

In a medium large sauté pan place the olive oil and heat it on medium high until it is hot. Add the garlic, yellow onions, and red bell peppers. Sauté the ingredients for 5 minutes, or until the onions are translucent.

Add the steamed squash, red chile powder, cumin, and salt. Stir the ingredients together.

In a medium large bowl place the blue cornmeal, flour, and baking powder. Mix the ingredients together. Add the squash mixture and fold it in.

In a medium bowl place the eggs and milk, and lightly beat them together. Add the mixture to the flour-squash mixture in the sauté pan and stir it in.

Form the batter into patties (3" in diameter and ⅓" thick).

In another large sauté pan place the vegetable oil and heat it on medium high until it is hot. Add the patties and cook them on each side for 3 minutes, or until they are golden brown and the batter is cooked.

serves 6

"Sometimes we jokingly call our restaurant the 'House of Pancakes', because we are always looking for new and different ways to make pancakes. This particular recipe is one of my favorites. It goes well with so many entrées, especially grilled fish. Although it is not overly spicy, it has just enough of a chile kick to keep your interest."

"I'm not much of a squash person, but I really love this dish. The spaghetti squash has a nutty flavor with a slightly crunchy texture. It is not overly sweet like a butternut or acorn squash. Try to buy them small, because the meat will be more tender."

"You want to cook these just like you would cook a regular pancake. Don't have your pan or griddle too hot, or you will burn the outside of the cakes while the dough on the inside will be raw."

"For a garnish we blend one half of a chipotle pepper with some sour cream and a little salt."

Rocky Packard
On Water

Red Bean Chipotle Chili

½	**can chipotle chile peppers** *(in adobo sauce)*
6	**cloves fresh garlic**
½	**cup olive oil**
2	**medium yellow onions, chopped small**
3	**tablespoons dried oregano**
1	**tablespoon ground cumin**
3	**16-ounce cans red kidney beans** *(with juice)*
2	**16-ounce cans white kernel corn** *(with juice)*
2	**16-ounce cans canned tomatoes** *(with juice)*
½	**cup tomato paste**
3	**tablespoons Dijon mustard**
2	**tablespoons molasses**
2	**tablespoons Worcestershire sauce**
¼	**cup red wine**
½	**tablespoon kosher salt**
2	**cups Monterey Jack cheese, grated**
1	**bunch fresh cilantro, stems discarded and leaves chopped**

In a food processor place the chipotle chile peppers and garlic, and coarsely purée them.

In a large stockpot place the olive oil and heat it on medium until it is hot. Add the chipotle purée, yellow onions, oregano, and cumin. Sauté the ingredients for 5 minutes, or until the onions are translucent.

Add the kidney beans, white corn, tomatoes, tomato paste, Dijon mustard, molasses, Worcestershire sauce, red wine, and kosher salt. Simmer the ingredients for 20 minutes, or until everything is heated through *(stir the chili often so that it does not burn)*.

Serve the chili garnished with the Monterey Jack cheese and cilantro.

serves 6 to 8

"This is a very hearty, spicy vegetarian chili that has sweet, smoky overtones. If you leave the cheese out, then it will also be non-dairy. It's very low in fat and is an excellent source of protein. Serve this with a green salad and some good bread."

"The menu at the Zia Diner is designed to reflect the diversified eating habits of Americans. Not only do we borrow from the many ethnic groups that exist in our country, but we also have a lot of 'comfort food' dishes....food like mom used to make when we were kids. In fact, our meat loaf and mashed potatoes are probably our best sellers."

Sarah Alvord
Zia Diner

Blue Corn Beer-Battered Chile Rellenos with Tomato Cinnamon Sauce

Blue Corn Beer-Battered Chile Rellenos

1   egg, well beaten
¼   pound smoked provolone cheese, grated
¼   pound jalapeño cheese, grated
¼   pound smoked gouda cheese, grated
¼   cup piñon nuts (pine nuts), toasted (see chef's comments on page 317)
2   tablespoons dried bread crumbs
2   cloves fresh garlic, finely chopped
2   tablespoons fresh cilantro, chopped
6   green chile peppers, roasted and peeled
1½   cups blue corn flour
3   egg yolks, lightly beaten
1   cup dark beer
1   pinch of salt
3   egg whites, beaten to stiff peaks
4   cups vegetable oil
¼   cup flour (or as needed)
       Tomato Cinnamon Sauce (recipe on next page)
6   cilantro sprigs

In a medium bowl place the beaten egg, provolone cheese, jalapeño cheese, gouda cheese, piñon nuts, bread crumbs, garlic, and cilantro. Stir the ingredients together.

Make a 2" slit, lengthwise, in each green chile pepper. Carefully remove the seeds.

Stuff each chile pepper with the cheese mixture and set it aside.

In another medium bowl place the blue corn flour. Make a well in the center of the flour. Place the egg yolks, beer, and salt in the well of the flour. Mix the ingredients together so that they are smooth. Fold in the egg whites.

In a large sauté pan place the vegetable oil and heat it on medium high until it is very hot.

(continued on next page)

"Here is an excellent recipe for homemade chile rellenos, which was a combined effort of myself, my mother, and my brother. It's a little different from most other relleno recipes in that it contains cilantro, piñon nuts, and three different cheeses."

"Chile rellenos don't take a lot of skill to make, but they are very time consuming. You have to slit the peppers open, stuff them, batter them, and deep-fry them. The key is to make sure that you make each one exactly the same, with the same amount of stuffing, the same amount of batter, and same amount of deep-frying time. If you follow this recipe carefully, then they should come out perfect."

"At one time we took these rellenos off our menu. But we had so many people complain that we decided to put them back on. They are very popular."

Lela Cross
La Plazuela

"The batter is a little tricky to make. If it is too thick, it won't cook through. If it is too thin, it won't adhere to the chile peppers. Also, make sure that the egg whites are well beaten so that there are stiff peaks. This will make the batter light."

Tomas Cross
La Plazuela

Dredge each stuffed chile pepper in the flour and then dip it in the batter *(allow the excess batter to drip off).*

Deep-fry the chile peppers for 3 to 5 minutes, or until they are golden brown. Drain them on paper towels.

On each of 6 individual serving plates spoon the Tomato Cinnamon Sauce. Place a chile relleño on top. Garnish the plate with a sprig of cilantro.

serves 6

Tomato Cinnamon Sauce

1¼	cups stewed tomatoes
1	bay leaf
2	teaspoons ground cinnamon
1	teaspoon ground nutmeg
1	teaspoon sugar
1	tablespoon fresh basil, chopped

"This is an unusual sauce that has a surprise taste because of the cinnamon and nutmeg. It goes really well with the rellenos. If you add some dill or rosemary, it also would go nicely with fish or steamed vegetables."

Lela Cross
La Plazuela

In a small saucepan place the tomatoes, bay leaf, cinnamon, nutmeg, and sugar. Simmer the ingredients on low heat for 30 minutes.

Remove the bay leaf from the tomato sauce.

Add the basil and stir it in.

makes approximately 1 cup

Roasted Ancho Peppers Stuffed with Butternut Squash

2	butternut squash, halved
¼	cup butter, melted
2	tablespoons brown sugar
1½	teaspoons ground cumin
½	teaspoon ground nutmeg
½	teaspoon white pepper
6	ancho chile peppers, roasted and peeled
2	tablespoons butter *(or as needed)*, melted

Preheat the oven to 350°.

On a baking sheet place the squash with the flesh side down. Bake them for 1 hour, or until the pulp is soft *(leave the oven on)*. Let the squash cool slightly. Remove the seeds. Scoop out the pulp and place it in a medium mixing bowl.

Add the ¼ cup of melted butter, brown sugar, cumin, nutmeg, and white pepper. Mix the ingredients together so that they are as smooth as possible.

Place the mixture in a pastry bag fitted with a large, round tip.

Make a slice, lengthwise, in the top of each ancho chile pepper. Very carefully remove the seeds.

Pipe a generous amount of the squash mixture inside each pepper. Brush the exposed squash with some of the 2 tablespoons of melted butter.

Place the stuffed peppers on a flat sheet. Bake them for 6 to 8 minutes, or until the squash is golden brown.

serves 6

"This dish is not for the weak of heart, because it is very spicy! Here in New Mexico we are pretty tough when it comes to eating hot food."

"You will find this dish to be beautiful to look at and easy to make. The key is to cook the squash very thoroughly. Some people don't like squash, so you can use any other kind of puréed vegetables that sound good, such as potatoes or carrots. Add some cheese to the vegetables if you like. The peppers should be viewed as little dishes to be stuffed with whatever your heart desires. A nice touch would be to stuff several peppers with different things and then serve them as an entrée."

Chris Arrison
Steaksmith

"I enjoy eating out more now than when I was new in the business. Back then, I was always very critical of the food and service, and drove my friends crazy! Fortunately, age does mellow one out, and now I just relax and enjoy the experience, flaws and all."

Herb Cohen
Steaksmith

Stuffed Poblano Peppers
with Tomatillo Salsa

Stuffed Poblano Peppers

1   **pound asiago cheese, grated**
1   **pound cream cheese, room temperature**
8   **poblano chile peppers**
    Tomatillo Salsa (recipe follows)

In a medium bowl place the asiago and cream cheeses, and mix them together well.

Make a slit, lengthwise, along the top of each poblano chile pepper. Very carefully remove the seeds.

Stuff each pepper with a generous portion of the cheese mixture.

Grill the peppers for 8 minutes, or until the chiles blacken and the cheese is melted.

Serve the peppers with the Tomatillo Salsa on the side.

serves 4

Tomatillo Salsa

3½   **pounds tomatillos, husks removed and skins scored, blanched, peeled and coarsely chopped**
1   **green bell pepper, seeded and diced medium**
1   **medium red onion, diced medium**
3   **avocados, peeled, pitted and diced medium**
2   **cloves fresh garlic, finely chopped**
1   **bunch fresh cilantro, chopped**
3   **teaspoons chile pequin** (hot red chile flakes)
⅛   **teaspoon ground cumin**
1   **cup lime juice, freshly squeezed**
⅛   **teaspoon white pepper** (or to taste)
⅛   **teaspoon black pepper** (or to taste)

Place the tomatillos in a food processor and coarsely purée them.

Add the rest of the ingredients and mix them together.

makes approximately 6 cups

Plazuela French Toast

6	eggs, well beaten
2	cups heavy cream
1	tablespoon fresh cilantro, chopped
1	teaspoon red chile powder
¼	teaspoon ground cinnamon
⅛	teaspoon ground nutmeg
1	tablespoon vanilla extract
¼	cup vegetable oil (or as needed)
12	thick slices bread
3	tablespoons powdered sugar
¼	cup melted butter, heated
1	cup maple syrup, heated

In a medium bowl place the beaten eggs, heavy cream, cilantro, red chile powder, cinnamon, nutmeg, and vanilla extract. Stir the ingredients together.

In a large sauté pan place some of the vegetable oil and heat it on medium high until it is hot.

Dip each bread slice into the egg mixture and cook it for 2 minutes on each side, or until it is golden brown.

Cut each piece in half, diagonally.

On each of 6 individual serving plates place four halves of the French toast. Sprinkle on the powdered sugar. Dribble on the melted butter and the maple syrup.

serves 6

"Fred Harvey used to own La Fonda hotel back in the 1930s, and this is one of his recipes. We added some cilantro and red chile to give it a surprise taste, but you can easily leave them out."

Lela Cross
La Plazuela

"Cooking runs in our family. My sister Lela is the Food and Beverage Manager of La Fonda, my brother is in the food service industry, my father is an excellent cook, and my mother, Vera, has her own catering business. It's called Tamales de Santa Fe. She is an expert in making classic northern New Mexico dishes."

Tomas Cross
La Plazuela

Dakota's Black Bean Chili

3	tablespoons olive oil
1	medium yellow onion, diced medium
1	medium red onion, diced medium
2	medium carrots, peeled and diced medium
2	stalks celery, diced medium
2	medium parsnips, peeled and diced medium
3	dried negro chile peppers, seeded and crushed
4	dried guajillo chile peppers, seeded and crushed
6	dried ancho chile peppers, seeded and crushed
2	tablespoons ground cumin
1	teaspoon ground fennel seed
1	teaspoon ground nutmeg
1	teaspoon ground cinnamon
1	teaspoon ground allspice
4	cups cooked black beans, drained
4	cups cooked black beans, drained and puréed
4	cups cooked black runner beans *(see chef's comments on this page)*, drained
2	quarts chicken stock *(recipe on page 311)*
	salt and black pepper *(to taste)*
1	cup sour cream
1	bunch fresh cilantro, chopped

In a large stockpot place the olive oil and heat it on medium high until it is hot. Add the yellow onions, red onions, carrots, celery, and parsnips. Sauté the ingredients for 5 minutes, or until the onions are translucent.

Add the negro, guajillo, and ancho chile peppers, cumin, fennel, nutmeg, cinnamon, and allspice. Sauté the ingredients for 2 minutes.

Add the black beans, puréed black beans, black runner beans, and chicken stock. Stir the ingredients together and simmer them for 30 minutes. Season the chili with the salt and black pepper.

Garnish each serving of chili with the sour cream and cilantro.

serves 10 to 12

"Here is a vegetarian dish that does not taste like a vegetarian dish. It's spicy and very hearty, and even meat eaters love it. There is no way to screw it up when you make it."

"Black runner beans may be hard to find. They are very large.....about the size of lima beans. I know you can order them from Elizabeth Berry (her address is on page 351). Otherwise, just use regular black beans."

Dakota
Piñon Grill

LP CALDWELL

Pasta

Southwestern Lasagna

1½	pounds boneless chicken, skin removed
1	bunch fresh cilantro, chopped
1	teaspoon ground cumin
4	teaspoons salt *(or to taste)*
½	teaspoon black pepper *(or to taste)*
3	cups ricotta cheese
1	cup corn kernels
½	cup fresh tomatoes, diced medium
½	cup zucchini, diced medium
¼	cup piñon nuts *(pine nuts)*
¼	cup green chile peppers, roasted, peeled, seeded and chopped
1	bunch fresh cilantro, chopped
4	teaspoons red chile powder
2	teaspoons salt *(or to taste)*
6	tablespoons butter
¾	cup flour
1¼	cups light cream
1½	pounds fresh red chile pasta *(see chef's comments on this page)*, blanched in boiling water for 2 minutes and then placed on a lightly oiled baking sheet
1	pound cheddar cheese, grated

In a large saucepan place the chicken, the first bunch of chopped cilantro, cumin, the 4 teaspoons of salt, and black pepper. Cover the ingredients with water and boil them for 1 hour *(add more water if necessary)*. Strain the ingredients through a fine sieve *(reserve 1 cup of the liquid)*. Let the chicken cool and then slice it thin.

Preheat the oven to 350°.

In a large bowl place the ricotta cheese, corn, tomatoes, zucchini, piñon nuts, green chile peppers, the second bunch of chopped cilantro, red chile powder, and the 2 teaspoons of salt. Mix the ingredients together and set them aside.

In a medium saucepan place the butter and heat it on medium until it is melted and hot. Add the flour and stir it in. While stirring constantly, cook the mixture for 3 minutes.

While whisking constantly, add the light cream and the reserved cooking liquid from the chicken.

(continued on next page)

"This is a fun alternative to a traditional Italian lasagna. The red chile pasta gives an extra zing to the flavor and makes the dish seem more festive. If you can't find it in your store, then regular pasta will suffice. Or, if you make your own pasta from scratch, just mix some red chile powder into the dough. Ground beef or chorizo sausage may be used instead of chicken."

"When I cook I like to use fresh ingredients, and I try to come up with combinations that are not too weird. I'm a fairly simple, down-to-earth, straightforward kind of a person, and I think that my style of cooking reflects this."

Dan Kelley
Peppers

"Dan is the greatest chef. He's a hard worker, gets along with everybody, doesn't cause any trouble, and is very responsible. But best of all, he doesn't have a big ego, which is really refreshing."

Patricia Helmick
Peppers

In the bottom of a 9"x13" baking dish place half of the pasta. Layer on half of the ricotta-vegetable mixture, half of the chicken, half of the cream sauce and half of the grated cheddar cheese. Repeat this process with the rest of the ingredients.

Bake the lasagna for 30 minutes, or until the cheese is melted and everything is hot and bubbly.

serves 6

"This dish was named after a character in the Pietro Mascagni opera, which was playing in the final scene of the movie, Godfather III."

"I like the flavors in this recipe, which is similar to a basic puttanesca sauce. Puttanesca means 'in the style of a whore'. In the south of Italy everyone always had garlic, olive oil, and hot peppers in their pantry. So, in between customers the prostitutes would throw these items together, along with tomatoes or whatever else they had on hand, to make a quick sauce for their pasta."

"Be careful not to overcook the garlic. It's the easiest to digest and the most flavorful when it begins to turn golden brown around the edges."

"Don't add cheese to this dish because it already has a high salt content with the capers, olives, and anchovies. Most Americans want to add cheese to their pasta, no matter what's in it.....even seafood. But if the seafood were served without the pasta, they wouldn't dream of adding cheese. However, overall, I think that Americans are becoming more sophisticated in their tastes. At least it seems so in my restaurant."

Ken Calascione
La Traviata

Spaghettini alla Turiddu

½   cup olive oil
2   tablespoons fresh garlic, chopped
½   cup tomatoes, chopped
4   anchovies, coarsely chopped
16 Calamata olives, pitted and chopped
4   tablespoons capers
2   dried pequin chile peppers, crushed
2   tablespoons fresh oregano, chopped
2   tablespoons fresh parsley, chopped
1   pound spaghettini, cooked al dente

In a large sauté pan place the olive oil and heat it on medium high until it is hot. Add the garlic and sauté it for 5 minutes, or until it begins to turn golden brown around the edges.

Add the tomatoes, anchovies, olives, capers, pequin chile peppers, oregano, and parsley. Stir the ingredients together.

Add the pasta and toss it in well.

serves 4

Tortellini with Smoked Cheddar Cheese & Chipotle Pepper Cream

1	tablespoon canola oil
2	cloves fresh garlic, finely chopped
1	shallot, finely chopped
4	tablespoons white wine
3	cups heavy cream
2	ounces chipotle chile peppers *(in adobo sauce)*, **finely chopped**
6	ounces smoked cheddar cheese, diced medium
1½	pounds tortellini, cooked al dente and drained
1	cup broccoli florets, blanched
1	red bell pepper, seeded and diced medium
	salt and white pepper *(to taste)*

In a large saucepan place the canola oil and heat it on medium until it is hot. Add the garlic and shallots, and sauté them for 2 minutes.

Add the white wine. Simmer the ingredients for 2 minutes, or until the wine is almost completely reduced.

Add the heavy cream and stir it in. Simmer the sauce for 10 to 15 minutes, or until it is reduced by ½ *(stir it occasionally)*.

Add the chipotle chile peppers and smoked cheddar cheese. Stir the ingredients together so that the cheese is melted.

Add the tortellini, broccoli, red bell peppers, salt, and white pepper. Toss the ingredients together well.

serves 6 to 8

"One night some of the other chefs and I were playing around in the kitchen, trying to come up with a new recipe for our dinner, and this was the result. It tastes wonderful, and can be put together in about fifteen minutes."

"For me, being a chef means that every day is an adventure. I am constantly dealing with 'Murphy's Law', which I find very challenging."

"I try to train the people around me to view basic food in new and original ways. For instance, if you take the idea of a ham sandwich, you can put the essential ingredients together in a slightly different way to come up with an elegant appetizer.....remove the crust from rye bread and cut the slices into triangles. Mix some mustard with cream cheese, pipe it on the bread pieces, add a twist of ham, and garnish it with a small piece of lettuce and tomato."

Rustin Newton
Staab House

Spicy Shrimp with Spaghettini

½	cup extra virgin olive oil
6	cloves fresh garlic, very thinly sliced
¾	pound medium shrimp, peeled and deveined
2	teaspoons chile pequin *(or to taste)*
3	ounces sundried tomatoes, rehydrated in hot water and thinly sliced
1½	cups peas
1	tablespoon fresh parsley, chopped
½	cup white wine
3	tablespoons butter
12	ounces spaghettini, cooked al dente and drained
⅓	cup Romano cheese, freshly grated

In a large sauté pan place the olive oil and heat it on medium high until it is hot. Add the garlic and sauté it for 5 minutes, or until it begins to brown around the edges.

Add the shrimp and chile pequin, and sauté them for 30 seconds.

Add the sundried tomatoes, peas, and parsley, and toss them in.

Add the white wine to deglaze the pan. Cook the ingredients for 2 minutes, or until the shrimp are done.

Add the butter and stir it in so that it is melted.

Remove the pan from the heat. Add the pasta and toss it in well.

Serve the pasta and shrimp with the Romano cheese sprinkled on top.

serves 4

"What's nice about this dish is that it is very light, with a lot of different flavors that all come through. You may use fresh or frozen peas, snow peas, or sugar snap peas. Some people may not like the idea of cheese with shrimp, but only a tiny bit is used. I find the sharpness of the cheese to go nicely with the sweetness of the shrimp and peas."

Steven Lemon
Pranzo Italian Grill

"This is one of my favorite recipes that took some experimentation to perfect. We serve it at Pranzo, although in a slightly altered form.....fresh lemon juice replaces the white wine. Both versions are excellent."

"I love to eat out at restaurants with my friends, but they claim that I am very critical. I may complain to them about something that is wrong, but I have to be in the right mood to send something back to the kitchen. Sometimes I just don't have the energy to do it."

Marta Mueller
Pranzo Italian Grill

Stir-Fry Pasta

¼   **cup olive oil**
1   **red bell pepper, seeded and cut into thin strips**
1   **yellow bell pepper, seeded and cut into thin strips**
1   **green bell pepper, seeded and cut into thin strips**
1   **small red onion, thinly sliced**
1   **cup button mushrooms, thinly sliced**
1   **cup broccoli florets**
1   **small yellow squash, sliced into half moons**
1   **zucchini, sliced into half moons**
3   **cloves fresh garlic, finely chopped**
1   **teaspoon chile pequin** (hot red chile flakes)
½   **cup soy sauce**
¼   **cup olive oil**
3   **tablespoons Chipotle Chile Butter** (recipe on page 192)
     salt and white pepper (to taste)
1   **pound linguini, cooked and drained**

In a large wok place the first ¼ cup of olive oil and heat it on medium high until it is hot. Add the red, yellow and green bell peppers, red onions, mushrooms, broccoli, yellow squash, zucchini, and garlic. Stir-fry the ingredients for 3 to 5 minutes, or until the vegetables are tender, but still crisp.

Add the chile pequin, soy sauce, the second ¼ cup of olive oil, Chipotle Chile Butter, salt, and white pepper. Stir the ingredients together.

On each of 4 individual serving plates place the linguini. Spoon the vegetables on top.

serves 4

"This recipe evolved from my restaurant experience in both Japanese and Santa Fe restaurants. I like the combination of Oriental and Southwestern ingredients in food."

Rubin Rodriquez
Guadalupe Cafe

"I find this dish to be very gratifying because of all of the fresh vegetables. People who love spicy, meatless food especially enjoy it."

"We have owned the Guadalupe Restaurant for eighteen years, and from the very beginning we have always made everything from scratch. Way back then most restaurants depended on mixes, frozen items, and prepared foods for their dishes. I think that our philosophy of using fresh ingredients as much as possible has paid off."

Isabelle Koomoa
Guadalupe Cafe

Pasta del Pirata Barbanera

¼ cup olive oil
1 medium yellow onion, diced medium
4 cloves fresh garlic, finely chopped
4 anchovy fillets
1 teaspoon chile pequin *(hot red chile flakes)*
1 teaspoon fresh rosemary, chopped
1 eggplant, peeled and diced small
4 cups Roma tomatoes, diced medium
1 pound spaghetti, cooked al dente and drained
1 cup parmesan cheese, freshly grated

In a large sauté pan place the olive oil and heat it on medium high until it is hot. Add the yellow onions, garlic, anchovy fillets, chile pequin, and rosemary. Sauté the ingredients for 2 minutes.

Add the eggplant and Roma tomatoes, and stir them in. Reduce the heat to low, cover the pan, and simmer the ingredients for 20 minutes.

In a large, warm bowl place the spaghetti. Add the sauce and toss it in well. Sprinkle the parmesan cheese on top.

serves 6

Spaghetti with Garlic & Arugula

½ cup olive oil
2 tablespoons fresh garlic, chopped
¼ cup dry white wine
2 bunches arugula, chopped
2 dried pequin chile peppers, crushed
  salt *(to taste)*
1 pound spaghetti, cooked al dente

In a large sauté pan place the olive oil and heat it on medium high until it is hot. Add the garlic and sauté it for 5 minutes, or until it begins to turn golden brown on the edges.

Add the white wine, arugula, pequin chile peppers, and salt. Stir the ingredients together.

Add the pasta and toss it in well.

serves 4

Capellini with Grilled Vegetables

2	**tablespoons butter**
1	**tablespoon fresh garlic, roasted** *(see chef's comments on page 60)* **and finely chopped**
1	**cup shiitake mushrooms, grilled and sliced**
1	**bulb fennel root, grilled and sliced**
1	**medium red onion, grilled and sliced**
4	**jalapeño chile peppers, grilled, seeded and sliced**
6	**poblano chile peppers, grilled, seeded and sliced**
1	**tablespoon fresh basil, finely chopped**
¼	**cup Reggiano cheese** *(parmesan)*, **freshly grated**
1	**cup chicken stock** *(recipe on page 311)*
¼	**teaspoon cayenne pepper** *(or to taste)*
	salt *(to taste)*
1	**pound capellini pasta** *(or angel hair)*, **cooked al dente**
2	**tablespoons extra virgin olive oil**

In a medium large saucepan place the butter and heat it on medium high until it is melted and hot. Add the roasted garlic, shiitake mushrooms, fennel root, red onions, jalapeño and poblano chile peppers, basil, half of the Reggiano cheese, and chicken stock. Bring the ingredients to a boil so that they are heated through.

Add the cayenne pepper and salt, and stir them in.

Add the capellini and fold it in.

Add the olive oil and toss it in.

Serve the pasta with the rest of the cheese sprinkled on top.

serves 4

"Here is a really clean, healthy, substantial meal that doesn't hit you over the head with being vegetarian. You can use oil instead of butter, although the butter gives the dish a nice velvety texture."

"I recommend that people be economical in their use of a gas grill. If you are going to barbecue some chicken for dinner, go ahead and grill the vegetables for a future recipe at the same time. That would work well here, because the extra vegetables could be served cold or at room temperature."

"It is understandably somewhat intimidating to be married to a chef. My wife used to get mad at me if I made a negative comment or suggestion on her dishes. So now she has turned all the cooking over to me, and that seems to work out fine."

Pete Zimmer
Inn of the Anasazi

Spicy Lasagna

2	tablespoons vegetable oil
1	medium yellow onion, diced medium
1	clove fresh garlic, finely chopped
1	pound hot Italian sausage
½	cup ground beef
2	green chile peppers, roasted, peeled, seeded and diced medium
4	cups crushed tomatoes
½	cup red wine
	salt and black pepper *(to taste)*
1	pound lasagna noodles, cooked al dente and drained
2	cups Bêchamel Sauce *(recipe on page 115)*
½	pound mozzarella cheese, grated

"If you like spicy food, you will like this lasagna better than the typical version. I really enjoy making Italian dishes with a Southwestern twist."

Kimo Castro
San Francisco St. Bar & Grill

Preheat the oven to 350°.

In a large saucepan place the vegetable oil and heat it on medium high until it is hot. Add the yellow onions and garlic. Sauté them for 5 minutes, or until the onions are translucent.

Add the Italian sausage, ground beef, and green chile peppers. Sauté the ingredients for 5 to 7 minutes, or until the meats are cooked. Drain off the grease.

Add the tomatoes, red wine, salt, and black pepper. Reduce the heat to low and simmer the ingredients for 45 minutes.

In a 9"x13" baking pan place ⅓ of the meat sauce. Layer on ½ of the noodles. Repeat this procedure, ending with the last ⅓ of the meat sauce.

Pour the Bêchamel Sauce on top. Sprinkle on the mozzarella cheese.

Bake the lasagna for 25 to 30 minutes, or until it is hot and the cheese is bubbly.

serves 8

Pasta

Pasta with Green Chile Champagne Beurre Blanc, Crab & Red Chile Fried Oysters

Pasta with Green Chile Champagne Beurre Blanc & Crab

2	large Anaheim chile peppers, seeded and thinly sliced
6	scallions, finely sliced
4	cups champagne
2	lemons, freshly squeezed
½	cup heavy cream
½	pound unsalted butter, chopped
1	pinch cayenne pepper
1½	teaspoons kosher salt *(or to taste)*
1	pound wide noodle pasta, cooked al dente and drained
1	tablespoon unsalted butter
¾	pound Dungeness crab meat, cleaned
	Red Chile Fried Oysters *(recipe on next page)*
1	bunch fresh cilantro, chopped

In a large saucepan place ½ of the Anaheim chile peppers, ½ of the scallions, the champagne, and lemon juice. Bring the ingredients to a boil and then simmer them for 15 minutes, or until the sauce is reduced by ½.

Add the heavy cream and simmer the ingredients for 5 minutes, or until the sauce is slightly reduced. Remove the pan from the stove. Add the ½ pound of butter and quickly whisk it in so that it is melted and hot. Strain the sauce through a fine sieve and return it to the saucepan.

Add the rest of the Anaheim chile peppers and scallions, cayenne pepper, and salt, and stir them in. Add the cooked pasta and toss the ingredients together.

In a small sauté pan place the 1 tablespoon of butter and heat it on medium until it is melted and hot. Add the crab and sauté it for 1 minute, or until it is heated.

On each of 6 individual serving plates place the pasta. Place the crab and Red Chile Fried Oysters on top. Sprinkle the cilantro on top.

serves 6

"When Gina first came up with this recipe I didn't say anything, but I really wondered if it would work. I mean, just look at the ingredients.....green chile, pasta, champagne beurre blanc, crab, red chile, and fried oysters. There's really a lot going on. Anyway, she went ahead and made it, I tasted it, and it was phenomenal!"

Cliff Skoglund
Geronimo

"This dish is a combination of different ingredients that I personally like. There is a wonderful contrast of tastes and textures, with the soft noodles, tangy sauce, crispy oysters, and sweet crab meat. I love to eat this with a glass of good white wine."

"Pasta is a wonderful medium, because it is so versatile. It can be a flat noodle or a stuffed pasta; it can be creamy or chunky; and it absorbs flavors really well."

Gina Ziluca
Geronimo

Red Chile Fried Oysters

1	tablespoon kosher salt
1½	cups flour
3	tablespoons red chile powder
½	cup cornmeal
24	small oysters, shucked
4	cups vegetable oil *(or as needed)*

In a medium bowl place the kosher salt, flour, red chile powder, and cornmeal. Mix the ingredients together well. Dredge the oysters in the mixture so that they are well coated.

In a large heavy pan place the vegetable oil and heat it on high until it is very hot.

Add the oysters and flash-fry them for 1 minute, or until they are golden brown.

Drain the oysters on paper towels.

serves 6

Spicy Noodles

1	cup peanuts, ground *(see chef's comments on this page)*
⅓	cup scallions, thinly sliced
1	tablespoon chile pequin *(hot red chile flakes)*
1	tablespoon sesame seeds, toasted
1	teaspoon ground coriander
½	teaspoon ground ginger
1	cup soy oil
2	tablespoons hot chile oil
½	cup soy sauce
1	pound vermicelli, cooked al dente, drained and cooled

In a large bowl place all the ingredients *(except for the vermicelli),* and whisk them together.

Add the vermicelli and toss it in well.

Cover the bowl with plastic wrap and refrigerate it for 1 hour.

Toss the ingredients together again before serving.

serves 4

Penne Pasta in
Green Chile Pesto Cream

7	cloves fresh garlic, roasted *(see chef's comments on this page)* and coarsely chopped
2	cups green chile peppers, roasted, peeled, seeded and chopped
¾	cup parmesan cheese, freshly grated
½	cup piñon nuts *(pine nuts)*, toasted *(see chef's comments on page 317)*
1	tablespoon fresh cilantro leaves, coarsely chopped
3	tablespoons olive oil
1	teaspoon lime juice, freshly squeezed
½	teaspoon salt
¼	teaspoon black pepper
1	quart heavy cream
2	pounds penne pasta *(see chef's comments on this page)*, cooked al dente
¼	cup piñon nuts, toasted

In a food processor place the garlic, green chile peppers, parmesan cheese, the ½ cup of piñon nuts, cilantro, olive oil, lime juice, salt, and black pepper. Blend the ingredients together so that they are smooth. Set the purée aside.

In a large saucepan place the heavy cream and heat it on medium for 5 minutes, or until it is reduced by ⅓.

Add the green chile purée to the cream and stir it in. Heat the sauce so that it simmers.

Add the pasta to the sauce and toss it in well.

Garnish each serving with a sprinkling of the ¼ cup of piñon nuts.

serves 8

"When I am working in the restaurant and need to come up with specials, I have a tendency to get stuck in ruts. For instance, I'll get stuck in always using tomatoes with pasta, or whatever. This particular recipe was created when I was in my pesto rut. It's a little spicy, but really delicious!"

"Penne pasta is a tubular pasta with slanted ends, which is a bit thicker than macaroni, but smaller than rigatoni. You may substitute any kind of substantial pasta shape."

"You can roast the garlic in a small pan on the stove. Add a little olive oil and roll them around until they are nicely brown. Or, you can roast them in the oven in a pan."

"I think that being a chef is a noble profession, because you are giving people one of the necessities of life. Cooking also is a wonderful creative outlet for me. There is something very satisfying about working in a smoothly running kitchen with a lot of creative people.....kind of like driving a finely tuned Porsche!"

"For me, when I eat spicy food, if my nose isn't running and my eyelids don't get sweaty, it's not hot enough!"

Rocky Durham
Zia Diner

Fettucine with Smoked Salmon, Mushrooms, Walnuts & Green Chile Cream Sauce

Fettucine with Smoked Salmon, Mushrooms & Walnuts

2	tablespoons olive oil
¼	pound mushrooms, sliced
1	pound fettucine, cooked al dente
½	pound smoked salmon, flaked into bite-size pieces
½	cup walnuts, coarsely chopped
½	cup Parmesan cheese, freshly grated
2	cups Green Chile Cream Sauce *(recipe follows)*

In a small sauté pan place the olive oil and heat it on medium high until it is hot. Add the mushrooms and sauté them for 5 minutes, or until they are tender.

In a large, warm bowl place the sautéed mushrooms and the rest of the ingredients. Toss everything together well.

serves 4

Green Chile Cream Sauce

¾	cup green chile peppers, roasted, peeled, seeded and diced
1¼	cups heavy cream
	salt and black pepper *(to taste)*

In a small saucepan place the green chile peppers and cream. Heat them on medium for 5 minutes, or until the sauce thickens. Season the sauce with the salt and black pepper.

makes 2 cups

"One night I had dinner at my sister's house, and she served a wonderful pasta with smoked salmon, mushrooms, and walnuts. So I borrowed that idea and decided to turn it into a Southwestern version. It's been a big hit with everyone."

Dorothy Charles
The Galisteo Inn

"Pastas are Dorothy's favorite thing to make, and she's wonderful at it. Her recipes sound so simple, but they always taste delicious. She is an excellent cook and I really enjoy having her around because she is so mellow. When she is cooking she appears to be casually throwing fresh ingredients together, and then suddenly a wonderful meal miraculously appears in the dining room."

Joanna Kaufman
The Galisteo Inn

White Lasagna with Green Chile Cheese Sauce

3   teaspoons olive oil
1   **head broccoli, divided into florets and blanched** (peel and chop
     the stems, and reserve them)
1   **head cauliflower, divided into florets and blanched**
1   **eggplant, peeled and diced medium**
1   **red bell pepper, seeded and thinly sliced**
⅓   **pound mushrooms, thinly sliced**
1   **cup green chile peppers, roasted, peeled, seeded and diced
     medium**
     salt and white pepper (to taste)
     Green Chile Cheese Sauce (recipe on page 119)
1   **pound lasagna pasta, cooked al dente, rinsed and drained**
1   **pound ricotta cheese**
¾   **pound mozzarella cheese, grated**
6   **tablespoons parmesan cheese, freshly grated**

Preheat the oven to 325°.

In a large sauté pan place the olive oil and heat it on medium
high until it is hot. Add the broccoli, cauliflower, eggplant, red
bell peppers, and mushrooms. Sauté the ingredients for 3
minutes. Add the green chile peppers, salt, and white pepper. Stir
the ingredients together.

Lightly oil a 9"x12" baking dish. Spread a thin layer of the Green
Chile Cheese Sauce on the bottom of the dish. In this order, layer
on enough of the lasagna noodles to cover the pan, more of the
cheese sauce, and ⅓ of the vegetable mixture. Dot on ⅓ of the
ricotta cheese. Sprinkle on ¼ of both the mozzarella and
parmesan cheeses. Repeat this process 2 more times, ending
with a fourth layer of the lasagna noodles.

In a food processor place the reserved broccoli stems and the
remaining cheese sauce. Purée the ingredients so that they are
smooth.

Spread the sauce over the top of the fourth layer of noodles.
Sprinkle on the remaining mozzarella and parmesan cheeses.

Bake the lasagna for 1 hour, or until everything is hot and bubbly.

serves 8

"This is a white lasagna because there is no tomato sauce in it. It's a wonderful, healthy dish with lots of different vegetables. The green chile peppers give it a delicious under flavor."

"When you prepare food for people in a deli where they watch you do it, you are like their mother. They want everything just so, with lots of special requests. Especially in Santa Fe, where there is a large health-conscious population, people will be really picky. They say, 'I would like that dish, but can I have it without the meat, without any oil, without any sugar, and without any salt?' So what's left? A piece of lettuce and a plate!"

Peter Raub
Santa Fe Market

"I love foods that are spicy to the point just short of making me cry."

Marsha Chobol
Santa Fe Market

Spaghetti Carbonara

"My understanding of the origins of this recipe is that it stems from a pre-socialist outlaw group in Italy called the 'Carbonaros'. They were always warring and hiding, and carried non-perishable food that was very easy to prepare. This is an Americanized version of the classic recipe. It contains butter, cream, eggs, and provolone cheese, all of which were lacking in the original."

Kimo Castro
San Francisco St. Bar & Grill

12	ounces spaghetti, cooked al dente and drained
⅓	pound bacon, diced medium, cooked and drained
1	clove fresh garlic, finely chopped
2	teaspoons chile pequin *(hot red chile pepper flakes)*
1	tablespoon white wine
1	teaspoon salt *(or to taste)*
½	cup provolone cheese, grated
2	tablespoons parmesan cheese, freshly grated
2	tablespoons Romano cheese, freshly grated
1	tablespoon butter
2	egg yolks, beaten
¾	cup heavy cream

In a large saucepan place the spaghetti, bacon, garlic, chile pequin, white wine, and salt. Heat the ingredients on medium and toss them together.

Add the provolone, parmesan, and Romano cheeses, butter, egg yolks, and heavy cream. Stir the ingredients together so that the cheeses melt.

serves 4

L P CALDWELL

Fish & Shellfish

Jalapeño Ginger Broiled Shrimp

3	inches fresh ginger root, peeled and thinly sliced
1½	cups water
½	medium red onion, finely diced
½	red bell pepper, seeded and finely diced
½	yellow bell pepper, seeded and finely diced
1	jalapeño chile pepper, seeded and finely diced
3	scallions, finely diced
3	limes, juiced
2	teaspoons salt
24	large shrimp, peeled and deveined

In a food processor place the ginger root and water, and purée them so that a paste is formed.

Place the ginger paste in a cheesecloth *(or a thin cotton cloth)*. Fold the cloth together and squeeze the juice out into a medium bowl.

Add the red onions, red and yellow bell peppers, jalapeño chile peppers, scallions, lime juice, and salt. Mix the ingredients together.

Preheat the oven to broil.

In a lightly oiled baking pan place the shrimp so that each one lies flat on the bottom of the pan. Broil them for 1 to 2 minutes. Turn the shrimp over and spoon the vegetable mixture on top. Broil the shrimp for 2 minutes more, or until they are done.

serves 4

"I love the flavor of shrimp and often use it in my recipes. The ginger flavor of this dish will depend on the youth of the ginger you use. If your ginger is fresh and young, it will be sweet, with a zing to the after-taste. Old ginger tends to be woody, with almost an astringent taste. You can store your ginger in sherry or oil in the refrigerator, and it will keep for months."

"I grill or broil shrimp to the point where they turn pink, and then I turn them over. There is nothing worse than eating an overcooked shrimp that tastes like a rubber band."

Rocky Packard
On Water

"I find owning a restaurant to be stressful, challenging, and rewarding. When I was in culinary school I took management classes, but they in no way prepared me for reality. I have to be a psychologist, a teacher, a coach, a disciplinarian, a big brother, a mother.....I have to be all of these different people to effectively deal with my employees."

Don Fortel
On Water

Shrimp & Shiitake Mushroom Sauté with Cracked Black Pepper & Tomato Salsa

Shrimp & Shiitake Mushroom Sauté

2	tablespoons olive oil
1½	pounds shiitake mushrooms, cleaned and quartered
2	shallots, finely chopped
1	clove fresh garlic, finely chopped
2	pounds large shrimp, peeled and deveined
3	tablespoons white wine
	salt *(to taste)*
	Cracked Black Pepper and Tomato Salsa *(recipe follows)*

In a large sauté pan place the olive oil and heat it on medium high until it is hot. Add the shiitake mushrooms, shallots, and garlic. Sauté them for 5 minutes.

Add the shrimp and sauté them for 2 minutes, or until they are just done.

Add the white wine and deglaze the pan.

Season the shrimp with the salt.

In a large bowl place the shrimp and the Cracked Black Pepper and Tomato Salsa. Toss the ingredients together.

serves 6

Cracked Black Pepper & Tomato Salsa

6	Roma tomatoes, diced medium
1	yellow bell pepper, roasted, peeled, seeded and finely diced
¼	cup fresh garlic, finely chopped
½	cup scallions, thinly sliced
¼	cup fresh cilantro, chopped
⅓	cup cracked black pepper
½	cup V-8 juice
4	limes, freshly squeezed and zested *(outer green part grated off)*

In a large bowl place all the ingredients and toss them together.

makes approximately 3 cups

"This is a very simple dish to make and it has a wonderful combination of flavors. Some 'prep' time is required in peeling and deveining the shrimp, and chopping the vegetables, but otherwise you basically just throw the ingredients together."

"I grew up in the Midwest, and fresh seafood was not available, so I didn't learn to like it. In fact, as recently as eight years ago the flavor of shrimp almost repulsed me, and I never ate any kind of fish at all. But I kept pushing myself to try it, and now I enjoy up to twenty-five varieties."

"The kick in this salsa comes from the cracked black pepper. I like to make it at least one day in advance so the flavors can marry. This will keep for up to three days."

Rustin Newton
Staab House

Ore House Grilled Shrimp with Chipotle Barbecue Sauce

Ore House Grilled Shrimp

36	large shrimp *(16 to 20 count),* **peeled and deveined**
	Chipotle Barbecue Sauce *(recipe follows)*
2	**medium tomatoes, diced small**
1	**medium red onion, diced small**
2	**large avocados, peeled, seeded and cubed small**

Place the shrimp on 6 small skewers. Grill them on one side for 2 minutes.

Turn them over and apply a thick layer of the Chipotle Barbecue Sauce. Grill the shrimp for 2 to 3 minutes more, or until the desired doneness is achieved.

On each of 6 individual serving plates sprinkle on the tomatoes, red onions, and avocados. Place the shrimp on top.

serves 6

Chipotle Barbecue Sauce

3	**dried ancho chile peppers, soaked in hot water for 2 hours, drained** *(reserve the soaking water),* **stems and seeds removed**
½	**can chipotle chile peppers** *(in adobo sauce)*
½	**cup tomatoes, diced**
3	**cloves fresh garlic**
¼	**cup balsamic vinegar**
¼	**cup brown sugar**
1	**pinch ground cinnamon**
1	**pinch ground cloves**
1	**pinch salt**

In a food processor place all of the ingredients *(except for the reserved soaking water)* and purée them together. Add ½ to 1 cup of the reserved soaking water so that the desired consistency is achieved.

makes 2 cups

"Both our customers and employees absolutely love this dish. The sweetness of the brown sugar combined with the smoky heat of the chiles really gives the sauce an outstanding flavor."

Daniella Croce Carr
Ore House

"A few years ago I told a friend that I wanted to change professions and do work that was more loving to people. She asked me what could be more loving than preparing food for others. That was a nice reminder for me."

"This is a hot recipe! The great thing about the sauce is that you can use it on almost anything you grill. It's wonderful with seafood, poultry, beef and pork. Baste it on as you are cooking the food, just as you would with any commercial barbecue sauce. You may need to thin it out with some water if you use it on foods that need to cook longer. Otherwise, it will burn."

Isaac Modivah
Ore House

Marinated Grilled Shrimp with Saffron Jalapeño Tarragon Sauce

Marinated Grilled Shrimp

24	large shrimp, peeled and deveined
1	cup olive oil
1	small yellow onion, sliced
1	teaspoon salt
½	teaspoon black pepper
	Saffron Jalapeño Tarragon Sauce *(recipe follows)*

In a medium bowl place the shrimp, olive oil, yellow onions, salt, and black pepper. Cover the bowl with plastic wrap and marinate the shrimp for 2 hours in the refrigerator.

Grill the shrimp for 2 minutes on each side, or until they are just done.

On each of 4 individual serving plates place the shrimp. Pour the Saffron Jalapeño Tarragon Sauce on top.

serves 6

Saffron Jalapeño Tarragon Sauce

1	pinch saffron
3	jalapeño chile peppers, seeded and finely chopped
¼	cup fresh tarragon, chopped
3	shallots, finely chopped
½	cup white wine
1	quart heavy cream
	salt and black pepper *(to taste)*

In a medium saucepan place the saffron, jalapeño chile peppers, tarragon, shallots, and white wine. Heat them on medium high for 10 to 15 minutes, or until the liquid is reduced by ½.

Add the heavy cream and bring the sauce to a boil. Season it with the salt and black pepper. Place the sauce in a blender and purée it so that it is smooth.

makes approximately 2 cups

Beer-Battered Shrimp Rellenos with Tomato Japone Chile Sauce & Tomatillo Green Chile Sauce

Beer-Battered Shrimp Rellenos

½	lemon, freshly squeezed
1	pinch salt
½	pound large shrimp, peeled and deveined
4	ounces mozzarella cheese, grated
	salt and black pepper *(to taste)*
6	poblano chile peppers, roasted and peeled
4	cups canola oil
	Beer Batter *(recipe on page 306)*
	Tomato Japone Chile Sauce *(recipe on next page)*
	Tomatillo Green Chile Sauce *(recipe on next page)*

Fill a medium saucepan half full of water. Add the lemon juice and the pinch of salt, and bring the water to a boil.

Place the shrimp in the water and bring them to a boil. Immediately remove the shrimp, place them in a chilled bowl, and refrigerate them.

Slice the chilled shrimp into ½" pieces and place them in a medium bowl. Add the mozzarella cheese and stir it with the shrimp. Season the mixture with the salt and black pepper.

Cut a 2" slit, lengthwise, in each of the poblano chile peppers. Carefully remove the seeds.

Stuff each pepper with an equal amount of the shrimp and cheese mixture.

In a large, heavy pan place the canola oil and heat it on medium high until it is hot.

Dip each of the stuffed poblano chile peppers in the Beer Batter.

Place them in the hot oil and deep-fry them for 3 minutes, or until they are golden brown. Drain them on paper towels.

On each of 6 individual serving plates place a chile relleno. Serve the Tomato Japone Chile Sauce and Tomatillo Green Chile Sauce on the side.

serves 6

"I like to make rellenos with different stuffings, from seafood to lamb. Shrimp seems to work especially well, judging by the reactions of people who eat this dish. The only tricky thing is the peeling of the chiles, which you might have to get the hang of. Don't wash the seeds out with water, because this will remove the oil and the wonderful smoky flavor of the chiles."

Tim Lopez
Rancho Encantado

"The late Betty Egan came to the Southwest from Ohio in the early 1960s with her children, looking for a place to convert to a guest ranch. She found this property in Tesuque and fell in love with it. The buildings were in a real mess, with as much grass growing inside as out, and cattle wandering through. She and her family started working on repairing and building the structures. A rumor started in town that there was this crazy old lady from the midwest trying to rebuild the old Rancho del Monte. Rancho Encantado opened in 1968, and its success is legendary. A television movie has been made about this story, starring Blair Brown as Betty Egan."

John Litton
Rancho Encantado

Tomato Japone Chile Sauce

7	**Roma tomatoes, roasted** *(see chef's comments on page 72)*
8	**dried japone chile peppers** *(see chef's comments on this page)*, **seeded**
½	**medium yellow onion, finely chopped**
2	**cloves fresh garlic, finely chopped**
5	**scallions, finely sliced**
½	**bunch fresh cilantro, chopped**
1	**teaspoon white vinegar**
	salt and black pepper *(to taste)*

Place the roasted Roma tomatoes and japone chile peppers in a food processor, and purée them so that they are somewhat smooth.

In a medium saucepan place the puréed ingredients, yellow onions, garlic, scallions, cilantro, white vinegar, salt, and black pepper. Stir the ingredients together and simmer them for 15 minutes *(add a little water if the sauce is too thick)*.

makes approximately 1 cup

Tomatillo Green Chile Sauce

8	**tomatillos, husks removed**
½	**medium yellow onion, thinly sliced**
½	**cup green chile peppers, roasted, peeled, seeded and diced**
2	**cloves fresh garlic, finely chopped**
1	**jalapeño chile pepper, seeded and finely chopped**
½	**bunch fresh cilantro, chopped**
1	**lime, freshly squeezed**
	salt and white pepper *(to taste)*

In a large saucepan place the tomatillos and enough water to cover them. Boil the tomatillos for 5 to 10 minutes, or until they discolor *(see chef's comments on this page)*, and drain them.

Place the tomatillos, yellow onions, green chile peppers, and garlic in a food processor. Purée the ingredients so that they are smooth.

Return the purée to the saucepan.

Add the jalapeño chile peppers, cilantro, lime juice, salt, and white pepper. Stir the ingredients together and simmer them for 15 minutes.

makes 3 cups

Shrimp in Chile Sauce

2	egg whites
2	teaspoons rice wine
3	tablespoons cornstarch
1	teaspoon salt
2	pounds medium shrimp, peeled and deveined
½	cup vegetable oil
4	tablespoons scallions, chopped medium
2	tablespoons fresh ginger root, peeled and finely chopped
4	tablespoons ketchup
2	tablespoons hot chile oil
6	tablespoons chicken stock *(recipe on page 311)*
1	teaspoon sugar
1	teaspoon salt *(or to taste)*
4	teaspoons cornstarch
4	teaspoons water
2	teaspoons toasted sesame oil

In a medium bowl place the egg whites, rice wine, the 3 tablespoons of cornstarch, and the first teaspoon of salt. Stir the ingredients together well. Add the shrimp and stir them in so that they are well coated with the mixture.

In a wok place the vegetable oil and heat it on high until it is very hot. Add the shrimp and stir-fry them for 30 seconds, or until they are opaque. Remove the shrimp and set them aside.

Discard all but about 4 tablespoons of the oil from the wok.

Add the scallions and ginger, and sauté them for 1 minute.

Add the ketchup, hot chile oil, chicken stock, sugar, and the second teaspoon of salt. Stir the ingredients together and bring them to a boil.

In a small bowl place the 4 teaspoons of cornstarch and the water. Stir the ingredients together well.

While whisking constantly, slowly add the cornstarch paste to the wok. Add the sesame oil and stir it in.

Return the shrimp to the pan. Simmer the ingredients for 2 minutes, or until the sauce thickens.

serves 4

"This is a very spicy dish. I love to eat it at the restaurant, and I also make it at home. Read the recipe through and have all of your ingredients ready before you start cooking."

"My father wanted my mother to make the dishes his mother made, so he was always telling her how to do things. If she made a dish he would taste it and be able to tell exactly what was wrong.....that she had put the sugar in too early, or whatever. He had an amazing palate."

Marta Hung
Imperial Wok

Scallops Santiago

2	tablespoons olive oil
4	tablespoons yellow onions, finely chopped
2	tablespoons scallions, thinly sliced
2	tablespoons red bell peppers, finely diced
1	tablespoon jalapeño chile pepper, seeded and finely chopped
2	cloves fresh garlic, finely chopped
1	pound scallops, muscles removed, washed and drained
1	dried red chile pepper, crumbled
2	tablespoons fresh Italian parsley, chopped
½	teaspoon dried thyme
	salt and white pepper *(to taste)*
2	tablespoons brandy, warmed
½	cup fresh tomatoes, puréed
½	cup white wine
3	cups cooked white rice

In a large sauté pan place the olive oil and heat it on medium high until it is hot. Add the yellow onions, scallions, red bell peppers, jalapeño chile peppers, and garlic. Sauté the ingredients for 5 minutes, or until the onions are translucent.

Add the scallops and sauté them for 2 minutes, or until they are opaque.

Reduce the heat to medium. Add the crumbled red chile pepper, Italian parsley, thyme, salt, and white pepper. Sauté the ingredients for 1 minute.

Add the warm brandy and flambé the ingredients.

Add the tomato purée and white wine. Stir the ingredients together and simmer them gently for 5 minutes.

Serve the scallops and sauce on top of the white rice.

serves 6

Red Chile Scallop & Spinach Cakes with Fried Corn Salsa

Red Chile Scallop & Spinach Cakes

1	pound scallops, muscles removed, and finely chopped
3	eggs, lightly beaten
1	cup spinach, washed, stems and veins removed, and chopped
2	cups dried bread crumbs
¼	cup red chile powder
1	tablespoon Dijon mustard
1	teaspoon salt
½	teaspoon black pepper
¼	cup olive oil *(or as needed)*
	Fried Corn Salsa *(recipe follows)*

In a medium large bowl place the first 8 ingredients and mix them together well. Chill the mixture for at least 1 hour. Form the mixture into small patties.

In a large skillet place the olive oil and heat it on medium high until it is hot. Add the scallop cakes and sauté them for 2 to 3 minutes on each side, or until they are golden brown. Serve the cakes with the Fried Corn Salsa on the side.

serves 4 to 6

Fried Corn Salsa

¼	cup olive oil
1	can corn *(16 ounces)*, drained
1	small red onion, diced small
1	jalapeño chile pepper, seeded and finely chopped
1	large red bell pepper, seeded and diced small
1	large green bell pepper, seeded and diced small
1	tablespoon fresh cilantro, finely chopped
	salt and black pepper *(to taste)*

In a medium large sauté pan place the olive oil and heat it on medium high until it is hot. Add the corn, red onions, jalapeño chile peppers, red and green bell peppers, and cilantro. Sauté the ingredients for 5 to 6 minutes, or until the peppers are slightly soft. Add the salt and black pepper.

makes approximately 4 cups

"This recipe is a favorite with our customers. It has a wonderful flavor and is quite easy to prepare. The only tricky part is in sautéing the cakes. You need to have a high heat, but you can't let them burn. It's hard to tell when they are done because you can't stick a toothpick in them. Just experiment, and you'll figure it out."

"We describe our cuisine as eclectic, modern, and international.....whatever that means! Basically, we do our own thing and don't follow food trends. We do try to have a healthy beat on what we serve, but otherwise we cook what we personally like."

"We put as much effort into the visual presentation of food as into the actual cooking of it. Each plate is built on its own, and not mass-produced like in a lot of large restaurants with a factory-like atmosphere. Here we are small, and very personal."

"Here is a straightforward salsa that tastes great and is very healthy. If we take it off the menu our customers come in and ask for it. You can use this with any kind of seafood."

Paul Hunsicker
Paul's Restaurant

Red Chile Seafood Stew

"I came up with this recipe during the winter when I wanted something hearty. It's so substantial that you can serve it as an entrée. A lot of my recipe ideas include seafood because I don't eat too much meat."

"It's easy to make a fish stock. Take about one pound of fish heads and bones, or a whole fish, and put them in a large pot. Add a chopped onion, carrot, three stalks of celery, a small bunch of parsley, and two quarts of water. Simmer the stock for one hour and then strain it. Also you can buy fish stock in the store. Knorr is a very good brand."

Gina Ziluca
Geronimo

"Gina is an expert at enhancing the flavor of a dish by adding chiles. The subtlety and complexity of chiles add such a wonderful quality to basic American food. Seafood stew is seafood stew, but when chiles are added it is elevated to another level."

Cliff Skoglund
Geronimo

3	tablespoons olive oil
1	large yellow onion, diced medium
2	cups leeks, thinly sliced
4	stalks celery, diced medium
2	poblano chile peppers, seeded and thinly sliced
3	jalapeño chile peppers, roasted, peeled, seeded and finely chopped
1	teaspoon fresh garlic, finely chopped
2	cups fish stock *(see chef's comments on this page)*
½	cup brandy
18	jumbo shrimp, peeled and deveined
12	sea scallops, muscles removed
6	new potatoes, peeled, diced medium and parboiled
4	ears corn, husks removed, grilled and kernels removed
¼	cup ancho chile peppers, roasted, peeled, seeded and puréed
1	teaspoon ground oregano
4	cups heavy cream
½	tablespoon kosher salt *(or to taste)*

In a large stockpot place the olive oil and heat it on medium high until it is hot. Add the yellow onions, leeks, celery, poblano and jalapeño chile peppers, and garlic. Sauté the ingredients for 5 minutes, or until the onions are translucent.

Add the fish stock and brandy. Simmer the ingredients for 5 minutes, or until the liquid is reduced by ¼.

Add the shrimp, scallops, and potatoes. Cook the ingredients for 2 minutes.

Add the corn, ancho chile purée, oregano, and heavy cream. Stir the ingredients together and simmer them for 5 minutes.

Season the stew with the kosher salt.

serves 6

Green Chile Piñon Paella
with Mango Kiwi Salsa

Green Chile Piñon Paella

3	cups uncooked long grain white rice
1	teaspoon saffron threads
¼	teaspoon paprika
1	teaspoon salt
6	cups chicken stock *(recipe on page 311)*
½	teaspoon olive oil
8	chicken wings
½	teaspoon cayenne pepper
¼	teaspoon white pepper
¼	teaspoon paprika
2	tablespoons olive oil
2	tablespoons olive oil
6	hot Italian sausages, cut into ½" slices
1	can Goya chickpeas, drained
2	7-ounce jars pitted green olives, drained
1	ear corn, husked, boiled and cut into 1" slices
1	2-ounce jar pimientos, drained and chopped
½	cup green chile peppers, roasted, peeled, seeded and diced medium
½	cup piñon nuts *(pine nuts)*, toasted *(see chef's comments on page 317)*
4	cloves fresh garlic, minced
	salt *(to taste)*
6	crab legs, cut into pieces at the joints and steamed
	Mango Kiwi Salsa *(recipe on next page)*

In a large stockpot place the rice, saffron, the first ¼ teaspoon of paprika, the teaspoon of salt, chicken stock, and the ½ teaspoon of olive oil. Bring the ingredients to a boil and then reduce heat to low. Simmer the ingredients for 20 minutes, or until the rice is tender. Set the ingredients aside.

Preheat the oven to 250°.

Sprinkle the chicken wings with the cayenne pepper, white pepper, and the second ¼ teaspoon of paprika.

(continued on next page)

"I'm a big fan of paella. To me, it's a big hodgepodge of all the good things in life that are thrown together in one dish. This recipe has a Southwestern twist because of the green chile and piñon nuts. It's foolproof, and can be made from scratch in two hours."

Pat Walter
Grant Corner Inn

"Pat has a Puerto Rican background and is a real paella person. Whenever we go out we try to order paella and see if it is up to his expectations.....and usually it's not. Pat designed this recipe for a dinner party we had, and he served it in a beautiful paella dish that his uncle had given us. The presentation was really magnificent.....rather like bringing out a beautiful roasted turkey on a platter. The crab legs were standing up and fanning out in a star pattern, and everyone helped themselves."

Louise Stewart
Grant Corner Inn

In a large sauté pan place the first 2 tablespoons of olive oil and heat it on medium high until it is hot. Add the chicken wings and sauté them for 3 to 4 minutes on each side, or until they are done. Remove the chicken and drain it on paper towels.

Add the second 2 tablespoons of olive oil to the pan and heat it on medium high until it is hot. Add the sausage and cook it for 10 minutes, or until it is done. Drain the sausage on paper towels.

In a large casserole dish place the cooked rice. Add the cooked sausage, chickpeas, green olives, corn pieces, pimientos, green chile peppers, piñon nuts, garlic, and salt. Stir the ingredients together. Place the chicken and crab on top.

Cover the pan and bake the paella for 30 minutes, or until it is heated through.

Serve the paella with the Mango Kiwi Salsa on the side.

serves 6

Mango Kiwi Salsa

2	**mangos, peeled, meat removed from the core and diced medium**
4	**kiwis, peeled and diced medium**
4	**scallions, chopped**
1	**bunch fresh cilantro, finely chopped**
1	**small white onion, finely diced**
1	**clove fresh garlic, finely chopped**
¼	**teaspoon sugar**
¼	**teaspoon cayenne pepper**
1½	**tablespoons balsamic vinegar**
½	**tablespoon red wine vinegar**
1	**lime, freshly squeezed**

In a medium bowl place all the ingredients and stir them together.

Cover the bowl with plastic wrap and refrigerate the salsa for 45 minutes.

makes approximately 3 cups

"With traditional paella there is no salsa, so this recipe makes it really special. You can use the salsa with crackers and cheese, pork, or whatever sounds good. All of the ingredients are so flavorful, how can you go wrong! It's sweet, spicy, tangy, and sour, all at the same time. You must use it up the day you make it, however, because it doesn't keep well."

Louise Stewart
Grant Corner Inn

Paella Tomas

½   **cup olive oil**
1½ **pounds chicken breast, skin and bones removed, and cut into 2" strips**
2   **cups uncooked rice**
¼   **cup red onion, finely chopped**
1   **small red bell pepper, seeded and diced medium**
1   **small green bell pepper, seeded and diced medium**
2   **cloves fresh garlic, finely chopped**
6   **links chorizo sausage, meat removed from casing, cooked and drained**
1½ **cups stewed tomatoes**
3   **artichoke hearts, quartered**
1   **cup green peas**
¾   **cup clam juice**
2   **teaspoons salt** *(or to taste)*
½   **teaspoon black pepper, freshly ground**
4   **cups chicken stock** *(recipe on page 311)*
1   **teaspoon saffron threads, pounded**
½   **cup green chile peppers, roasted, peeled, seeded and diced medium**
¼   **cup fresh cilantro, chopped**
2   **tablespoons fresh oregano, chopped**
12   **large shrimp, peeled and deveined**

Preheat the oven to 350°.

In a large sauté pan place the olive oil and heat it on medium high until it is hot. Add the chicken strips and sauté them for 5 minutes, or until they are almost done. Remove the chicken from the pan and set it aside.

Add the rice to the pan and sauté it for 2 minutes, or until it looks shiny.

Add the red onions, red and green bell peppers, and garlic. Sauté the ingredients for 5 minutes, or until the onions are translucent.

Add the cooked chorizo, cooked chicken strips, stewed tomatoes, artichoke hearts, peas, clam juice, salt, and black pepper. Stir the ingredients together.

In a medium saucepan place the chicken stock and saffron, and bring them to a boil. Pour the stock over the chicken and vegetables, and stir it in.

(continued on next page)

"Paella is a Spanish dish, but I turned the classic recipe into a Southwestern version. Although it is time-consuming to make, it is well worth the effort. Read through the directions several times before you start."

"Be sure that you don't overcook the shrimp, or they will turn into rubber bands. You can add any kind of shellfish that you want, such as lobster, clams, and mussels."

Tomas Cross
La Plazuela

"When I was in high school I spent some time in Spain, and that's when I was introduced to paella. At first I didn't think I would like it, but it was really good. I remember thinking that the saffron gave it an unusual flavor. Also, the different shellfish, like the mussels, took some getting used to. Now, of course, I am very familiar with all of these ingredients, and paella is one of my favorite dishes."

Lela Cross
La Plazuela

Cover the pan, reduce the heat to low, and simmer the ingredients for 10 minutes. Transfer the mixture to a large baking dish.

Add the green chile peppers, cilantro, and oregano. Stir the ingredients together. Place the shrimp on top.

Cover the dish with a lid. Bake the paella in the oven for 10 to 15 minutes, or until the shrimp is cooked and the rice is done. Remove the lid and bake the ingredients for 6 to 8 minutes more, or until the paella slightly browns.

serves 6

Rosemary Red Chile Grilled Salmon Steaks

6	cloves fresh garlic
2	dried red chile peppers
2	sprigs fresh rosemary
1	cup olive oil
4	5-ounce salmon steaks

In a medium jar place the garlic, red chile peppers, rosemary, and olive oil. Cover the jar with a lid and let it sit for 48 hours at room temperature.

Brush the salmon on both sides with the flavored oil. Grill the salmon for 4 to 5 minutes on each side, or until it is done.

serves 4

La Tertulia's Marinated Salmon Steaks with Poblano Salsa

La Tertulia's Marinated Salmon Steaks

2   cloves fresh garlic, finely chopped
½   bunch fresh cilantro, chopped
¼   cup olive oil
2   tablespoons red wine vinegar
     salt and black pepper *(to taste)*
6   6-ounce salmon steaks
     Poblano Salsa *(recipe follows)*

In a large bowl place the garlic, cilantro, olive oil, and red wine vinegar. Add the salmon steaks and cover them well with the marinade. Cover the bowl with plastic wrap and let the fish sit for 1 hour at room temperature.

Season the salmon steaks with the salt and black pepper. Grill them for 4 to 6 minutes on each side, or until the desired doneness is achieved.

On each of 6 individual serving plates place a salmon steak. Top each piece of fish with the Poblano Salsa.

serves 6

Poblano Salsa

4   poblano chile peppers, roasted, peeled, seeded and diced medium
1½   medium tomatoes, seeded and diced medium
1   can pitted black olives, drained and sliced
2   jalapeño chile peppers, seeded and finely chopped
2   scallions, thinly sliced
1   tablespoon red wine vinegar
1   tablespoon olive oil

In a medium bowl place all the ingredients and mix them together well.

makes approximately 2 cups

"The marinade is very simple and yet it gives the salmon a wonderful flavor. People love this dish because it tastes good and is very healthy."

"I have been eating most of my meals at La Tertulia for over twenty-one years. Even though the food is excellent, I sometimes get tired of it and crave something else."

"We serve this salsa with fish at the restaurant and it is very popular. I eat it at home with chips, meat, chicken, and eggs. It's very versatile and tastes delicious. I think the black olives are what makes it special."

Joy Ortiz-Nashan
La Tertulia

Citrus Poached Salmon with Cherry Cascabel Chile Sauce

Citrus Poached Salmon

1	lime, halved
1	orange, halved
1	lemon, halved
4	8-ounce salmon steaks
	Cherry Cascabel Chile Sauce *(recipe follows)*

Fill a large saucepan half full of water and bring it to a boil. Add the limes, oranges, and lemons.

Place the salmon steaks in the boiling citrus water and let the water return to a boil. Cook the salmon for 1 minute, or until it is just done.

On each of 4 individual serving plates place the salmon steaks. Top each steak with the Cherry Cascabel Chile Sauce.

serves 4

Cherry Cascabel Chile Sauce

1	ounce cascabel chile peppers, stemmed and seeded
6	ounces dried cherries, stemmed and seeded
1	lemon, freshly juiced
1	orange, freshly juiced
1	tablespoon honey
½	cup water

In a medium saucepan place all of the ingredients and stir them together. Bring the mixture to a boil and then reduce the heat to a simmer. Cook the ingredients for 10 minutes, or until the liquid is reduced by ½. Remove the pan from the heat and let it cool slightly.

Place the mixture in a food processor and purée it. Strain the purée through a fine sieve and discard the pulp.

Place the sauce in a small saucepan and reheat it on low heat.

makes approximately 1 cup

"In this recipe we poach the salmon in citrus water, which gives it a wonderful, subtle fruit flavor. The salmon will be cooked to the correct point when it starts to float to the top of the water."

"I like to eat out, but I'm not much of a restaurant goer. I know a lot of chefs in town and if I ever want to try a new cuisine I'll just sneak in the back door to visit, and ask them what's cooking."

"Cascabel chiles are also known as 'rattlesnake' chiles, because the dried seeds inside the pods make a rattling noise when the wind blows. It's a little round chile about the size of a plum. The flavor is sweet and hot, and it goes well with fruits. If you can't find them, you may use another sweet dried red chile, such as a guajillo."

"I get many compliments on this sauce. The citrus flavors help to tone down the heat of the chiles. It's delicious with all kinds of seafoods."

Tim Lopez
Rancho Encantado

Habanero Tequila Cured Salmon with Pineapple Cascabel Salsa

Habanero Tequila Cured Salmon

½	cup sugar
1	teaspoon ground allspice
1	teaspoon ground cinnamon
1	teaspoon ground mace
½	cup coarse salt
1	tablespoon coarsely ground black pepper
1	whole salmon *(10 to 12 pounds)*, cut into 2 fillets
5	dried habanero chile peppers, crumbled
1	teaspoon olive oil
2	bunches fresh cilantro, chopped
1	bottle tequila
1	loaf french bread, thinly sliced
	Pineapple Cascabel Salsa *(recipe on next page)*

In a small bowl place the sugar, allspice, cinnamon, mace, salt, and black pepper. Stir the ingredients together.

Rub the spice mixture on both sides of each fillet. Place the fillets on a wire rack and let them sit for 20 minutes.

In a food processor place the habanero chile peppers, olive oil, and the first bunch of chopped cilantro. Purée the ingredients so that they are smooth.

Rub the chile pepper purée over both sides of each fillet.

In a large shallow pan place one of the fillets *(skin side down)*. Sprinkle the second bunch of chopped cilantro on top of the fish. Place the other fillet on top of the first fillet *(skin side up)*.

Pour the tequila over the fish and cover the pan with plastic wrap. Place 10 to 15 pounds of weight on top of the fish and refrigerate it for 5 days *(turn the fish over on the 2nd and 4th days)*.

Remove the fish from the pan and thinly slice it on the bias.

Serve the salmon on top of the french bread slices with the Pineapple Cascabel Salsa on the side.

serves 12

"Prior to my coming to Santa Fe, I used to do a lot of curing and smoking of meats and fish. So, when I moved here I wanted to come up with a South-western version of gravlox, which is a cured, dried salmon. The tequila flavor is very subtle and it takes some of the sharpness out of the habanero chiles, which are really hot."

"Weight the fish down with something heavy. At work I use #10 cans of food that weigh about eight pounds each. At home you could use books with an iron on top."

"This dish is wonderful as an entrée or appetizer. It will serve about twenty-four people if you use it as an appetizer."

"I never reconstitute dried chiles in water because I think that you lose too much flavor that way. Instead, I wear rubber gloves and rub them between my hands so that they crumble and flake. If the chiles are extremely dry, I put them in a 350° oven for a few minutes until they soften a bit."

Dakota
Piñon Grill

"I used to work in the Caribbean, and we would combine fruit and chiles together all of the time. The cascabel chiles have a wonderful smoky flavor. This salsa is excellent with all kinds of seafood and it keeps well in the refrigerator."

"To me the secret of cooking is to get the best ingredients you can find, and then do as little as possible to them. I used to like complicated French cooking, but now I like the simple approach, with marinades, grilling, and salsas."

Dakota
Piñon Grill

"This is a great recipe that takes no time at all to prepare. Just throw everything in the blender and your glaze is ready. The flavor is a combination of hot and sweet.....it's delicious! We also use this glaze as a dressing over grilled sliced chicken with baby greens and roasted pecans."

"Chipotle peppers can be pretty fickle. Sometimes just one pepper will knock your socks off, and other times you can use three and the glaze still won't be hot enough. So I advise you to add one pepper at a time, and taste the result before adding more."

Paul Hunsicker
Paul's Restaurant

Pineapple Cascabel Salsa

15	dried cascabel chile peppers, seeded and crushed
½	fresh pineapple, peeled, cored and coarsely diced
¼	cup red wine vinegar
1½	fresh pineapples, peeled, cored and diced medium
1	red bell pepper, seeded and diced medium
1	medium red onion, diced medium
1	bunch fresh cilantro, chopped
½	cup olive oil
	salt and white pepper *(to taste)*

In a food processor place the cascabel chile peppers, the ½ diced pineapple, and the red wine vinegar. Purée the ingredients so that they are smooth.

In a large bowl place the puréed ingredients, the 1½ diced pineapples, red bell peppers, red onions, cilantro, olive oil, salt, and white pepper. Stir the ingredients together.

makes 8 cups

Grilled Tuna with Honey Apricot Chipotle Glaze

¾	cup apricot jam
2	chipotle chile peppers *(in adobo sauce)*
1	tablespoon fresh cilantro, chopped
2	tablespoons honey
1	lime, freshly squeezed
2	tablespoons olive oil
6	8-ounce tuna steaks, brushed with oil
2	limes, cut into 12 wedges

In a blender place the apricot jam, chipotle chile peppers, cilantro, honey, lime juice, and olive oil. Purée the ingredients so that they are smooth. Set the sauce aside.

Grill the tuna steaks for 5 minutes on each side, or until the desired doneness is achieved.

On each of 6 individual serving plates place a tuna steak. Pour the sauce on top. Garnish the dish with the lime wedges.

serves 6

Pan-Seared Rare Tuna with Red Pepper Vinaigrette

Pan-Seared Rare Tuna

6	6-ounce tuna steaks
2	tablespoons fennel seeds, toasted *(see chef's comments on this page)* **and ground**
2	tablespoons olive oil
	Red Pepper Vinaigrette *(recipe follows)*

Cover the tuna steaks with the ground fennel seeds.

In a large sauté pan place the olive oil and heat it on medium high until it is hot. Cook the tuna steaks for 1 to 2 minutes on each side, or until they are rare.

Serve the tuna steaks with the Red Pepper Vinaigrette dribbled on top.

serves 6

Red Pepper Vinaigrette

2	tablespoons olive oil
1	red bell pepper, seeded and finely diced
1	teaspoon chile pequin *(hot red chile flakes)*
10	fresh basil leaves, chopped
2	tablespoons champagne vinegar
3	tablespoons olive oil
	salt and black pepper *(to taste)*

In a medium sauté pan place the 2 tablespoons of olive oil and heat it on medium high until it is hot. Add the red bell peppers and sauté them for 5 minutes, or until they begin to soften. Add the chile pequin and cook it for 1 minute.

In a medium bowl place the sautéed bell pepper mixture, basil, champagne vinegar, the 3 tablespoons of olive oil, salt, and black pepper. Whisk the ingredients together.

Cover the bowl with plastic wrap and refrigerate the vinaigrette overnight.

makes approximately 1 cup

"I really like this dish because the different flavors work so well together. You can taste the fennel, you can taste the tuna, and you can taste the Red Pepper Vinaigrette. It's a dish that doesn't create a brand new taste, but rather has flavors that complement each other."

"We use fennel seeds in a lot of our dishes at Pranzo. Fennel has a very unique flavor that cannot be substituted. Toast the seeds in a dry pan on the stove (keep tossing them) until they are slightly brown and the aroma is released. By toasting the seeds the flavor is greatly enhanced."

"This recipe calls for champagne vinegar, which is lightly sweet. I suggest that you buy the very best quality of vinegar that you can find (or afford), because it will make all the difference in the flavor of your sauce. Vinegars are like wines. There is a tremendous difference in their quality and price. At home I have a bottle of one-hundred-year-old balsamic vinegar which was very expensive, but I only need to use a couple of drops at a time, because the flavor is so concentrated."

Steven Lemon
Pranzo Italian Grill

Ore House Grilled Tuna with Caribbean Curry Sauce

"I like for tuna to be cooked on the outside and rare to medium rare on the inside. I don't want the middle to be cold, just warm. It takes some experience to know the exact moment the tuna should be removed from the heat."

"Have fun with food! When you cook, don't be too uptight about how things are going to turn out. Turn on the radio, have a glass of wine, and get into the pleasure of putting a dish together. And don't forget to enjoy yourself when you eat it."

"This curry sauce goes well with all kinds of fish, chicken, and pork. It's quite fiery, but if you prefer, you can add some crushed tomatoes to tone down the heat."

Isaac Modivah
Ore House

Ore House Grilled Tuna

	Caribbean Curry Sauce *(recipe follows)*
6	**8-ounce tuna steaks**
1½	**cups white rice, cooked with chicken broth** *(recipe on page 311)*
2	**large avocados, peeled, pitted, and sliced**

Brush the Caribbean Curry Sauce on both sides of the tuna steaks. Grill them for 3 to 4 minutes on each side, or until the desired doneness is achieved *(keep basting the fish with more sauce during the cooking time)*.

On each of 6 individual serving plates place the tuna. Place the rice and avocados on the side. Serve the fish with extra Caribbean Curry Sauce on the side.

serves 6

Caribbean Curry Sauce

1	**small red onion, coarsely chopped**
2	**cloves fresh garlic, coarsely chopped**
2	**teaspoons chile pequin** *(hot red chile flakes)*
1	**tablespoon ground turmeric**
1	**tablespoon ground coriander**
1	**tablespoon ground cumin**
1	**tablespoon black pepper**
1	**tablespoon fresh ginger root, peeled and grated**
1	**cup fish stock** *(recipe on page 171)*
½	**cup lime juice, freshly squeezed**
1	**large pinch salt** *(to taste)*

In a food processor place the red onions, garlic, chile pequin, turmeric, coriander, cumin, and black pepper. Purée the ingredients so that a paste is formed.

Place the paste in a medium saucepan. Add the ginger and fish stock. Cook the ingredients on medium heat for 10 minutes, or until the sauce begins to thicken. Add the lime juice and stir it in. Season the sauce with the salt.

makes approximately 1½ cups

Fish and Shellfish

Sesame Seed Tuna with Jalapeño Fruit Salsa

Sesame Seed Tuna

1	**cup parmesan cheese, freshly grated**
1	**cup sesame seeds** *(unbleached)*
4	**8-ounce tuna steaks**
1	**cup flour**
4	**eggs, well beaten**
4	**tablespoons olive oil** *(or as needed)*
	Jalapeño Fruit Salsa *(recipe follows)*

In a medium bowl place the parmesan cheese and sesame seeds, and stir them together.

Dredge each tuna steak first in the flour, next in the beaten eggs, and then in the parmesan-sesame seed mixture.

In a large sauté pan place the olive oil and heat it on medium high until it is hot. Add the coated tuna steaks and cook them for 4 to 5 minutes on each side, or until they are just done.

On each of 4 individual serving plates place a tuna steak. Serve the Jalapeño Fruit Salsa on the side.

serves 4

Jalapeño Fruit Salsa

1	**kiwi, peeled and diced medium small**
¼	**cup fresh pineapple, peeled and diced medium small**
¼	**cup strawberries, stemmed and diced medium small**
¼	**cup cantaloupe, peeled, seeded and diced medium small**
2	**yellow jalapeño chile peppers, seeded and finely diced**
¼	**cup orange juice, freshly squeezed**
⅛	**cup lemon juice, freshly squeezed**

In a medium bowl place all the ingredients and stir them together.

makes approximately 2 cups

"When you grill the fish with the parmesan cheese and sesame seeds, the coating turns a nice brown color and the fish stays white. This, together with the different colors from the fruit salsa, makes a wonderful presentation."

Darrell Hedgecoke
Mañana

"Darrell is a wonderful chef because he's talented, he's a team player, he's even tempered, he's good with his staff, and he is very honest. These are traits that are hard to come by in employees."

"As the manager of the Inn of the Governors, I love my job. I have the opportunity to serve people when they are on vacation, which means they usually are in a good frame of mind. Even on those rare occasions when someone has a complaint, I have an opportunity to turn a negative situation into a positive one, and hopefully make a new friend in the process."

Charlotte Silva
Mañana

Sage & Black Pepper Crusted Tuna with Walnut Oil Vinaigrette

"This is an excellent fish entrée that has a very spicy crust. If you are worried about the heat you can reduce the amount of cayenne, but don't eliminate it entirely. Serve this with a nice pilaf that has toasted piñon nuts and fresh sage in it, along with steamed vegetables. This makes a delicious, simple but elegant meal."

"To make cracked black pepper you can use your coffee grinder. Wipe it out with a paper towel, add the peppercorns, and grind them. You also could use a pepper mill, but it would take quite a while to grind out a tablespoonful."

"This is a rich vinaigrette that really complements the heat of the black pepper and cayenne. It has an interesting buttery flavor, and is wonderful to use instead of a cream sauce. You can use this on a salad of bitter greens, such as arugula or radicchio, or as a marinade for fish."

Pete Zimmer
Inn of the Anasazi

Sage & Black Pepper Crusted Tuna

¼	cup fresh sage, finely chopped
1	tablespoon fresh thyme, finely chopped
1	tablespoon cayenne pepper
1	tablespoon cracked black pepper
4	8-ounce tuna steaks
2	tablespoons olive oil *(or as needed)*
	salt and black pepper *(to taste)*
	Walnut Oil Vinaigrette *(recipe follows)*

In a small bowl place the sage, thyme, cayenne pepper, and cracked black pepper. Mix the spices together.

Dredge the tuna steaks in the spice mixture so that they are very well coated.

In a large skillet place the olive oil and heat it on medium high until it is very hot. Sauté the tuna steaks for 1 to 2 minutes on each side, or until they are medium rare. Season them with the salt and black pepper.

On each of 4 individual serving plates pour on some of the Walnut Oil Vinaigrette. Place a tuna steak on top.

serves 4

Walnut Oil Vinaigrette

1	cup walnuts, finely chopped
1	tablespoon fresh thyme, finely chopped
1	cup walnut oil
¼	cup olive oil
4	lemons, juiced
	salt and black pepper *(to taste)*

In a small bowl place all of the ingredients and whisk them together so that they are well blended.

makes approximately 2 cups

Catfish Po' Boy

1	tablespoon red chile powder
1	tablespoon paprika
2½	teaspoons garlic powder
1½	teaspoons onion powder
1½	teaspoons ground oregano
1½	teaspoons ground thyme
1	tablespoon salt *(or to taste)*
2½	teaspoons black pepper *(or to taste)*
1	cup flour
2	eggs, lightly beaten
1	cup milk
2	tablespoons Dijon mustard
3	cups cornmeal
6	catfish fillets
¼	cup vegetable oil
6	sourdough sandwich rolls, halved lengthwise
	Jalapeño Tartar Sauce *(recipe on page 111)*
1	head romaine lettuce
2	tomatoes, thinly sliced
1	medium red onion, thinly sliced

In a small bowl place the red chile powder, paprika, garlic powder, onion powder, oregano, thyme, salt, and black pepper. Stir the ingredients together.

In a medium bowl place ⅓ of the spice mixture and the flour, and mix them together.

In a second medium bowl place the beaten eggs, milk, and Dijon mustard. Mix the ingredients together.

In a third medium bowl place another ⅓ of the spice mixture and the cornmeal, and mix them together.

Sprinkle each catfish fillet with the remaining ⅓ of the spice mixture.

Dredge each fillet first in the flour-spice mixture, next in the eggwash, and then in the cornmeal-spice mixture.

In a large sauté pan place the vegetable oil and heat it on medium high until it is very hot *(to the point of smoking)*. Add the coated fish fillets and sauté them for 3 to 4 minutes on each side, or until they are golden brown.

(continued on next page)

"Generations of cajun cooks have made this dish. It's a great way to prepare fish. Not only is it very spicy and flavorful, but it also is easy. The spice mixture that you use is a good thing to keep on hand as a seasoning for other meats and fish. When you dredge the fish in the cornmeal, use a firm hand so that it won't fall off. This way you will get a really crisp catfish that won't be greasy at all."

"There is an on-going argument amongst catfish lovers, which is.....what's better? Farm raised catfish or catfish caught from rivers, streams, lakes and ponds? I believe that the farm raised ones are the best, because they live in clean, fresh water and they are harvested, iced, and then trucked out to the markets immediately."

Harry Shapiro
Harry's Road House

On the inside of each sourdough roll spread on the Jalapeño Tartar Sauce. Add the lettuce, tomatoes, red onions, and a catfish fillet.

serves 6

Sweet & Sour Sambal Swordfish

1	**cup sugar**
½	**cup red wine vinegar**
3	**cloves fresh garlic, pressed**
¼	**cup soy sauce**
2	**tablespoons sambal** *(see chef's comments on this page)*
4	**6-ounce swordfish steaks**
1	**tablespoon olive oil** *(or as needed)*
	salt and black pepper *(to taste)*

In a small saucepan place the sugar and red wine vinegar, and bring them to a gentle boil. Cook the liquid for 10 minutes, or until it is reduced by ½.

Add the garlic, soy sauce, and sambal. Cook the sauce for 5 to 8 minutes, or until it is thick enough to coat a wooden spoon. Keep the sauce warm.

Rub the swordfish steaks with the olive oil. Grill them for 1½ to 2 minutes on each side, or until they are just done.

Season the fish with the salt and black pepper. Spoon the sauce on top.

serves 4

Chile Trout with Papaya Salsa

Chile Trout

2	tablespoons fresh sage, finely chopped
4	tablespoons ancho chile powder
1	tablespoon Chimayo red chile powder
1	tablespoon unsweetened cocoa powder
1	tablespoon sugar
1	tablespoon salt *(or to taste)*
4	whole boneless trout
4	sprigs fresh rosemary
	Papaya Salsa *(recipe follows)*

In a medium bowl place the sage, ancho chile powder, Chimayo red chile powder, cocoa powder, sugar, and salt. Mix the ingredients together.

Skewer a rosemary sprig along the backbone of each trout *(use a sharp knife tip to make several small holes).*

Dredge each trout in the chile-spice mixture so that it is well coated.

Grill the trout for 3 minutes on each side, or until they are just done. Place the Papaya Salsa on top of the trout.

serves 4

Papaya Salsa

4	papayas, peeled, seeded and finely diced
2	poblano chile peppers, roasted, peeled, seeded and finely diced
2	jalapeño chile peppers, seeded and finely diced
1	jicama, peeled and finely diced
1	bunch scallions, finely sliced
2	tablespoons fresh ginger root, peeled and finely chopped
2	tablespoons toasted sesame oil
2	tablespoons olive oil

In a large bowl place all the ingredients and mix them together well.

makes approximately 4 cups

"One day I had some beautiful, long sprigs of rosemary, and got the idea to skewer them in the backbone of each trout. They burn when you grill the trout and get a very delicious smoky, rosemary flavor. The cocoa powder in the spice mixture that you rub on the trout darkens their color and enhances the flavor of the anchos."

"If you can't find ancho chile powder, you can take dried anchos and grind them up. Otherwise, use any medium hot chile powder that you have."

"Visually this is a very pretty salsa, and it has a refreshing, fruity, hot, and gingery flavor. I put it on top of the head of the trout to disguise it."

Dakota
Piñon Grill

Trucha Española

½	cup peanut oil
1	small red onion, cut into small cubes
½	red bell pepper, seeded and cut into small cubes
½	yellow bell pepper, seeded and cut into small cubes
1	cup green chile peppers, roasted, peeled, seeded and chopped medium
½	cup Roma tomatoes, chopped medium
3	tablespoons fresh cilantro, chopped
¼	teaspoon ground cumin
½	teaspoon salt
¼	teaspoon ground coriander
1	cup flour
4	tablespoons peanut oil *(or as needed)*
4	8-ounce trout, boned
½	cup white wine

Preheat the oven to 200°.

In a medium large sauté pan place the ½ cup of peanut oil and heat it on medium until it is hot. Add the red onions and bell peppers. Sauté them for 5 minutes, or until the onions are translucent.

Add the green chile peppers, Roma tomatoes, cilantro, cumin, and salt. Simmer the ingredients for 5 minutes. Set the mixture aside.

In a flat dish place the coriander and flour, and mix them together.

In a medium large, non-stick sauté pan place 1 tablespoon of peanut oil for each trout and heat it on medium high until it is very hot.

One at a time, spread open each trout. Dredge each trout on both sides in the flour mixture. Place it in the pan, inside flesh down, and sauté it for 3 minutes. Turn the trout over. Pour 2 tablespoons of the white wine over the trout and shake the pan. Add ¼ of the reserved chile mixture. Cook the trout for 2 minutes, or until the sauce begins to bubble.

Transfer the trout and sauce to an individual serving plate and place it in the oven to keep it warm. Repeat this process for the rest of the trout.

serves 4

"This is my favorite way to eat trout. The recipe was named after the town of Española, New Mexico, just north of Santa Fe, which is where my friends, Shelley and David Smith-Henne lived when they developed it. Other than using a little oil, it is a very healthy dish, with lots of vegetables and chiles. The only tricky part to making it is to have your pan hot enough so that the trout doesn't stick. Also, you have to cook the trout one at a time, which is a minor bother compared to the wonderful end result."

"I like to cook at home for friends, but there's also a stack of six Swanson's pot pies in my freezer. Some nights that's all I can manage."

"I think that food can satisfy hunger on many different levels. Not only does it satisfy our physical hunger, it can also satisfy our emotional hunger as well. For instance, there are times when nothing will do except for your mother's chicken soup. In my particular case, however, it was my father's chicken soup."

Sarah Alvord
Zia Diner

188

Spicy Marinated Swordfish
with Rapini & Pico de Gallo

Spicy Marinated Swordfish with Rapini

4	6-ounce swordfish steaks
	Chile Paste *(recipe on page 305)*
2	teaspoons olive oil
2	shallots, finely chopped
12	ounces rapini *(see chef's comments on this page)*, **bottom inch cut off**
	Pico de Gallo *(recipe follows)*
4	lime wedges

In a shallow dish place the swordfish steaks. Rub each piece of fish with the Chili Paste. Cover the dish with plastic wrap and let the fish marinate in the refrigerator for 4 hours.

Grill the fish for 4 to 5 minutes on each side, or until it is just done.

In a large sauté pan place the olive oil and heat it on medium high until it is hot. Add the shallots and sauté them for 2 to 3 minutes, or until they are translucent. Add the rapini and cover the pan. Let the rapini sweat for 3 to 4 minutes, or until it is al dente.

On each of 4 individual serving plates place the swordfish. Spoon the Pico de Gallo on ½ of each piece of fish. Place the rapini and a lime wedge on the side.

serves 4

Pico de Gallo

1	medium red onion, finely chopped
2	cups Roma tomatoes, seeded and finely chopped
1	jalapeño chile pepper, seeded and finely chopped
2	tablespoons fresh cilantro, finely chopped
1	lime, freshly squeezed and pulp finely chopped
	salt and white pepper *(to taste)*

In a medium bowl place all the ingredients and mix them together well.

makes approximately 3 cups

"Rapini is wild broccoli. It's long and thin, with a tiny floret on top. The flavor is mild and it is so tender that you can eat the whole thing. When I lived in California I was able to find it in the supermarket, and I have also seen it in Santa Fe. Your produce man could special order it for you. Otherwise, use spinach, and cook it in the same way."

"My philosophy of cooking is that I like everything to be fresh and tasty, with the items recognizable on the plate. I don't like food that is disguised with heavy flavorings and sauces."

"I'm from England, which is a country that does not have a good reputation for fine dining. Although this used to be true, things are really changing now. They have some excellent restaurants and they are getting better all of the time."

Jim Makinson
Bishop's Lodge

Spicy Fish Fillets in Parchment

6	12" squares parchment paper
6	5-ounce orange roughy fillets
18	slices ripe tomato
1	tablespoon chile pequin *(hot red chile flakes)*
¼	cup pitted black olives, finely chopped
1	orange, zested *(outer orange part grated off)*
1	cube butter, chopped medium
6	sprigs fresh thyme
	salt and black pepper *(to taste)*

Preheat the oven to 450°.

Oil the top of each square of parchment paper with vegetable oil spray.

In the center of each square place, in this order, a fish fillet, 3 slices of tomato, a sprinkling of the chile pequin, olives, orange zest, butter, a sprig of thyme, and the salt and black pepper.

Fold each end of the parchment over the fish, so that all 4 sides are folded in.

Place the packets, seam side down, on a lightly oiled baking sheet.

Bake the fish for 12 minutes, or until it is done *(if needed, open a packet to check the doneness)*.

On each of 6 individual serving plates place a packet of the fish. Cut an opening in the top of the packet.

serves 6

"I've always liked to cook foods in parchment paper, because they steam inside and none of the nutrients or flavor are lost. When you serve this on a plate and cut the paper open, you get a burst of the steam and aromas. It's a very sensory presentation. Serve it with the Potato Strudel (recipe on page 135)."

"The secret to this dish is the orange zest. I don't understand the physiology of foods, but whatever the orange peel does to enhance the flavor of some dishes is truly a miracle."

"Parchment paper is sold at grocery stores in the section where you find the plastic wrap and foil."

Sylvia Johnson
Celebrations

Santa Fe Rolled & Stuffed Sole with Pineapple Habanero Ginger Salsa

Santa Fe Rolled & Stuffed Sole

2	cloves fresh garlic, finely chopped
2	teaspoons fresh cilantro, chopped
1	teaspoon fresh rosemary, chopped
2	teaspoons parmesan cheese, freshly grated
¼	cup balsamic vinegar
¼	cup olive oil
8	bunches fresh spinach, washed, dried and stems removed
16	small Dover sole fillets
2	red bell peppers, roasted, peeled, seeded and very thinly sliced
2	green bell peppers, roasted, peeled, seeded and very thinly sliced
½	cup butter, melted
	Pineapple Habanero Ginger Salsa (recipe on next page)
1	pound baby greens

In a large bowl place the garlic, cilantro, rosemary, parmesan cheese, balsamic vinegar, and olive oil. Whisk the ingredients together. Add the spinach leaves and toss them in so that they are well coated.

Cover the bowl with plastic wrap and marinate the spinach in the refrigerator overnight.

Preheat the oven to 350°.

On top of each fish fillet, place in this order, the spinach leaves (reserve the marinade), red and green bell pepper strips, another fish fillet, spinach leaves, and red and green bell pepper strips. Roll the fish up and place it in a baking dish.

Pour the marinade from the spinach leaves and the melted butter over the rolled fish fillets.

Bake the fish for 40 minutes, or until it is done.

On each of 8 individual serving plates place 2 of the rolled and stuffed fish fillets. Place the Pineapple Habanero Ginger Salsa on top of the fish. Sprinkle the baby greens around the edges.

serves 8

"I like Dover sole because it has a very mellow flavor. Also, it is thin and easy to work with. In this dish you can taste the fish, the marinated spinach, and the ever-present bell pepper. I fillet the peppers very, very thin, so they don't overwhelm the delicate flavor of the other ingredients."

"When I was growing up, my mother insisted on serving our family a seven-course meal every night. However, everything was out of a box, a can, or the freezer. She cooked the food for five hours, so that everything was a faded gray. Still, because there were so many courses, I was able to experience many different flavors. After I was older and out on my own, I realized it was possible to use fresh ingredients, and that's when I really got interested in food."

Pat Walter
Grant Corner Inn

"We like to serve this fish on top of pasta that is tossed with butter, olive oil, garlic, and scallions. This provides a full-balanced meal as well as a beautiful presentation."

Louise Stewart
Grant Corner Inn

Pineapple Habanero Ginger Salsa

1	small fresh pineapple, peeled, cored and diced medium
2	tablespoons red onion, finely chopped
4	smoked and dried habanero chile peppers, finely chopped
2	tablespoons fresh ginger root, peeled and finely chopped
2	tablespoons fresh cilantro, chopped
1	tablespoon balsamic vinegar

In a medium bowl place all the ingredients and mix them together well. Cover the bowl with plastic wrap and refrigerate the ingredients for 30 minutes.

makes approximately 2 cups

Lime Marinated Red Snapper with Chipotle Chile Butter

Lime Marinated Red Snapper

2   limes, freshly juiced
4   tablespoons olive oil
½   teaspoon white pepper
6   6-ounce red snapper fillets
     Chipotle Chile Butter *(recipe follows)*

In a small bowl place the lime juice, olive oil, and white pepper. Whisk the ingredients together.

In a large, shallow dish place the red snapper. Pour on the marinade so that it covers both sides of the fish. Let the fish marinate for 30 minutes at room temperature.

Grill the fish for 3 to 4 minutes on each side, or until they are just done.

On each of 6 individual serving plates place a fish fillet. Place a slice of the Chipotle Chile Butter on top.

serves 6

Chipotle Chile Butter

10   dried chipotle chile peppers
2   pounds unsalted butter, softened
¼   cup dry red wine
2   tablespoons fresh thyme, chopped
1   tablespoon fresh basil, chopped
½   teaspoon Worcestershire sauce

In a small saucepan place the chipotle chile peppers and the red wine. Bring the ingredients to a boil. Remove the pan from the heat and let the chiles soak for 1 hour.

Place the chiles, butter, red wine, thyme, basil, and Worcestershire sauce in a food processor. Coarsely purée the ingredients.

Form the butter mixture into a log and wrap it in plastic wrap. Freeze the butter. Cut off slices as they are needed.

makes 2 pounds

"I have one standard at our restaurant that I am firm about. I refuse to serve our New Mexican dishes with the chile eliminated, or on the side. The chile belongs on top of the enchiladas, or whatever, and that is where it goes. Tourists are often frightened by our chile (especially since we have a sign at our entry, warning about the heat of the chile), but most of them are good sports and are willing to try it. Almost always, they love it! Although I must admit that once when I was eating out in another restaurant I overheard some people at a nearby table complaining about the Guadalupe Cafe because they couldn't get dishes without chile. I say to people like this, 'If you don't want to try our chile, then don't order a New Mexican dish. Order a hamburger, pasta salad, sandwich, or any of the numerous other items on our menu.' I may sound stubborn about this, but I am the boss!"

Isabelle Koomoa
Guadalupe Cafe

"When I get home from work I am too tired to cook. Usually, I just fall asleep. If I have time, I really do love to eat out at different restaurants."

Rubin Rodriquez
Guadalupe Cafe

Marinated Halibut with Chipotle Aioli

Marinated Halibut

1	clove fresh garlic, finely chopped
2	tablespoons fresh basil, finely chopped
½	cup olive oil
2	limes, freshly squeezed
4	6-ounce halibut steaks
	Chipotle Aioli *(recipe follows)*

In a large bowl place the garlic, basil, olive oil, and lime juice. Whisk the ingredients together.

Add the halibut steaks and cover them well with the marinade.

Cover the bowl with plastic wrap and let the fish sit for 1 hour at room temperature.

Grill the halibut for 4 to 5 minutes on each side, or until the desired doneness is achieved.

Serve the halibut with the Chipotle Aioli on the side.

serves 4

Chipotle Aioli

2	egg yolks
3	cups olive oil
4	dried chipotle chile peppers, rehydrated, seeded and puréed
1	clove fresh garlic, finely chopped
2	teaspoons fresh parsley, chopped
	salt and white pepper *(to taste)*

In a food processor place the egg yolks and beat them well. With the food processor constantly running, slowly dribble in the oil so that a mayonnaise consistency is achieved.

Add the chipotle chile peppers, garlic, parsley, salt, and white pepper. Stir the ingredients together well.

makes approximately 3 cups

"After college I went to Europe and worked as a cook in Italy and Switzerland for over three years. I was young and energetic then, and it was lots of fun."

"We try to make this mayonnaise so that its spiciness does not overpower the fish. The safest thing to do is to add the peppers gradually, and keep tasting the sauce. What you want is a nice, subtle Southwestern punch."

Robbie Day
San Francisco St. Bar & Grill

Fish and Shellfish

Whole Fish in Hot Bean Sauce

1	cup vegetable oil
1	2-pound whole fish, cleaned, scaled and boned *(head and tail left intact)*, and ¼" deep slashes made on each side
2	tablespoons fresh garlic, finely chopped
2	tablespoons fresh ginger root, peeled and finely chopped
4	tablespoons hot bean paste *(see chef's comments on page 256)*
4	tablespoons soy sauce
2	tablespoons rice wine
2	teaspoons sugar
4	teaspoons salt *(or to taste)*
2	cups water
1	tablespoon cornstarch
1	tablespoon water
1	tablespoon cider vinegar
2	teaspoons toasted sesame oil
4	tablespoons scallions, chopped medium

In a large sauté pan place the vegetable oil and heat it on medium high until it is hot. Add the fish and sauté it for 1 minute on each side.

Add the garlic, ginger, and hot bean paste. Stir-fry the ingredients for 1 minute *(push the fish to the side)*.

Add the soy sauce, rice wine, sugar, salt, and the 2 cups of water. Stir the ingredients together. Cook the fish for 5 minutes, or until the sauce is reduced by ½.

In a small bowl place the cornstarch and the 1 tablespoon of water, and whisk them together.

Add the cornstarch paste to the pan and stir it in well.

On a serving plate place the fish with the sauce. Dribble the cider vinegar and sesame oil on top of the fish. Sprinkle on the scallions.

serves 4

"The traditional Chinese way to make this recipe is to use the whole fish, with the head, eyes, and tail all left intact.....the whole works. Americans are used to being served fish in steaks or fillets, so this presentation may give some of you the willies. If so, feel free to use any cut of fish you want. The kind of fish you use is not important.....just make sure it is very fresh."

"I love the New Mexico green chile, but to me it is not very spicy. I am used to food that is much, much hotter."

Marta Hung
Imperial Wok

Southwestern Bouillabaisse

2	**pounds mussels**
2	**pounds clams**
3	**pounds large shrimp, peeled and deveined**
2	**pounds scallops** *(20 to 30 count)*, **muscles removed**
½	**cup leeks, grilled and sliced**
3	**cups French green beans, ends cut off**
3	**cups yellow squash, grilled and sliced**
4	**cups Roma tomatoes, quartered and grilled**
6	**serrano chile peppers, grilled**
2	**medium red onions, quartered and grilled**
2	**tablespoons fresh garlic, chopped**
5	**cups chicken stock** *(recipe on page 311)*
4	**cups dry white wine**
2	**tablespoons fresh basil, chopped**
2	**tablespoons fresh Italian parsley, chopped**
	salt and black pepper *(to taste)*

In a large stockpot place all of the ingredients *(except for the basil, parsley, salt, and black pepper)*. Bring the liquid to a boil on high heat and cover the pot with a lid. Steam the ingredients for 3 to 5 minutes, or until the mussels and clams begin to open their shells.

Add the basil and parsley, and steam the ingredients for 3 minutes more. Season the soup with the salt and black pepper.

In each of 8 serving bowls arrange the seafood. Pour the broth and vegetables on top.

serves 8

"This recipe differs from a typical bouillabaisse in that it is much more hearty and robust. The vegetables are grilled and then cut into chunky pieces, so you have a real earthy, peasant-like dish."

"It's important to properly season this soup. Don't be afraid to taste the broth to insure that it has all the characteristics needed for a full-bodied flavor. Add more herbs, salt and pepper as you see fit."

"People in Santa Fe are landlocked, so when they get to eat a delicious seafood dish like this, it is truly a special treat."

Pete Zimmer
Inn of the Anasazi

LP CALDWELL

Fowl

Ancho Chile Chicken with Caribbean Chutney

Ancho Chile Chicken

1	pound dried ancho chile peppers
4	ounces sundried tomatoes *(not packed in oil)*
1	red bell pepper, halved, cored and seeded
½	cup tomato sauce
2	tablespoons olive oil
3	cloves fresh garlic, minced
1	tablespoon ground cinnamon
1½	tablespoons ground cumin
2	teaspoons ground coriander
½	teaspoon ground cloves
½	teaspoon salt
½	teaspoon black pepper
12	pieces chicken *(breasts, thighs and drumsticks)*
	Caribbean Chutney *(recipe on next page)*

In a medium large pot place the ancho chile peppers, sundried tomatoes, and red bell pepper. Cover the ingredients with water and bring them to a boil. Cover the pot and remove it from the heat. Let the ingredients sit for at least 2 hours, or until they are very tender. Remove the stems from the ancho chile peppers. Strain out the water and reserve it.

Preheat the oven to 400°.

Place the softened ingredients and tomato sauce in a food processor and purée them. Add enough of the reserved water so that a thick sauce is formed.

In a medium skillet place the olive oil and heat it on medium high until it is hot. Add the garlic and sauté it for 2 minutes. Add the cinnamon, cumin, coriander, cloves, salt, and black pepper. Sauté the mixture for 1 minute. Add the sautéed spices to the puréed sauce and stir them in.

Place the chicken in a baking dish and cook it for 40 minutes, or until it is about two-thirds done. Spread the sauce over the chicken and bake it for 20 more minutes, or until it is done *(baste the chicken frequently)*.

Serve the chicken with the Caribbean Chutney on top.

serves 6

"It seems that there is an ongoing dilemma in households and most restaurants which is.....what to do with chicken. Because of its low fat content, chicken is one of the most popular foods in America. But it is hard to keep coming up with exciting new recipes. In this case, however, I think we have hit the jackpot!"

"The sauce that you cook the chicken in is different from the basic New Mexican red chile sauce. It has a delicious smoky, cinnamon flavor, which gives it an interesting twist. It's similar to a mole sauce, but without the chocolate or fruit."

Daniella Croce Carr
Ore House

"I do not enjoy garnishes on a plate. I want the food to look good and to be its own garnish. Sometimes I'll see a color photograph in a food magazine and there will be this little piece of food in the center of a plate, with all the rest of the items being garnish. To me, this doesn't look that good. And it certainly doesn't make me think that eating the dish will be a sensual and fulfilling experience."

Isaac Modivah
Ore House

Caribbean Chutney

⅓	cup raisins
3	pounds ripe bananas, peeled and coarsely chopped
3	cups pineapple, crushed
1	medium red onion, coarsely chopped
3	cloves fresh garlic, coarsely chopped
1	cup tomato sauce
½	cup ketchup
1	cup honey
1	cup white wine vinegar
1	cup dark rum
2	cups water
2	cups brown sugar
1	teaspoon cayenne pepper
1½	teaspoons allspice
1½	teaspoons ground nutmeg
1	teaspoon ground cloves
2	teaspoons ground ginger
1	teaspoon salt
1	teaspoon black pepper

Note: For best results, this recipe must be made at least 2 days in advance.

In a food processor purée all of the ingredients in batches so that the desired consistency is achieved *(smooth or chunky)*.

Place the mixture in a saucepan and cover it with a lid. Cook the mixture on low heat for 30 to 45 minutes, or until it is reduced to a paste. *(Stir it frequently so that it doesn't burn, especially at the end.)*

Remove the chutney from the heat and let it cool. Store it in the refrigerator for at least 2 days.

makes approximately 6 cups

"This chutney is a variation of what is called a 'Spicy Banana Ketchup' in the Yucatan. I was vacationing near Cancun, and really enjoyed the fruit salsas in the area. The combination of sweet and spicy is wonderful."

"The chutney will burn pretty easily if you don't watch it. You have to keep stirring it.....not constantly, but every minute or two. When the chutney gets to be thick and gloppy, be extra careful. There are sugars that are caramelizing, and you don't want the hot sugar to get on your skin and burn you. This is why chefs always wear jackets with long sleeves."

"You can store this chutney in the refrigerator for up to six months. It gets better with age."

Isaac Modivah
Ore House

Santa Fe Chicken Breasts with Roasted Chile Black Bean Sauce

Santa Fe Chicken Breasts

1	clove fresh garlic, finely chopped
1	tablespoon fresh rosemary, chopped
1	teaspoon chile pequin *(hot red chile flakes)*
½	cup olive oil
1	lemon, freshly squeezed
4	chicken breasts, skin removed
	Roasted Chile Black Bean Sauce *(recipe on next page)*

In a medium bowl place the garlic, rosemary, chile pequin, olive oil, and lemon juice. Whisk the ingredients together.

Add the chicken breasts and cover them well with the marinade.

Cover the bowl with plastic wrap and let the chicken marinate for 2 hours at room temperature.

Grill the chicken for 5 to 7 minutes on each side, or until it is just done.

On each of 4 individual serving plates place the Roasted Chile Black Bean Sauce. Place a grilled chicken breast on top.

serves 4

"We are trying to have more diversity in our menu by having interesting daily specials, and this dish is one of our creations. It's easy to make, it's healthy, and the sauce has a wonderful, complex flavor. Make this for friends and they will be amazed at what a good cook you are."

Robbie Day
San Francisco St. Bar & Grill

Roasted Chile Black Bean Sauce

2	tablespoons butter
2	poblano chile peppers, roasted, peeled, seeded, diced and puréed
1	cup dark beer
3	tomatillos, husks removed, chopped and roasted
1	cup cooked black beans, puréed
1	teaspoon brown sugar
½	cup chicken stock *(recipe on page 311)*
3	ancho chile peppers, roasted, peeled, seeded, diced and finely ground
1	mulato chile pepper, roasted, peeled, seeded, diced and finely ground
½	cup pumpkin seeds, toasted *(see chef's comments on page 317)* and finely ground

In a large saucepan place the butter and heat it on medium until it is melted and hot. Add the poblano chile peppers and sauté them for 2 minutes.

Add the dark beer and deglaze the pan. Lower the heat and simmer the ingredients for 5 minutes.

Add the tomatillos, black beans, brown sugar, and chicken stock. Stir the ingredients together and simmer them for 3 minutes.

Add the ancho chile peppers, mulato chile peppers, and ground pumpkin seeds. Stir the ingredients together and simmer them for 5 minutes.

makes approximately 3 cups

"Our customers really love this sauce. The different chiles, black beans, beer, tomatillos, and toasted pumpkin seeds all combine to create a terrific new flavor. It's also delicious served with pork."

Robbie Day
San Francisco St. Bar & Grill

"Everybody cooks in El Salvador, which is where I come from. My mother and grandmother both were wonderful cooks, so maybe some of their talent wore off on me."

Hijinio Magana
San Francisco St. Bar & Grill

Chinese Chicken in Hot Pepper Sauce

3 tablespoons cornstarch
2 tablespoons soy sauce
3 tablespoons water
2 whole chicken breasts, skin and bones removed, and cut into 1" cubes
2 teaspoons cornstarch
2 tablespoons sugar
4 tablespoons soy sauce
2 tablespoons rice wine
2 teaspoons toasted sesame oil
1 teaspoon salt *(or to taste)*
4 cups vegetable oil
16 dried Chinese hot red chile peppers, stems and seeds removed
2 teaspoons fresh ginger root, peeled and finely chopped
1 cup raw peanuts, roasted

In a medium bowl place the 3 tablespoons of cornstarch, the 2 tablespoons of soy sauce, and the water. Stir the ingredients together.

Add the chicken cubes and toss them in so that they are well coated with the mixture. Cover the bowl with plastic wrap and let the chicken marinate for 30 minutes at room temperature.

In a small bowl place the 2 teaspoons of cornstarch, sugar, the 4 tablespoons of soy sauce, rice wine, toasted sesame oil, and salt. Whisk the ingredients together and set them aside.

In a large wok place the vegetable oil and heat it on medium high until it is very hot. Add the chicken cubes and deep-fry them for 30 to 45 seconds, or until they are golden brown. Drain the chicken on paper towels.

Remove all but 4 tablespoons of the vegetable oil from the wok and heat it on high until it is very hot. Add the hot red peppers and stir-fry them for 1 minute, or until they blacken.

Add the chicken, ginger, and the reserved cornstarch mixture. Stir the ingredients together and simmer them for 2 minutes.

Garnish the chicken with the roasted peanuts.

serves 4

"In Chinese cooking we use a lot of Chinese hot red chile peppers. They are about as long as a jalapeño, but they are skinnier. They also are a lot spicier. I like to eat them whole, although they are probably too hot for most Americans. We warn our customers about them."

"If you are cooking Chinese food in a wok, a gas range is best, because once you turn the heat off, it's off. The secret to good Chinese food is to stir-fry the food quickly and not to overcook it."

Marta Hung
Imperial Wok

Hack Chicken

4	teaspoons sugar
6	tablespoons soy sauce
2	tablespoons toasted sesame oil
2	tablespoons hot red pepper oil
2	tablespoons brown vinegar *(see chef's comments on this page)*
1	tablespoon brown peppercorns *(see chef's comments on this page)*, ground
1	English hothouse cucumber, peeled and thinly sliced
1	teaspoon salt
2	pounds chicken breast, skin and bones removed, cooked, cooled and thinly sliced
1	tablespoon fresh garlic, finely chopped
1	tablespoon fresh ginger root, peeled and finely chopped
1	teaspoon brown peppercorns, ground

In a small bowl place the sugar, soy sauce, toasted sesame oil, hot red pepper oil, brown vinegar, and the 1 tablespoon of ground brown peppercorns. Whisk the ingredients together and set the sauce aside.

In a medium bowl place the cucumbers and sprinkle them with the salt. Let the cucumbers sit for 10 minutes. Rinse and drain them well.

On a decorative serving plate artfully arrange the cucumber slices. Place the chicken strips on top. Sprinkle the garlic, ginger, and the 1 teaspoon of the ground brown peppercorns on top of the chicken. Dribble the sauce on top.

serves 4

"Brown vinegar is made from dark rice. It has a unique flavor that cannot be duplicated. You might have to go to an Oriental grocery store to find it. Otherwise, use cider vinegar."

"You should be able to find brown peppercorns in your market. They have a different flavor than black peppercorns. If you can't find the exact ingredients you need for Chinese dishes, you can substitute other things. The dishes won't taste exactly the same, but they will still be delicious."

Marta Hung
Imperial Wok

Tangy Chicken
with Salsa Endiablada

Tangy Chicken

4	**dried pequin chile peppers, crushed**
1	**cup olive oil**
¼	**cup white wine vinegar**
1	**teaspoon epazote** *(see chef's comments on page 123)*
6	**chicken breasts, skin removed**
	Salsa Endiablada *(recipe follows)*

In a large bowl place the crushed pequin chile peppers, olive oil, white wine vinegar, and epazote. Whisk the ingredients together. Add the chicken breasts and cover them well with the marinade. Refrigerate the chicken for 2 hours.

Grill the chicken for 5 to 7 minutes on each side, or until it is just done. Serve it with the Salsa Endiablada on top.

serves 6

Salsa Endiablada

2	**tablespoons olive oil**
8	**tomatillos, husks removed, and diced medium**
1	**small carrot, peeled and diced medium**
2	**strips bacon, diced, cooked and drained**
2	**rings fresh pineapple, peeled and diced medium**
1	**stick cinnamon**
2	**chipotle chile peppers** *(in adobo sauce)*
4	**pasilla chile peppers, seeded and chopped**
½	**cup raisins**
1	**2-ounce bar Ibarra** *(Mexican)* **chocolate**
5	**cups chicken stock** *(recipe on page 311)*
2	**teaspoons white vinegar**

In a large saucepan place the olive oil and heat it on medium high until it is hot. Add the tomatillos, carrots, bacon, pineapple, and cinnamon stick. Sauté the ingredients for 5 minutes.

In a food processor place the chipotle and pasilla chile peppers, raisins, Ibarra chocolate, chicken stock, and white vinegar. Coarsely purée the ingredients. Add the purée to the saucepan and simmer it for 30 minutes.

makes approximately 6 cups

"I grew up in El Salvador, although I am now an American citizen. My mother was a teacher in the countryside, so my brothers and I took turns cooking for each other. During the civil war most of us escaped to the United States. It was very scary."

"This sauce is an excellent alternative to a basic enchilada sauce. It's very spicy, and is similar to a mole. The name means 'devilish sauce' and it's a favorite in Mexico. Be sure that you use a good quality chocolate, like Ibarra."

Kimo Castro
San Francisco St. Bar & Grill

Southwestern Stuffed Chicken Breast

"The heat in this recipe comes from the chorizo sausage. It is very greasy, so wring it out in a cheesecloth after you cook it. If you don't, then when you cook the chicken all of the oil will leak out and turn everything orange."

"Visually this dish is very beautiful, because when you slice the chicken you see the stuffing inside."

"Most people don't know the possibilities of jicama.....they only know it as a raw salad condiment. But it also makes a wonderful cooked vegetable. It absorbs other flavors well, and maintains a crisp texture."

Rustin Newton
Staab House

2	tablespoons vegetable oil
2	medium apples, peeled, cored and diced small
1	jicama, peeled and diced small
1	small white onion, diced small
2	tablespoons brandy
½	pound chorizo sausage, meat removed from casing, cooked and drained
½	pound turkey sausage, diced medium
8	6-ounce boneless chicken breasts, skin removed, and pounded thin
¼	cup butter, melted
	salt and black pepper *(to taste)*

Preheat the oven to 350°.

In a large sauté pan place the vegetable oil and heat it on medium high until it is hot. Add the apples, jicama, and white onions. Sauté the ingredients for 3 to 5 minutes, or until the onions are translucent.

Add the brandy and deglaze the pan. Remove the pan from the heat.

In a large bowl place the cooked chorizo and sautéed ingredients, and mix them together. Cover the bowl with plastic wrap and refrigerate the mixture for 10 minutes.

Add the turkey sausage and mix it in.

In the center of each chicken breast place the filling mixture. Roll the chicken breast around the filling and secure it with a toothpick.

On a large baking sheet place the rolled, stuffed chicken breasts. Brush them with the melted butter. Sprinkle on the salt and black pepper.

Bake the chicken for 20 to 25 minutes, or until it is just done. Remove the chicken from the oven and let it sit for 5 minutes.

Cut each stuffed breast into slices.

serves 8

Pollo Barbacoa
with Pipian Verde Sauce

Pollo Barbacoa

3   **serrano chile peppers, finely chopped**
3   **tablespoons lime juice, freshly squeezed**
1   **tablespoon sherry vinegar**
1   **tablespoon honey**
6   **tablespoons olive oil**
     salt and black pepper *(to taste)*
1   **whole chicken, cut into pieces**
     Pipian Verde Sauce *(recipe on next page)*

In a large bowl place the serrano chile peppers, lime juice, sherry vinegar, honey, olive oil, salt, and black pepper. Whisk the ingredients together.

Add the chicken pieces and coat them well with the marinade. Cover the bowl with plastic wrap and refrigerate it overnight.

Grill the chicken for 5 to 8 minutes on each side, or until it is done.

On each of 4 individual serving plates place the chicken. Pour the Pipian Verde Sauce on top.

serves 4

"This is a barbecued chicken dish that has a wonderful flavor from the marinade. The same recipe will work equally well with pork."

Peter Raub
Santa Fe Market

"My husband is learning how to cook and he is really enjoying it. It is such a treat for me to have someone else cook. As a chef, I find that people are afraid to invite me over for dinner, because they are intimidated. But professional chefs appreciate other people cooking for them more than most, because they really understand what kind of care goes into it."

Marsha Chobol
Santa Fe Market

Pipian Verde Sauce

1	pound tomatillos, husks removed and peeled
4	serrano chile peppers
2	tablespoons peanut oil
1½	medium yellow onions, chopped medium
3	cloves fresh garlic, finely chopped
3	tablespoons peanut oil
1	cup pumpkin seeds, toasted *(see chef's comments 317)* **and finely ground**
4	tablespoons fresh cilantro, chopped
1	teaspoon sugar
	salt and black pepper *(to taste)*

In a large saucepan place the tomatillos and serrano chile peppers, and cover them with water. Simmer the ingredients for 10 minutes, or until the tomatillos are soft. Remove the tomatillos and serrano chile peppers from the pan *(reserve the cooking liquid)*.

In a food processor place the tomatillos and serrano chile peppers. Cover the ingredients with the reserved cooking liquid and coarsely purée them.

In a medium sauté pan place the 2 tablespoons of peanut oil and heat it on medium high until it is hot. Add the yellow onions and garlic, and sauté them for 5 minutes.

Add the 3 tablespoons of peanut oil and heat it so that it is hot. Add the tomatillo-chile purée, ground pumpkin seeds, cilantro, and sugar. Sauté the ingredients for 5 minutes, or until the sauce begins to thicken.

Add the salt and black pepper. Place the mixture in the food processor and purée it for 1 minute.

makes 3 cups

Chicken Enchiladas
with Mexico D.F. Red Mole

Chicken Enchiladas

1   **pound chicken, cooked, skin and bones removed, and shredded**
2   **cups mozzarella cheese, grated**
      Mexico D.F. Red Mole *(recipe on next page)*
12   **corn tortillas**

In a medium bowl place the chicken and 1 cup of the mozzarella cheese, and mix them together.

In the bottom of a 9"x12" baking dish spread on some of the Mexico D.F. Red Mole.

In a shallow bowl place the rest of the mole. Dip each tortilla in the mole and fill it with the chicken and cheese mixture. Roll up the tortillas and place them in the baking dish.

Pour the remaining sauce over the enchiladas. Sprinkle on the remaining mozzarella cheese.

Bake the enchiladas for 30 minutes, or until the cheese is melted and everything is hot and bubbly.

serves 6

"Here is a tasty, straightforward recipe for chicken enchiladas. We serve it at the Santa Fe Market and it is very popular. If you prefer, beef may be substituted for the chicken."

Marsha Chobol
Santa Fe Market

"Visual presentation becomes less important to me the longer I cook. I used to be very impressed by a fancy plate, but now I'm much more concerned with really good food."

Peter Raub
Santa Fe Market

Mexico D.F. Red Mole

6	ounces dried guajillo chile peppers, pods saved, seeds toasted and ground
2	dried chipotle chile peppers
2	tablespoons peanut oil
1	large yellow onion, finely chopped
2	cloves fresh garlic, finely chopped
¼	cup pumpkin seeds, toasted *(see chef's comments on page 317)* and ground
6	tablespoons chile caribe *(crushed red chile peppers)*
½	teaspoon ground Mexican oregano
1	tablespoon coriander seeds, ground
1	teaspoon ground cinnamon
¼	teaspoon ground cloves
2	teaspoons sugar
2	tablespoons sherry vinegar
2	tablespoons peanut oil
2¼	cups chicken stock *(recipe on page 311)*
	salt and black pepper *(to taste)*

In a medium saucepan place the guajillo chile and chipotle chile peppers. Cover them with water. Simmer the ingredients for 10 minutes, or until they are soft. Remove the chile peppers from the liquid and set them aside.

In a large sauté pan place the first 2 tablespoons of peanut oil and heat it on medium high until it is hot. Add the yellow onions and garlic, and sauté them for 5 minutes, or until the onions begin to brown.

In a food processor place the softened chile peppers, toasted chile seeds, onions, and garlic. Purée them so that they are smooth. Strain the ingredients through a fine sieve into a medium bowl *(use a rubber spatula to press the mixture through)*.

In the food processor place the strained pepper-onion mixture, pumpkin seeds, chile caribe, Mexican oregano, coriander, cinnamon, cloves, sugar, and sherry vinegar. Purée the ingredients so that they are very smooth.

In the same sauté pan place the second 2 tablespoons of peanut oil and heat it on medium high until it is hot. Add the puréed ingredients and sauté them for 5 minutes. Add the chicken stock and stir it in well. Season the sauce with the salt and black pepper.

makes approximately 1 quart

"Mole recipes can be very complicated or very simple, and this version falls in the latter category. It's delicious, and can be used with many different Mexican dishes. I came up with the recipe when I was in Mexico City. The 'D.F.' in the title stands for 'District Federal', which is the name of the state that Mexico City is in."

Peter Raub
Santa Fe Market

"I really believe that you have to put love into your cooking. If a person is happy with their life, they love people, and they love to cook, this will be evident in the end product. When you are at your personal best, you create your best."

Marsha Chobol
Santa Fe Market

Pollo y Nopales

½	**cup olive oil**
2	**cups yellow onions, coarsely chopped**
1½	**cups prickly pear cactus** *(see chef's comments on this page)*, **diced medium**
1½	**cups celery, sliced medium**
1	**cup red bell peppers, seeded and diced medium**
4	**tablespoons fresh garlic, finely chopped**
4	**boneless chicken breasts, skins removed, and cut into ½" cubes**
½	**cup Calamata olives, pitted and coarsely chopped**
2	**tablespoons** *(or to taste)* **chipotle chile peppers** *(in adobo sauce),* **finely chopped**
¼	**cup fresh cilantro, chopped**
1½	**teaspoons ground cumin**
2½	**cups chicken stock,** *(recipe on page 311)*
½	**teaspoon salt** *(or to taste)*
	black pepper *(to taste)*
6	**slices garlic bread**

In a large saucepan place the olive oil and heat it on medium high until it is hot. Add the yellow onions and sauté them for 10 minutes, or until they are golden brown.

Add the cactus, celery, red bell peppers, and garlic. Sauté the ingredients for 5 minutes, or until the cactus is soft.

Add the chicken, Calamata olives, chipotle chile peppers, cilantro, cumin, chicken stock, salt, and black pepper. Stir the ingredients together and then simmer them for 15 minutes.

Serve the stew with the garlic bread.

serves 6

"I learned about cactus from the Mexican guys who work in our kitchen. They would feed themselves by making a stew with leftover chicken scraps and cactus. By talking to them, I found out that cactus not only is a staple in Mexico, but it also is used as a home remedy. Apparently it is a leveler of blood sugar for hypoglycemics and diabetics. I've noticed that people calm down when they eat this dish, so maybe the cactus really does have special powers."

"The tricky thing with cactus is removing the spines. You can grab the cactus leaves with tongs and cut off each nib, or you can hold them over an open flame and burn the spines off. Once Joan Baez was eating cactus in our restaurant and she got a couple of spines in her mouth. They had been scraped off, but a few were stuck to the cactus. The owner was in a panic, fearing Ms. Baez was permanently injured and would never sing again. Fortunately, she was okay, and was very gracious about the whole thing. The moral of this story, however, is to be very careful!"

Kit Baum
El Farol

Grilled Chicken Breast with Bell Pepper-White Wine Sauce

½	**cup red bell pepper, roasted, peeled, seeded and diced medium**
½	**teaspoon chile pequin** (*hot red chile flakes*)
1	**cup heavy cream**
⅛	**cup dry white wine**
	salt and white pepper (*to taste*)
4	**chicken breasts, skin and bones removed**

In a medium saucepan place the red bell peppers, chile pequin, heavy cream, and white wine. Bring the ingredients to a boil on high heat. Reduce the heat to low and simmer the sauce for 10 minutes, or until it is reduced by ⅓.

Add the salt and white pepper, and stir them in. Keep the sauce warm.

Grill the chicken breasts for 5 to 7 minutes, or until they are just done.

On each of 4 individual serving plates place a grilled chicken breast. Pour the sauce on top.

serves 4

"One day I had some red bell peppers that I roasted. I needed to come up with a nice sauce for a chicken dish, so I decided to use the roasted peppers with some cream and wine, and it tasted delicious. Because it is light and subtle, it should be served with delicately flavored items such as fish, veal, or chicken."

"My first experience working in a restaurant kitchen was disastrous. I was only fifteen years old and the chef started me in the middle of the lunch rush hour. There were thirty tickets in front of me and I was totally panicked, with no idea of what to do. He told me I'd never make it as a chef and kicked me out. Later on he was fired, so I came back. This time I was started off slowly, the way I should have been the first time, and I did really well."

Tony Trujillo
Inn at Loretto

Green Chile Vinaigrette Marinated Chicken with Corn & Goat Cheese Relish

Green Chile Vinaigrette Marinated Chicken

8   8-ounce chicken breasts *(free range chicken)*
1   cup Green Chile Vinaigrette *(recipe on page 115)*
2   cups Corn and Goat Cheese Relish *(recipe follows)*

In a large bowl place the chicken and the Green Chile Vinaigrette. Cover the bowl with plastic wrap and let the chicken marinate for 1 hour at room temperature.

Grill the chicken for 6 to 7 minutes on each side, or until it is just done.

Serve the chicken with the Corn and Goat Cheese Relish on the side.

serves 8

Corn & Goat Cheese Relish

2   ears corn, roasted in husks and kernels removed
1   poblano chile pepper, roasted, peeled, seeded and diced medium
3   tomatillos, husks removed, blanched, peeled and finely diced
½   medium red onion, finely diced
2   medium tomatoes, seeded and finely chopped
¾   cup feta cheese, crumbled
¼   cup fresh cilantro, chopped
⅛   cup Green Chile Vinaigrette *(recipe on page 115)*
1   teaspoon lime juice, freshly squeezed
    salt and white pepper *(to taste)*

In a large bowl place all the ingredients and mix them together well.

makes approximately 1 quart

"One day I needed to come up with a new chicken recipe, and this is what developed. It is a nice, nice dish, with a lot of strong flavors happening at the same time. Shrimp or scallops both work well as substitutes."

"When I was in junior high school I enrolled in a Home Economics course so that I could cook. I got straight A's in that part of the course, but I ditched the sewing part, so I never ended up with a good grade."

"The goat cheese gives this relish a tangy pungent flavor that is nicely complemented by the Green Chile Vinaigrette. It's really delicious and very different tasting. Because of all the vegetables, it's almost like eating a salad."

Scott Shampine
El Nido

"I love going out to eat. I don't care how good or bad the food and service are. As long as I'm not cooking the food, serving it, or washing dishes, I'm happy!"

Dennis Dampf
El Nido

Citrus Marinated Chicken Breasts with Salsa Verde Cruda

Citrus Marinated Chicken Breasts

2	cloves fresh garlic, finely chopped
1	tablespoon lime juice, freshly squeezed
½	cup orange juice, freshly squeezed
½	cup pineapple juice
½	cup olive oil
4	6-ounce chicken breasts
	Salsa Verde Cruda *(recipe follows)*

In a medium bowl place the garlic, lime juice, orange juice, pineapple juice, olive oil, and chicken breasts. Cover the bowl with plastic wrap and marinate the chicken overnight in the refrigerator.

Grill the chicken breasts for 4 to 6 minutes on each side, or until they are just done.

On each of 4 individual serving plates place a chicken breast. Serve the Salsa Verde Cruda on the side.

serves 4

Salsa Verde Cruda

4	cups chicken stock *(recipe on page 311)*
¾	pound tomatillos, husked, washed and cut into quarters
2	cloves fresh garlic
1½	bunches fresh cilantro
2	serrano chile peppers, seeded
1	pinch sugar

In a medium saucepan place the chicken stock and bring it to a boil. Reduce the heat to low and simmer the stock for 45 minutes, or until it is reduced to approximately ½ cup.

In a food processor place the reduced chicken stock and the rest of the ingredients, and coarsely purée them.

makes 2 cups

Roast Turkey with
Mole Negro Oaxaqueño

4	cups peanut oil
½	ripe plantain, peeled and sliced into ⅜" wide pieces
1	corn tortilla
2	teaspoons raisins
2	tablespoons unsalted peanuts
2	tablespoons sliced blanched almonds
2	slices sourdough bread, cubed
1	small yellow onion, coarsely chopped
6	cloves fresh garlic
6	dried pasilla chile peppers
4	dried mulato chile peppers
6	fresh thyme sprigs
6	fresh marjoram sprigs
1½	tablespoons fresh Mexican oregano
1	3" long canela (cinnamon) stick, broken up
3	whole cloves
3	whole allspice
1	large tomato, roasted (see chef's comments on page 72)
¼	cup vegetable oil
1	cup water
1	ounce Ibarra (Mexican) chocolate, finely chopped
2	cups chicken stock (recipe on page 311)
1	8-pound turkey breast

Note: Drain all of the deep-fried items on paper towels.

In a large, heavy pan place the peanut oil and heat it on medium high until it is very hot. Deep-fry the plantain slices for 1 minute, or until they turn golden brown. Deep-fry the tortilla for 1 minute, or until it is crisp. Deep-fry the raisins for 15 seconds, or until they are puffy. Deep-fry the peanuts and almonds for 5 seconds. Deep-fry the bread cubes for 30 seconds, or until they are golden brown. Deep-fry the yellow onions and garlic for 30 seconds, or until they are golden brown.

Remove the stems and the seeds from the pasilla and mulato chile peppers (discard the stems). In a small dry sauté pan place the seeds and toast them on medium high for 2 minutes, or until they begin to blacken. Set the seeds aside.

(continued on next page)

"People love this mole and are always asking us how we make it. The secret to a good mole is that each ingredient must be toasted or deep-fried separately. This seals the flavor in so that you can taste each ingredient, even though everything is cooked together."

"I love moles! When I first went to Mexico about ten years ago I tasted a mole for the first time. My initial reaction was shock, but then I immediately became addicted to it. Each Mexican family has a different way of making mole, and each family is very proud of its own version. Some of the recipes are simple, and others are extremely complex, with subtle undertones that are deep and rich."

"If you know the chocolate is in the mole, you will taste it. If you don't know, you will have a surprise flavor. The chocolate blends beautifully with the smoky flavors of the chiles."

Margueritte Meier
Old Mexico Grill

In the same dry sauté pan place the thyme, marjoram, and Mexican oregano. Cook them on medium high for 1 minute, or until they are lightly toasted. Remove the herbs from the pan, let them cool, and then coarsely grind them.

Place the cinnamon stick, cloves, and allspice in the hot sauté pan and toast them for 3 minutes. Remove the spices from the pan, let them cool, and then coarsely grind them.

In a food processor place the roasted tomato, plantain, tortilla, raisins, peanuts, almonds, bread cubes, yellow onions, garlic, the pasilla and mulato chile pepper seeds, thyme, marjoram, Mexican oregano, cinnamon, cloves, and allspice. Purée the ingredients together.

In another large heavy saucepan place the vegetable oil and heat it on medium until it is hot. Add the puréed mixture and cook it for 15 minutes *(scrape the bottom of the pan occasionally)*.

Place the reserved pasilla and mulato chile peppers and the water in the food processor. Purée them together.

Add the puréed chile peppers and the chocolate to the saucepan, and stir them in. Cook and stir the ingredients for 5 minutes, or until the chocolate is melted.

Add the chicken broth and stir it in well. Cook the mole for 25 minutes.

Preheat the oven to 325°.

Place the turkey breast in a deep pan and roast it for 1½ to 2 hours, or until it is almost done. Pour ½ of the mole over the turkey and cook it for 30 minutes more, or until it is done.

Slice the turkey and serve it topped with the rest of the mole.

serves 8

Chicken in Hot Tomato Sauce

¼	cup olive oil
1	chicken, cut up
1	medium yellow onion, diced medium
2	tablespoons fresh garlic, chopped
¼	cup dry white wine
2	large tomatoes, chopped
4	tablespoons fresh Italian parsley, chopped
2	dried pequin chile peppers, crushed
	salt *(to taste)*

In a large sauté pan place the olive oil and heat it on medium high until it is hot. Add the chicken pieces and sauté them for 3 minutes on each side, or until they are golden brown.

Add the yellow onions and garlic. Sauté them for 5 minutes, or until the garlic begins to turn golden brown around the edges.

Add the rest of the ingredients and stir them together. Cover the pan and simmer the chicken for 15 minutes, or until it is done.

serves 4

"The Italian name for this chicken dish is 'Pollo All'arrabbiata', which means agitated or angry, because of the hot peppers. It's a very simple, fresh-tasting dish, and you can put it together in fifteen minutes. The sauce is basic and you can add different items, like olives or capers. Or, you can make it sweet by adding golden raisins, a pinch of cinnamon, and a pinch of chocolate."

"Serve this with couscous or grilled polenta."

"Cooking is not a perfect science.....you can't corner it into a complete, logical form. To me, it is always a spontaneous, creative process. I throw logic out of the window when I cook and often try bizarre sounding combinations. This often works because you don't really taste the individual ingredients..... what you taste is every-thing all together, which is a brand new taste. It's quite remarkable!"

"I like food that is fresh, simple and subtle, but intense."

Ken Calascione
La Traviata

Chorizo Chicken Hash

4	**links chorizo sausage, meat removed from the casings**
1	**tablespoon butter**
1	**large yellow onion, chopped medium**
2	**cups cooked chicken, skin and bones removed, and shredded**
¼	**cup green chile peppers, roasted, peeled, seeded and diced medium**
1	**jalapeño chile pepper, finely chopped**
¼	**cup fresh cilantro, chopped**
4	**eggs, poached**
4	**slices tomatoes**
2	**potatoes, sliced and grilled**

In a medium sauté pan place the chorizo sausage and break it up with a spatula. Sauté the chorizo for 10 minutes on medium high heat, or until it is done. Drain it well on paper towels and set it aside.

In a large sauté pan place the butter and heat it on medium until it is melted and hot. Add the yellow onions and sauté them for 10 minutes, or until they begin to brown.

Add the chicken and chorizo, and sauté them for 5 minutes.

Add the green chile peppers, jalapeño chile peppers, and cilantro. Stir the ingredients together.

On each of 4 individual serving plates place the hash. Place a poached egg and a tomato slice on top. Serve the grilled potatoes on the side.

serves 4

"Brunch is my favorite meal, and this recipe is my favorite brunch dish to serve. In fact, it is the most popular item on our early-in-the-day menu."

"We have an outdoor patio at the restaurant, and in the winter time we have heaters and the fireplace going. About eleven o'clock the sun streams into the patio, and everyone is nice and toasty warm, eating brunch or lunch. And when they eat this Chorizo Chicken Hash, they get a lot warmer, because it is hot!"

Sylvia Johnson
Celebrations

"I'm originally from Finland, although I have lived in many places in the United States. Santa Fe is one of the best places in the world, especially if you like to ski. Before I moved to Santa Fe I had never tasted green chile. At first it took some getting used to, but now I actually crave it."

Veikko Antilla
Celebrations

Marinated Chicken with Siafun Noodles, Sate Sauce & Cucumber Yogurt Sauce

Marinated Chicken with Siafun Noodles

3	**cloves fresh garlic, finely chopped**
2	**tablespoons fresh ginger root, peeled and finely chopped**
2	**teaspoons chile pequin** *(hot red chile flakes)*
1	**cup soy sauce**
1	**cup sake** *(rice wine)*
8	**8-ounce chicken breasts** *(free range chicken)*
1	**cup Sate Sauce** *(recipe on next page),* **heated**
4	**cups vegetable oil** *(or as needed)*
1	**package Siafun Noodles** *(Chinese cellophane noodles)*
	Cucumber Yogurt Sauce *(recipe on next page)*

In a large bowl place the garlic, ginger, chile pequin, soy sauce, and sake. Whisk the ingredients together. Add the chicken breasts and coat them well with the marinade.

Cover the bowl with plastic wrap and refrigerate the chicken for 8 hours.

Grill the chicken breasts for 5 to 7 minutes on each side *(baste them with the Sate Sauce),* or until they are just done .

In a wok place the vegetable oil and heat it on high until it is very hot. Add the Siafun Noodles and cook them for 10 seconds, or until they are puffed up.

On each of 8 individual serving plates place a chicken breast. Place the Siafun Noodles and the Cucumber Yogurt Sauce on the side. Serve the remaining Sate Sauce in a small bowl on the side.

serves 8

"This is one of those great recipes that is simple to make and tastes just wonderful. Chicken can be boring, but the marinade turns it into something really special."

"Siafun Noodles are really good. The instructions on the package usually say to boil them, but I think they are much better deep-fried."

Scott Shampine
El Nido

"I love to take leftover Sate Sauce and mix it with cold linguini to make a pasta salad. The flavors of the peanut butter, chile, cilantro, ginger, and scallions all come through."

Dennis Dampf
El Nido

"I've lived in Santa Fe for twenty-four years and I love it here. I love the architecture, the wide open spaces, the history, and the tri-cultural aspect of it. The weather is great and the people are wonderful."

Don Scharhag
El Nido

"Someday I hope to own my own restaurant where I plan to have everything natural and wholesome. I will grow my own herbs, make my own yogurt and butter, and grind my own flour. The ambiance will be light and airy, where people will feel equally comfortable in shorts or a tuxedo."

"The cucumbers and yogurt are cool, and help to tone down the spiciness from the Sate Sauce. And for some reason, yogurt and peanuts go really well together."

Scott Shampine
El Nido

Sate Sauce

1	tablespoon peanut oil
4	dried chile pequin peppers
1	tablespoon fresh ginger root, peeled and finely chopped
2	cloves fresh garlic, finely chopped
1	bunch scallions, finely sliced
½	bunch fresh cilantro, chopped
½	teaspoon Chinese 5-spice powder
2	cups chicken stock *(recipe on page 311)*
¼	cup sake *(rice wine)*
¼	cup soy sauce
1	tablespoon rice wine vinegar
½	pound creamy peanut butter
1	tablespoon coconut milk *(see chef's comments on page 113)*
1	medium tomato, seeded and diced medium
½	bunch scallions, coarsely chopped

In a large sauté pan place the peanut oil and heat it on medium high until it is hot. Add the chile pequin peppers, ginger, garlic, the 1 bunch of scallions, cilantro, and Chinese 5-spice powder. Sauté the ingredients for 3 minutes.

Add the chicken stock, sake, soy sauce, and rice wine vinegar. Reduce the heat to low and simmer the ingredients for 30 minutes. Strain the ingredients through a fine sieve and return the liquid to the sauté pan *(discard the pulp)*.

Add the peanut butter and coconut milk, and stir them in. Simmer the sauce for 25 minutes. Add the tomatoes and the ½ bunch of scallions, and stir them in.

makes approximately 1 quart

Cucumber Yogurt Sauce

1	large cucumber, peeled, seeded and diced small
2	tomatoes, diced
½	bunch fresh cilantro, chopped
1	lemon, freshly squeezed
1	cup plain yogurt
¼	teaspoon ground cumin

In a medium bowl place all of the ingredients and mix them together well.

makes approximately 3 cups

Jalapeño Smoked Chicken with Cornmeal Crêpes & Avocado Relish

Jalapeño Smoked Chicken

8	**Cornmeal Crêpes** *(recipe on page 306)*
2	**pounds boneless chicken breast, smoked and cut into ½"** **cubes**
½	**pound watercress, chopped**
2	**jalapeño chile peppers, seeded and thinly sliced**
	Avocado Relish *(recipe follows)*
1	**cup farmer's cheese, crumbled**

In the middle of each crêpe place some of the chicken, watercress, and jalapeño chile peppers. Roll each crêpe up.

On each of 4 individual serving plates place 2 of the crêpes. Garnish them with a dollop of the Avocado Relish and some of the crumbled farmer's cheese.

serves 4

Avocado Relish

2	**avocados, peeled, pitted and finely diced**
1	**medium tomato, seeded and finely diced**
1	**scallion, finely sliced**
1	**tablespoon fresh cilantro, chopped**
1	**tablespoon capers, drained**
1	**lime, freshly squeezed**
	salt and white pepper *(to taste)*

In a medium bowl place all the ingredients and stir them together.

makes approximately 1¼ cups

"We make this recipe with shrimp as well as with chicken, and they are both equally good. I smoke the chicken with hickory wood in a professional smoker. I put it in a pot with a little water, mustard seed, garlic, and salt. At home you can use an outside grill. Put the chicken in a disposable aluminum pan and poke a few holes in it so that the smoke can get through to the chicken."

"This avocado relish is very nice. It is not spicy, just flavorful, so you can really taste the smoked chicken. I don't like to serve dishes where all the components are hot.....I like a nice balance."

Martin Rios
Old House

Chicken Satay with
Avocado Fruit Relish

"I used to make this recipe at another restaurant and we served it with mole. When I came to work here I got the idea that it would be good with a tropical fruit salsa. It's a great example of combining flavors of the East with the Southwest, which is a very popular trend these days."

"When I first came to the United States from El Salvador, there were only two ways I could make a living as an unskilled worker.....in construction or in the restaurant business. The construction work was too hard for me and I didn't like it, so I started working in the kitchen. My bosses were very nice and taught me almost everything I know, except for the knowledge I brought with me from El Salvador."

Kimo Castro
San Francisco St. Bar & Grill

Chicken Satay

1   teaspoon fresh garlic, finely chopped
1   teaspoon fresh ginger root, peeled and finely chopped
1   teaspoon chile pequin *(hot red chile flakes)*
2   cups light sesame oil
2   cups olive oil
1   tablespoon soy sauce
2   pounds boneless chicken tenderloins
      Avocado Fruit Relish *(recipe folows)*

In a large bowl place the garlic, ginger root, chile pequin, sesame oil, olive oil, and soy sauce. Whisk the ingredients together.

Add the chicken tenderloins and cover them well with the marinade.

Cover the bowl with plastic wrap and refrigerate the chicken for 2 hours.

Grill the tenderloins for 2 to 3 minutes on each side, or until they are just done.

Serve the chicken with the Avocado Fruit Relish on the side.

serves 6

Avocado Fruit Relish

1   avocado, pitted, peeled and finely diced
1   mango, peeled, meat removed from the core and finely diced
1   papaya, peeled, seeded and finely diced
2   tomatillos, husks removed, peeled and finely diced
2   jalapeño chile peppers, seeded and finely diced
2   teaspoons fresh cilantro, chopped

In a medium bowl place all of the ingredients and mix them together.

makes approximately 2 cups

Sautéed Chicken Livers with Tecolote Salsa

Sautéed Chicken Livers

4	tablespoons butter
8	ounces chicken livers, drained, fat and membranes removed
1	teaspoon tabasco sauce
	Tecolote Salsa *(recipe follows)*
	salt and black pepper *(to taste)*
12	eggs

Preheat the oven to 425°.

In a large sauté pan place the butter and heat it on medium high until it is melted and hot. Add the chicken livers and sauté them for 5 minutes, or until they are browned. Add the tabasco sauce, 1½ cups of the Tecolote Salsa, salt, and black pepper. Cook the ingredients for 2 minutes more, or until everything is heated and the chicken livers are slightly pink on the inside.

In each of 6 individual, buttered shirred egg dishes *(or small, individual baking dishes)* place the chicken liver mixture. Crack two eggs on top. Bake the eggs for 5 to 6 minutes, or until they are set. Garnish each dish with the rest of the salsa.

serves 6

Tecolote Salsa

4	tablespoons lard *(or oil)*
2	medium white onions, chopped medium
10	medium tomatoes, blanched, peeled and diced
⅓	cup green chile peppers, roasted, peeled, seeded and diced
1	teaspoon cracked black pepper
	salt *(to taste)*

In a large saucepan place the lard and heat it on medium high until it is melted and hot. Add the white onions and sauté them for 5 minutes, or until they are translucent. Add the tomatoes, green chile peppers, and cracked black pepper. Simmer the ingredients for 5 minutes. Season the salsa with the salt.

makes approximately 3 cups

"If you like chicken livers, these will be the best you've ever eaten. They are hot, spicy, and delicious. If you don't like chicken livers, forget it. I got the basic recipe from my mess sergeant when I was in the army in Iceland. Tons of chickens were shipped to us and the livers were always thrown out. He was from Puerto Rico and would save them and cook them up for the kitchen crew to eat."

"Ever since I was a kid I have loved to cook. My first memory is making orange chiffon cakes with lots of eggs."

"My philosophy of cooking is to keep it simple and don't make anything that you yourself wouldn't like to eat."

"Lard or bacon drippings make this salsa taste really, really good. But, if you are concerned about your health, it's okay to use oil. The recipe came from a Tesuque Pueblo woman who used to work for my mother-in-law, so it's very authentic. I like to put it inside omelettes as a filling."

Bill Jennison
Tecolote Cafe

Encantado Chicken Breast with Poblano Cream Sauce

"This is an extremely delicious way to prepare chicken and everyone who eats it just loves it. Because of the cream sauce and cheese, it is a rich dish that you would not want to serve to your family every day. Rather, it's something that would be perfect for a special dinner party."

Encantado Chicken Breast

3	tablespoons vegetable oil
4	8-ounce chicken breasts
2	cups Poblano Cream Sauce *(recipe follows)*
12	ounces mozzarella cheese, grated

Preheat the oven to 350°.

In a large sauté pan place the vegetable oil and heat it on medium high until it is hot. Add the chicken breasts and sauté them for 3 minutes on each side, or until they are golden brown.

Place the chicken breasts in a lightly oiled baking dish. Pour the Poblano Cream Sauce on top. Sprinkle on the mozzarella cheese. Cover the pan with foil and bake the chicken for 20 to 30 minutes, or until just done.

On each of 4 individual serving plates place a chicken breast. Spoon some of the Poblano Cream Sauce from the baking pan on top.

serves 4

"Depending on the time of year, the poblano chiles will vary in their heat. Overall, they have a spicy, peppery flavor. The real heat comes from the jalapeño peppers."

"This sauce is wonderful with pasta. Don't overcook it, or it might break. If this happens you can add more cream and whisk it in."

Tim Lopez
Rancho Encantado

Poblano Cream Sauce

1	tablespoon butter
1	medium yellow onion, thinly sliced
3	jalapeño chile peppers, seeded and finely chopped
2	cloves fresh garlic, finely chopped
3	poblano chile peppers, roasted, peeled, seeded and diced small
1	quart heavy cream

In a medium sauté pan place the butter and heat it on medium high until it is hot and melted. Add the yellow onions, jalapeño chile peppers, and garlic. Sauté the ingredients for 5 minutes, or until the onions are translucent. Add the poblano chile peppers and the cream, and stir them in. Simmer the sauce for 5 minutes.

makes approximately 1 quart

Chicken Poblano
with Red Chile Sauce

Chicken Poblano

2½   pounds boneless chicken breasts, skins removed, and cut
         into 1" cubes
2   poblano chile peppers, seeded and cut into ¾" squares
         Red Chile Sauce *(recipe follows)*

On each of 8 bamboo skewers alternately place the chicken and
poblano chile peppers.

Grill the chicken for 6 to 8 minutes, or until it is just done.

On each of 4 individual serving plates spread the Red Chile
Sauce. Place 2 of the chicken skewers on top.

serves 4

Red Chile Sauce

½   cup olive oil
3   cloves fresh garlic, finely chopped
½   pound beef scraps
½   cup flour
3½   cups water
½   cup Chimayo red chile powder
½   teaspoon salt *(or to taste)*

In a large saucepan place the olive oil and heat it on medium
high until it is hot. Add the garlic and sauté it for 5 minutes, or
until it is golden brown. Add the beef scraps and sauté them for
10 minutes, or until they are done.

While stirring constantly, slowly add the flour. Cook and stir the
ingredients for 1 minute.

While continuing to stir, add the water.

Add the Chimayo chile powder and salt, and whisk them in.
Simmer the sauce for 10 minutes, or until the lumps are gone.

Strain the sauce through a fine sieve *(to remove the beef scraps)*.

makes approximately 3 cups

"Be sure to first soak the bamboo skewers in water for about twenty minutes, or else they might catch on fire when you grill the chicken."

"I love to eat out at other restaurants. If the food or service is not perfect, I am more forgiving than most of my friends, because I understand what happens behind the scenes and why things go wrong."

"One day another cook and I decided we were bored with always eating green chile for lunch, so we started to fool around and came up with this red chile sauce recipe. The beef scraps are what give it such a good flavor. Buy a really cheap cut of beef that has fat in it."

"A lot of times our appetizer cook, Luigi, will pass out tortillas and this chile sauce for customers to nibble on at the bar for free. Herb (the owner) may not know that he does this, but I guess he'll find out when this book is published!"

Chris Arrison
Steaksmith

Chile Oil Marinated Chicken Sandwich

"Flavored oils are very popular in current American cuisine, from basil oil to garlic oil to chile oil. This recipe calls for red chile pods that are deep-fried, which greatly enhances their flavor and removes that 'hack' feeling at the back of your throat."

"I like to marinate the chicken for one to three days. The longer it sits in the chile oil the hotter it gets. If you are sensitive to fiery foods you should remove it after one day and try it. If there is not enough punch to it, then marinate it longer."

Rustin Newton
Staab House

3	cups canola oil
12	dried red chile peppers, stemmed
4	cloves fresh garlic, chopped
1	tablespoon red chile powder
1	teaspoon dried Mexican oregano
	salt *(to taste)*
6	6-ounce boneless chicken breasts, skin removed
6	onion rolls, split in half lengthwise
	mayonnaise *(to taste)*
6	large leaves lettuce
2	tomatoes, thinly sliced

In a large saucepan place the canola oil and heat it on medium high until it is very hot. Add the red chile peppers and deep-fry them for 5 to 7 minutes, or until they begin to discolor *(reserve the oil and let it cool)*. Drain them on paper towels.

In a food processor place the cooled oil, chile peppers, garlic, red chile powder, Mexican oregano, and salt. Purée the ingredients so that they are smooth.

In a large bowl place the chicken breasts and cover them with the puréed mixture. Cover the bowl with plastic wrap and refrigerate the chicken for 24 hours.

Grill the chicken breasts for 5 to 7 minutes on each side, or until they are just done.

On each onion roll spread the mayonnaise. Add the lettuce, tomatoes, and a grilled chicken breast.

serves 6

Fowl

Green Chile Duck Hash

2	**tablespoons olive oil** *(or as needed)*
1	**2-pound duck, roasted** *(see chef's comments on this page for roasting instructions)*, **bones removed, and diced medium**
2	**medium baking potatoes, washed and diced small**
½	**cup green chile peppers, seeded and finely chopped**
1	**small white onion, finely chopped**
2	**cloves fresh garlic, finely chopped**
½	**teaspoon fresh sage, finely chopped**
½	**teaspoon fresh thyme, finely chopped**
½	**teaspoon ground cumin**
½	**teaspoon ground coriander**
2	**cups duck stock** *(see chef's comments on this page)*
2	**limes, freshly squeezed**
1	**pinch cayenne pepper**
	salt and black pepper *(to taste)*
8	**eggs, poached**
8	**flour tortillas, warmed**
1	**cup hot salsa** *(your favorite)*

In a large sauté pan place the olive oil and heat it on medium until it is hot. Add the duck, potatoes, green chile peppers, white onions, and garlic. Sauté the ingredients for 8 to 10 minutes, or until the potatoes are crispy and the onions begin to caramelize.

Add the sage, thyme, cumin, and coriander. Sauté the ingredients for 1 minute.

Add the duck stock to deglaze the pan. Add the lime juice and cayenne pepper, and stir them in. Season the hash with the salt and black pepper.

In each of 4 individual bowls place the hash. Place 2 poached eggs on top. Fold 2 tortillas into quarters and tuck them into the sides of each bowl. Serve the dish with the salsa on the side.

serves 4

"I once worked for a boss who insisted that we serve sautéed chicken livers with eggs for breakfast. Somehow I just couldn't see how that would be appealing to people, so I created this recipe as an alternative. Fortunately, my boss loved it and gave up his chicken liver idea."

"This dish is a gourmet hash. The flavor is so excellent that when you taste it you will feel you have died and gone to heaven. You don't pass GO, you don't collect $200, you are just there! And, it's fun to eat, because you can use the tortillas like a spoon."

"To make the duck stock, simmer a couple of duck legs from the butcher, an onion, celery stalk, carrot, and bay leaf in a gallon of water for an hour or so. Or, you could use a beef bouillon instead."

"When I cook duck, I first grill it on low heat for fifteen to twenty minutes, and then roast it in the oven at 375° for ten to fifteen minutes."

"A lot of people have trouble getting all the juice out of limes. Roll the lime on a counter and press down hard to loosen it. Then stick a fork in it when you squeeze it."

Pete Zimmer
Inn of the Anasazi

Taos Chile Honey Glazed Duck with Poblano Mango Salsa

"Every time I go to a Chinese restaurant and have Peking duck I get upset because it never tastes as good as this recipe. The vinegar, honey, chile flakes and soy in the glaze give the duck such an incredible flavor."

"When you add the glaze to the duck it will start to pop and splat inside the oven, and the duck will turn a dark brown color. Don't be afraid of the screaming noises in the oven and don't think that the duck is burning, because it isn't. Make sure that you roast it deeply. And, if you have a deep roasting dish it shouldn't make too big a mess. Thank God I have people to clean out my oven!"

"This is a simple, straightforward salsa that is an excellent complement to the duck. It's also good as a relish for grilled chicken, or as a dipping sauce for Chinese egg rolls or won-tons. Another idea is to toss it with some baby greens and serve warm, sliced duck on top."

Pete Zimmer
Inn of the Anazazi

Taos Chile Honey Glazed Duck

1	cup honey
½	cup chile pequin *(hot red chile flakes)*
¼	cup toasted sesame oil
¼	cup soy sauce
½	cup champagne vinegar
½	cup water
2	2-pound ducks
	Poblano Mango Salsa *(recipe follows)*

Preheat the oven to 400°.

In a medium bowl place the honey, chile pequin, toasted sesame oil, soy sauce, champagne vinegar, and water. Mix the ingredients together.

Place the ducks on a sheet pan with a cooling wire rack and roast them for 20 minutes. Brush the chile honey glaze all over the ducks, both inside and out. Roast them for 20 to 30 minutes more, or until they are nicely darkened and done *(baste them frequently with the glaze)*.

Remove the ducks from the oven and split them in half.

Serve the duck halves with the Poblano Mango Salsa on top.

serves 4

Poblano Mango Salsa

1	cup mango, diced medium
2	poblano chile peppers, seeded and finely diced
1	medium red onion, diced small
1	red bell pepper, seeded and diced small
1	bunch fresh cilantro, chopped
1	tablespoon honey
1	tablespoon olive oil
	salt *(to taste)*

In a medium bowl place all of the ingredients and gently mix them together.

makes approximately 2 cups

Southwestern Crêpes Suisse with Jalapeño Melon Salsa

Southwestern Crêpes Suisse

2	tablespoons butter
1	medium yellow onion, finely diced
1½	cups green chile peppers, roasted, peeled, seeded and diced medium
1½	cups tomatillos, husks removed, and diced medium
4	scallions, thinly sliced
1	jalapeño chile pepper, seeded and finely chopped
2	cloves fresh garlic, finely chopped
1	cup chicken stock *(recipe on page 311)*
	salt and white pepper *(to taste)*
5	boneless chicken breasts, skin removed, cooked and diced
16	Crêpes *(recipe on page 307)*
2	cups heavy cream
1	cup Monterey Jack cheese, grated
	Jalapeño Melon Salsa *(recipe on next page)*

Preheat the oven to 350°.

In a large saucepan place the butter and heat it on medium high until it is melted and hot. Add the yellow onions and sauté them for 5 minutes, or until they are translucent.

Add the green chile peppers, tomatillos, scallions, jalapeño chile peppers, garlic, chicken stock, salt, and white pepper. Bring the ingredients to a boil. Reduce the heat to low and simmer them for 10 minutes.

Add the diced chicken and mix it in.

In the center of each crêpe place some of the chicken mixture. Roll the crêpe up and place it in a lightly greased baking pan. Pour the heavy cream over the crêpes and sprinkle on the grated cheese.

Bake the crêpes for 15 to 20 minutes, or until the cheese is melted and bubbly.

Serve the crêpes with the Jalapeño Melon Salsa on the side.

serves 6 to 8

"This is a perfect recipe for large groups because people love it, and it can be assembled the day before and then baked at the last minute. I serve this at an annual picnic, and people are always requesting the recipe. You can make this with tortillas instead of crêpes if you don't want to go to the trouble of making them, but I really like their delicate flavor."

Louise Stewart
Grant Corner Inn

"To me, a really great dish is when the different flavors are all exciting on their own, but they also blend together to create a different flavor that is equally as exciting. When this happens, you know you are hitting something really lucky! Cooking is sort of a game I play, weaving in and out of the flavor maze."

Pat Walter
Grant Corner Inn

Jalapeño Melon Salsa

2 cups cantaloupe, seeded and diced medium
1 cup honeydew melon, seeded and diced medium
1 medium red bell pepper, seeded and diced medium
2 jalapeño chile peppers, seeded and finely chopped
½ cup scallions, thinly sliced
½ cup fresh cilantro, chopped
1 lemon, freshly squeezed

In a medium bowl place all the ingredients and mix them together. Cover the bowl with plastic wrap and refrigerate the salsa for 30 minutes.

makes approximately 5 cups

Chicken Breasts Verde

2 tablespoons butter
1 large yellow onion, thinly sliced
1 cup green chile peppers, roasted, peeled, seeded and diced medium
½ pound button mushrooms, thinly sliced
4 chicken breasts, skins removed
4 large slices Swiss cheese

In a large sauté pan place the butter and heat it on medium high until it is melted and hot. Add the yellow onions and sauté them for 5 minutes, or until they are translucent.

Add the green chile peppers and mushrooms. Sauté them for 3 to 4 minutes, or until the mushrooms are tender. Set the ingredients aside.

Grill the chicken breasts for 4 to 5 minutes on each side, or until they are two-thirds done.

On top of each chicken breast place some of the green chile-mushroom mixture. Place a slice of Swiss cheese on top. Grill the chicken 2 to 3 minutes more, or until it is just done and the cheese is melted.

serves 4

El Nido Enchiladas with Raspberry Red Chile Sauce

El Nido Enchiladas

8	blue corn tortillas, softened in hot vegetable oil and drained on paper towels
2	cups Refried Jalapeño Black Beans *(recipe on page 294)*
4	chicken breasts, skin and bones removed, cooked and shredded
2	cups Raspberry Red Chile Sauce *(recipe on next page)*
4	poblano chile peppers, roasted, peeled, seeded and diced medium
1	cup feta cheese, crumbled
1	cup Monterey Jack cheese, grated
2	cups head lettuce, shredded
2	tomatoes, diced medium
½	cup sour cream

Preheat the oven to 450°.

To assemble each enchilada, place one of the softened blue corn tortillas on a large baking sheet. On top of each tortilla place, in this order, the refried black beans, shredded chicken, Raspberry Red Chile Sauce, poblano chile peppers, and feta cheese. Place another tortilla on top. Sprinkle on the Monterey Jack cheese.

Bake the enchiladas for 15 to 20 minutes, or until they are hot and the cheese is melted.

Cut each enchilada into 4 wedges. Garnish each serving with the lettuce, tomatoes, and sour cream.

serves 4

"The flavor of this dish is a little strange, but neat! People are not used to tasting raspberries with red chile. Once they get over the initial shock, however, they really like it."

Scott Shampine
El Nido

"This is a very unique enchilada dish that we serve at the restaurant. I really love it because of the sweet and spicy tastes. Both the raspberry and red chile flavors are very well balanced, with neither one overwhelming the other."

"I don't consider myself to be a chef, although I do know my way around a kitchen. My grandmother was a fantastic cook and I spent a lot of time with her as a child. I remember our going outside to rake leaves together and she would stop and make a little fire, and we would cook salami and eggs. She was a great woman."

Dennis Dampf
El Nido

Raspberry Red Chile Sauce

1	pound dried mild red chile peppers, soaked in water overnight and seeded
4	cloves fresh garlic
2	cups raspberry jam
½	bunch fresh cilantro, stems tied together with kitchen string
1	tablespoon garlic powder
1	tablespoon salt *(or to taste)*

In a medium stockpot place the chile peppers and cover them with water. Boil the chile peppers for 30 minutes *(reserve the cooking liquid)*.

Place the boiled chile peppers, the cooking liquid, and the garlic in a food processor. Purée the ingredients so that they are smooth.

Strain the ingredients through a fine sieve into a medium saucepan.

Add the raspberry jam, cilantro, garlic powder, and salt. Simmer the ingredients for 1½ to 2 hours, or until the sauce is the consistency of heavy cream *(add more water if needed)*.

Remove the cilantro.

makes 1 quart

"I thought that it would be fun to try a sauce with chiles and fruit, and this is what I came up with. It took me a while to get the exact proportions and ingredients right, but I'm glad I persevered because it is an outstanding sauce. I find it very gratifying to come up with a successful recipe like this."

"Be sure to cook the sauce long enough. Otherwise, it will be bitter. You also can ruin the sauce by cooking it too long. The key is to keep tasting the sauce along the way."

Scott Shampine
El Nido

Chile Grilled Chicken

½	cup chile molido *(ground red chile peppers)*
2	dried chipotle chile peppers, finely crushed
½	teaspoon fresh thyme, finely chopped
4	whole chicken breasts, skin and bones removed

In a small bowl place the chile molido, chipotle chile peppers, and thyme. Mix the ingredients together.

Dredge each chicken breast in the mixture so that it is well coated.

Grill the chicken *(over mesquite chips if possible)* for 3 to 4 minutes on each side, or until it is done.

serves 4

"This recipe is very spicy, with a great smoky flavor. If you are worried about the heat, leave out the chipotle chiles. You can use these spices on any poultry or fowl. And, as you can see, it only takes minutes to prepare."

Pete Zimmer
Inn of the Anasazi

Southwestern Marinated Chicken Breasts

12	dried red chile peppers
6	cloves fresh garlic, coarsely chopped
3	shallots, coarsely chopped
1	bunch fresh cilantro, chopped
½	teaspoon ground cumin
1	cup dry white wine
1	cup olive oil
	salt and white pepper *(to taste)*
4	whole chicken breasts, skin removed

In a food processor place all the ingredients *(except the chicken breasts)* and purée them so that they are smooth.

In a large bowl place the chicken breasts. Pour the puréed marinade over the chicken so that it is well coated. Cover the bowl with plastic wrap and let the chicken marinate for 24 hours in the refrigerator.

Grill the chicken breasts for 5 to 8 minutes on each side, or until they are just done.

serves 4

"I came up with this recipe several years ago together with a friend. It's really a wonderful, simple way to prepare chicken. Although it is only mildly spicy, the chile flavor definitely comes through."

Tony Trujillo
Inn at Loretto

Sambal Chile Chicken Cakes

4	8-ounce boneless chicken breasts, skin removed, and ground
2	tablespoons sambal chile paste *(see chef's comments on this page)*
1	orange, zested *(outer orange part grated off)* and finely chopped
1	lemon, zested and finely chopped
1	lime, zested and finely chopped
	salt *(to taste)*

In a medium bowl place all the ingredients and mix them together well.

Form the mixture into small patties.

Grill the patties for 3 to 4 minutes on one side. Turn the patties over and grill them for 2 to 3 minutes more, or until they are done.

serves 8

"Sambal is an extremely hot, Asian chile that is converted into a paste. It gives an authentic flavor to many Eastern dishes, and should not be too hard to find."

"These make a great appetizer. For a simple dipping sauce mix some orange juice concentrate together with a little cornstarch and water, and cook it until it is slightly thickened."

Rustin Newton
Staab House

Honey Chipotle Chicken

4	chipotle chile peppers *(in adobo sauce),* **drained and chopped**
2	cloves fresh garlic, finely chopped
2	tablespoons fresh cilantro, chopped
¼	cup honey
2	tablespoons stoneground mustard
2	teaspoons ground cumin
3	limes, freshly squeezed
1	tablespoon balsamic vinegar
2	tablespoons vegetable oil
12	5-ounce boneless chicken breasts, skins removed

Place the chipotle chile peppers, garlic, cilantro, honey, stoneground mustard, cumin, lime juice, and balsamic vinegar in a food processor. With the processor constantly running, slowly dribble in the oil.

Brush the sauce on both sides of the chicken breasts. Grill them for 6 to 7 minutes on each side, or until they are just done. Serve the chicken with the sauce on top.

serves 6

"This is definitely a unique dish that has a wonderful sweet and spicy flavor. It doesn't burn deeply like a jalapeño, but rather it heats just the surface of your tongue. Use the sauce on whatever you are barbecuing. Once I had it with grilled shrimp and it was dynamite!"

"Be sure you get the chipotle peppers well puréed, because if you bite into any big chunks, it can be lethal."

Chris Arrison
Steaksmith

Green Curry Thai Chicken & Eggplant Stew

3	pounds chicken breasts, skin and bones removed, and cut into 2" cubes
1	large eggplant, cut into 1" cubes
1	medium red onion, cut lengthwise into ¼" wide strips
1	3" long piece fresh ginger root, peeled and cut diagonally into ¼" wide pieces
3	tablespoons fresh garlic, coarsely chopped
6	kaffir lime leaves *(see chef's comments on this page)*
8	Thai chile peppers *(see chef's comments on this page),* **stemmed**
1⅔	cups coconut milk *(see chef's comments on page 113)*
1½	cups milk
1	quart Green Curry Sauce *(recipe on page 113)*

In a large stockpot place all of the ingredients and simmer them for 45 minutes on medium heat.

serves 8

"Kaffir lime leaves come dried from the Far East. They have a beautiful, exotic flavor for which there is no substitute. The limes in Thailand are very small, like a cherry tomato, and the leaves are also much smaller. Like a bay leaf or cinnamon stick, they are not to be eaten. If you can't find them, you can use lime zest."

"Thai chiles can be found at Oriental stores and at many large markets. There really is no substitute for the special flavor they have. By the way, don't eat these chiles. They are too hot for most people."

Katharine Kagel
Cafe Pasqual's

LP CALDWELL

Meat

Spicy Steak Rellenos
with Smoked Mozzarella

1	tablespoon garlic, finely chopped
4	tablespoons Sriracha hot chile sauce *(see chef's comments on this page)*
1	teaspoon ground cumin
2	limes, freshly squeezed
1	10-ounce beef tenderloin, thickly sliced
1½	cups piñon nuts *(pine nuts),* toasted *(see chef's comments on page 325)* and chopped
¼	cup scallions, finely chopped
6	Anaheim chile peppers, roasted and peeled
½	pound smoked mozzarella cheese, cut into thin strips
3	eggs, well beaten
½	cup milk
1	cup flour
2	cups tortilla chips, finely ground
6	cups vegetable oil *(or as needed)*
1	cup sour cream
1	lime, cut into wheels

In a medium bowl place the garlic, Sriracha hot chile sauce, cumin, and lime juice. Whisk the ingredients together.

Add the beef slices and cover them completely with the marinade. Cover the bowl with plastic wrap and let it sit for 1 hour at room temperature.

Grill the beef for 1 to 2 minutes on each side, or until it is rare.

Place the beef in a food processor and coarsely purée it.

In another medium bowl place the puréed beef, toasted piñon nuts, and scallions. Mix the ingredients together well.

Make a slit, lengthwise, down each Anaheim chile pepper.

Stuff each pepper with the beef mixture and the mozzarella cheese. Press the cut edges of the pepper together.

In a small bowl place the beaten eggs and milk, and whisk them together.

Dredge each stuffed pepper in the flour, dip it in the egg-milk mixture, and then roll it in the ground tortilla chips so that it is well coated.

(continued on next page)

"This is one of our lunch items and I absolutely love it. The smoky flavor of the mozzarella cheese enhances the flavor of the marinated grilled beef, which is limey and tangy. The outside of the relleno is crispy because it is coated in tortilla chips and deep-fried. It's a really fun thing to eat, and it's very different from a typical chile relleno."

Gina Ziluca
Geronimo

"Sriracha hot chile sauce is a bright red sauce made from hot Asian chiles. You can find it in Asian stores, or else you can substitute any hot red chile sauce that you like."

Amy Eldridge
Geronimo

"We leave the seeds in the peppers so you get a lot more heat. If you would like the dish to be milder, remove them."

Cliff Skoglund
Geronimo

Meat

In a large heavy saucepan place the vegetable oil and heat it on high until it is very hot. Add the chile peppers and deep-fry them for 2 minutes, or until they are golden brown. Drain the rellenos on paper towels.

On each of 6 individual serving plates place a chile relleno. Garnish each relleno with the sour cream and a lime wheel.

serves 6

Tecolote Green Chile Stew

1	pound lean beef, diced into bite-size pieces
1	cup flour
2	tablespoons vegetable oil
1	cup green chile peppers, roasted, peeled, seeded and diced
1	quart beef stock
1	large yellow onion, diced medium
1	cup carrots, diced
1	large potato, peeled and diced medium
	salt and black pepper *(to taste)*

Dredge the beef in the flour so that it is well coated.

In a large, heavy stockpot place the vegetable oil and heat it on medium high until it is hot. Add the coated beef pieces and sauté them for 5 minutes, or until they are browned.

Add the green chile peppers and beef stock. Bring the ingredients to a boil, cover the pot with a lid, and reduce the heat to low. Simmer the ingredients for 1 hour.

Add the yellow onions and simmer the ingredients for 1 hour.

Add the carrots and potatoes. Simmer the ingredients for 30 minutes, or until they are tender.

Season the stew with the salt and black pepper.

serves 4

Meat

Beef Filet with Ancho Chile Portabella Mushroom Steak Sauce

¼	cup fresh sage, chopped
½	cup extra virgin olive oil
1	lemon, freshly squeezed
2	teaspoons kosher salt *(or to taste)*
1	teaspoon black pepper, freshly ground *(or to taste)*
3	cups Portabella mushrooms, sliced ¼" thick
1	tablespoon extra virgin olive oil
1	medium yellow onion, diced medium
1	tablespoon fresh garlic, finely chopped
8	Roma tomatoes, grilled and diced medium
1	cup ancho chile peppers, roasted, peeled, seeded and puréed
2	limes, freshly squeezed
¼	cup extra virgin olive oil
1	tablespoon honey
6	8-ounce beef filets
	salt and black pepper *(to taste)*

In a medium bowl place the sage, the ½ cup of olive oil, lemon juice, kosher salt, and black pepper. Whisk the ingredients together.

Add the Portabella mushrooms and toss them in well. Cover the bowl with plastic wrap and marinate the mushrooms for 1 hour at room temperature.

Grill the mushrooms for 1 minute and set them aside.

In a medium sauté pan place the 1 tablespoon of olive oil and heat it on medium high until it is hot. Add the yellow onions and garlic. Sauté them for 5 minutes, or until the onions are translucent.

In a medium bowl place the sautéed onions, garlic, Roma tomatoes, ancho chile peppers, lime juice, the ¼ cup of olive oil, and the honey. Stir the ingredients together.

Add the grilled mushrooms and toss them in well.

Rub the beef with the salt and black pepper.

Grill the steaks for 4 minutes on each side, or until the desired doneness is achieved.

On each of 6 individual serving plates place the steaks. Spoon the sauce on top.

serves 6

"This sauce is quite substantial because of the Portabella mushrooms, which are very meaty. A lot of my sauces are so substantial that you don't need a vegetable on the plate, because the sauce acts as a vegetable. This sauce would also be excellent with a pasta."

Gina Ziluca
Geronimo

"I think that Portabellas are the best mushrooms that you can consume, and you can find them almost anywhere. They really taste delicious with the ancho chile peppers."

Cliff Skoglund
Geronimo

"Geronimo is the kind of place you would go if you had a fantasy about the perfect dining out experience. It's elegant, homey, friendly, with impeccable service and outstanding food. The ambiance is one of the finest in Santa Fe."

Keith Mayton
Geronimo

Short Ribs with Mole Verde

8	tomatillos, roasted *(see chef's comments on page 72)*
1	small yellow onion, roasted and chopped
2	cloves fresh garlic, roasted and finely chopped
6	serrano chile peppers, roasted and finely chopped
2	bunches fresh cilantro, chopped
1	bunch radish leaves, chopped
½	head romaine lettuce, chopped
1	teaspoon epazote *(see chef's comments on page 123)*
10	cups chicken stock *(recipe on page 311)*
¼	cup vegetable oil
4	pounds short ribs

Preheat the oven to 300°.

In a food processor place the tomatillos, yellow onions, garlic, serrano chile peppers, cilantro, radish leaves, romaine lettuce, and epazote. Coarsely purée the ingredients.

With the food processor constantly running, slowly add ½ of the chicken stock. Purée the ingredients well.

In a large saucepan place the purée and simmer it on low for 1 hour *(add more of the chicken stock as it is needed to keep the sauce of the same consistency)*.

In a large sauté pan place the vegetable oil and heat it on medium high until it is hot. Add the short ribs and fry them for 5 minutes on each side, or until they are brown.

In a large, shallow baking pan place the short ribs. Pour the sauce over the ribs. Bake them for 2 hours, or until they are very tender.

serves 4

Cowboy Cornbread Casserole

1	cup cornmeal
⅓	cup all purpose flour
2	teaspoons baking powder
1	teaspoon sugar
½	teaspoon salt
1	egg, beaten
1	tablespoon vegetable oil
1	cup buttermilk
½	cup green chile peppers, roasted, peeled, seeded and diced medium
2	tablespoons vegetable oil
1	green bell pepper, seeded and diced medium
1	red bell pepper, seeded and diced medium
1	medium red onion, finely diced
1	pound ground beef
1	cup cooked pinto beans, drained
2	teaspoons red chile powder
2	tablespoons ground cumin
	salt and white pepper *(to taste)*
1	bunch fresh cilantro, chopped
1	cup Monterey Jack cheese, grated

Preheat the oven to 325°.

In a large bowl place the cornmeal, flour, baking powder, sugar, and salt. Mix the ingredients together.

In a small bowl place the egg, the 1 tablespoon of vegetable oil, and the buttermilk. Whisk the ingredients together. Add the mixture to the flour mixture and stir it in so that it is well combined.

Pour ½ of the batter in another bowl and set it aside.

To the remaining batter add the green chile peppers and mix them in well.

In a 9"x12" greased pan place the green chile batter. Bake it for 20 minutes, or until it is barely firm *(do not overcook)*.

In a large sauté pan place the 2 tablespoons of vegetable oil and heat it on medium high until it is hot. Add the green bell peppers, red bell peppers, and red onions. Sauté the ingredients for 5 minutes, or until the onions are translucent.

(continued on next page)

"This is a fun recipe to make for parties because it's a real crowd pleaser. It's kind of like a giant sloppy joe sandwich that's a meal in itself. We serve it on Super Bowl Sunday and people just love it."

"I grew up in an ethnically diverse neighborhood. There were Sicilians, Italians, Puerto Ricans, and Blacks, all living in the same area. My friends were of all different races and we would always eat at each others' houses, so at a young age I was exposed to many different kinds of food."

Dakota
Piñon Grill

Add the ground beef and sauté it for 6 to 7 minutes, or until it is browned.

Add the pinto beans, red chile powder, cumin, salt, and white pepper. Stir the ingredients together.

Spread the beef-bean mixture evenly over the baked cornbread. Sprinkle on the cilantro. Spread the remaining batter over the top. Sprinkle the Monterey Jack cheese on top. Bake the bread for 30 minutes, or until it is firm.

serves 8

Ropa Sucia

2	tablespoons vegetable oil
1	medium white onion, thinly sliced
5	poblano chile peppers, roasted, peeled, seeded and thinly sliced
8	tomatoes, roasted *(see chef's comments on page 72)* **and diced**
2	cups corn kernels
2	teaspoons achiote paste *(see chef's comments on page 36)*
5	cups beef stock
1	teaspoon white vinegar
2	pounds roast beef, cooked until tender and shredded
4	cups cooked white rice

In a large saucepan place the vegetable oil and heat it on medium high until it is hot. Add the white onions and poblano chile peppers. Sauté them for 5 minutes, or until the onions are translucent.

Add the tomatoes, corn, achiote paste, beef stock, and white vinegar. Stir the ingredients together and simmer them for 15 minutes.

Add the shredded beef and stir it in. Simmer the sauce for 10 to 15 minutes, or until it has thickened.

On each of 6 individual serving plates place the rice. Spoon the sauce on top.

serves 6

Barbecued Brisket Tamales with Smoky Barbecue Sauce

Barbecued Brisket Tamales

1	pound beef brisket
4	cups Smoky Barbecue Sauce *(recipe on next page)*
2	cups masa harina *(ground corn flour)*
1½	tablespoons butter, melted
¾	teaspoon sugar
¾	teaspoon baking powder
¾	teaspoon salt *(or to taste)*
8	large dried corn husks, soaked in hot water for 30 minutes *(or until pliable),* drained and patted dry

Preheat the oven to 275°.

In a large, heavy dutch oven with a tight lid place the beef brisket and the Smoky Barbecue Sauce. Cover the pot and place it in the oven. Braise the beef brisket for 2 hours, or until it is very tender *(add some water if needed to keep the brisket moist)*. Remove the meat from the pan *(reserve the sauce)*. Let the meat cool, shred it, and set it aside.

In a medium large mixing bowl place the masa harina, ½ cup of the reserved liquid from the cooked beef brisket, butter, sugar, baking powder, and salt. Cream the ingredients together with an electric mixer *(use the paddle attachment)* for 10 minutes, or until the mixture is light and fluffy.

Tear 2 of the corn husks into a total of 12 thin strips.

Flatten out the 6 remaining corn husks. Spread a thin layer of the masa dough mixture on top of each corn husk *(leave 1" of the husk bare at each end)*. Place some of the shredded beef on top of the masa. Cover the beef with another thin layer of the masa dough. Roll the corn husk up lengthwise, and fold the ends in toward the center. Use 2 of the thin corn husk strips to tie each tamale securely shut.

In a steamer over boiling water place the tamales. Cover the pan and let the tamales steam for 30 minutes, or until the dough comes away easily from the corn husk.

On each of 6 individual serving plates spread the reserved Smoky Barbecue Sauce. Place a tamale on top.

serves 6

"I like to use beef brisket in tamales because it's inexpensive, it shreds well, the flavor is good, and it has just the right amount of fat in it."

"Both of my grand-mothers were really good cooks, but in different ways. One was a Southern preacher's daughter, and did a lot of baking, with greens and fried chicken. The other was the daughter of a doctor, and had more formal meals, with elegant place settings and impeccable table manners."

Mark Kiffin
Coyote Cafe

Smoky Barbecue Sauce

1	cup rice wine vinegar
1	cup cider vinegar
1	tablespoon ground allspice
½	tablespoon ground cloves
2	tablespoons coriander seeds
½	cup olive oil
1	medium yellow onion, finely chopped
4	cloves fresh garlic, roasted *(see chef's comments on page 60)*
1	cup dark brown sugar
¼	cup molasses
1	cup chipotle chile peppers *(in adobo sauce)*, puréed
1½	bottles ketchup
1	tablespoon Worcestershire sauce
1	cup water
1	tablespoon salt *(or to taste)*

In a medium saucepan place the rice wine vinegar, cider vinegar, allspice, cloves, and coriander seeds. Simmer the ingredients on medium for 15 minutes, or until they are reduced by ½. Strain the mixture through a fine sieve, and set the liquid aside.

In a large sauté pan place the olive oil and heat it on medium until it is hot. Add the yellow onions and garlic, and sauté them for 10 minutes, or until the onions are lightly browned.

Add the brown sugar, molasses, and the reserved vinegar-spice mixture. Cook the ingredients for 1 minute to deglaze the pan.

Add the chipotle chile purée, ketchup, Worcestershire sauce, water, and salt. Stir the ingredients together and then simmer them for 30 minutes.

Place the mixture in a food processor and purée it so that it is smooth.

makes 2 quarts

"The smoky flavor comes from the chipotles, which are jalapeño chile peppers that have turned red and then have been smoked over mesquite for seventy-two hours. This sauce is delicious with all kinds of meat, chicken, and shrimp."

"I have great respect and admiration for Mark Miller. He is extremely creative when it comes to food. We work great together as a team and he is always very respectful of me. The restaurant and its cuisine are his concept, so I always try to stay within the parameters of his vision."

Mark Kiffin
Coyote Cafe

Beef Fajitas with Guacamole & Pico de Gallo

Beef Fajitas

1	pound lean beef, cut into thin strips
	Fajita Marinade *(recipe on page 303)*
4	tablespoons corn oil
1	large yellow onion, thinly sliced
1	large red onion, thinly sliced
1	green bell pepper, seeded and thinly sliced
1	red bell pepper, seeded and thinly sliced
8	cherry tomatoes, halved and seeds removed
1	teaspoon garlic salt
1	lime, halved and seeds removed
8	flour tortillas, warmed
1	cup **Guacamole** *(recipe on next page)*
1	cup **Pico de Gallo** *(recipe on next page)*
1	cup sour cream

In a medium bowl place the beef and the Fajita Marinade. Toss the ingredients together so that the beef is well coated. Cover the bowl with plastic wrap and let the beef marinate overnight in the refrigerator.

In a large, heavy skillet place the corn oil and heat it on high until it is very hot. Add the marinated beef, yellow and red onions, green and red bell peppers, cherry tomatoes, and garlic salt. Sauté the ingredients for 3 to 5 minutes, or until the onions are translucent.

Squeeze the lime juice over the meat and vegetables. Serve the fajitas with the tortillas, Guacamole, Pico de Gallo, and sour cream on the side.

serves 4

"Fajitas are fun to serve because their presentation is so festive. They are brought out hissing and sizzling in a cast iron skillet, and everybody can hear and smell them. They are very healthy to eat. You don't have to fry the meat and vegetables if you would rather not use any oil. Instead you can steam them with a little water. Both shrimp and chicken can be used with this recipe."

Jennifer Nelson
Old Mexico Grill

"The chile peppers in Mexico are incredible. They have so many different types, and each one has its own unique flavor. They probably have more varieties than any other country in North or South America. I know of eighteen kinds, but there are many more."

Marc Greene
Old Mexico Grill

"This is a classic Mexican recipe for making guacamole. In America, some people like to add sour cream, and others prefer to use nothing but avocados, salt, and pepper."

Guacamole

8	**small Haas avocados, halved, peeled and pitted**
2	**tomatoes, seeded and finely diced**
½	**medium yellow onion, finely diced**
½	**jalapeño chile pepper, seeded and finely chopped**
½	**bunch fresh cilantro, finely chopped**
	salt *(to taste)*

In a large bowl place the avocados and mash them well with a fork.

Add the tomatoes, yellow onions, jalapeño chile peppers, and cilantro. Mix the ingredients together.

Season the guacamole with the salt.

makes approximately 2 cups

"Some pico de gallo recipes are very hot, but this one is mild. To increase the heat, add more jalapeños."

Jennifer Nelson
Old Mexico Grill

Pico de Gallo

12	**tomatoes, seeded and coarsely chopped**
½	**large yellow onion, finely chopped**
3	**jalapeño chile peppers, finely chopped**
½	**bunch fresh cilantro, finely chopped**
1	**teaspoon salt** *(or to taste)*

In a medium bowl place all the ingredients and mix them together.

makes approximately 2 cups

Grilled Pepper Steak
with Tampiqueño Salsa

Grilled Pepper Steak

¼ cup olive oil
2 cups red wine
2 tablespoons cracked black peppercorns
6 7-ounce sirloin steaks
   Tampiqueño Salsa (recipe follows)

In a large bowl place the olive oil, red wine, and black peppercorns. Whisk the ingredients together.

Add the sirloin steaks and cover them well with the marinade.

Cover the bowl with plastic wrap and refrigerate the steaks overnight.

Grill the steaks for 5 to 6 minutes on each side, or until the desired doneness is achieved.

On each of 6 individual serving plates place a steak. Spoon the Tampiqueño Salsa on top.

serves 6

Tampiqueño Salsa

2 tablespoons olive oil
4 poblano chile peppers, seeded and thinly sliced
1 medium yellow onion, diced medium
2 jalapeño chile peppers, seeded and thinly sliced
4 medium tomatoes, diced medium

In a large sauté pan place the olive oil and heat it on medium high until it is hot. Add the poblano chile peppers and yellow onions, and sauté them for 2 minutes.

Add the jalapeño chile peppers and tomatoes. Sauté the ingredients for 5 minutes.

makes approximately 1 quart

"In Mexico the beef is often tough, because the cattle are grass fed instead of grain fed. So to counteract the toughness, the meat is marinated and then served with a delicious sauce. This recipe is a classic example."

Kimo Castro
San Francisco St. Bar & Grill

"I love to cook when I can just create. The managing of the staff and money is more of a headache. Most people who work in a restaurant will tell you the same thing."

Robbie Day
San Francisco St. Bar & Grill

Grilled Sliced Filet Mignon with Ancho Roasted Pepper Sauce

4	red bell peppers, roasted, peeled and seeded
2	ounces dried ancho chile peppers, seeded
1	small yellow onion, diced
¼	cup red wine
¼	cup water
1	teaspoon salt
¼	teaspoon black pepper
1½	pounds filet mignon, sliced into 12 pieces

In a medium saucepan place all of the ingredients *(except for the filet mignon)* and simmer them for 15 minutes.

Purée the ingredients in a blender. Keep the sauce warm.

Grill the filet mignon slices for 2 to 5 minutes on each side, or until the desired doneness is achieved.

Serve the meat with the sauce on top.

serves 4

"One day at the restaurant I needed to come up with a filet recipe for that evening's meat special. I saw these ingredients lying around and so I put them together for the sauce..... and, it was wonderful! I used canned roasted bell peppers instead of roasting fresh ones, and they worked really well. If you can't find ancho peppers, then you can use chipotle chile peppers in adobo sauce. Use this sauce with fish, chicken, or pasta."

"Men and women have a different beat when it comes to cooking. My experience is that women are more organized and logical, as strange as this may sound. Sometimes I think that I just stumble through my cooking, with nothing planned. Also, in addition to being good businesspeople, most women seem to have a very artistic aspect to their cooking."

Paul Hunsicker
Paul's Restaurant

Dry Rub Sirloin

1	tablespoon ground cinnamon
1	tablespoon coriander seeds, freshly ground
1½	teaspoons cayenne pepper
1	tablespoon paprika
1	tablespoon sugar
1	tablespoon salt
4	12-ounce New York strip steaks

In a small bowl place all of the spices and mix them together.

Dredge the steaks in the spice mixture so that they are very well coated.

Grill the steaks over high heat for 3 to 5 minutes on each side, or until the desired doneness is achieved.

serves 4

"The spice ingredients in this recipe make what I call my 'magic spice mix'. It is a spice mixture that you can rub on anything that you grill, and it will turn an ordinary piece of meat or fish into something spectacular."

"The spice mixture will turn very dark when it is cooking because of the sugar and paprika, so don't be alarmed. Try to use a good quality, dark paprika, like Hungarian. And it's much preferable to grind coriander seeds as opposed to buying ground coriander. Use your coffee bean grinder, but wipe it out first."

Pete Zimmer
Inn of the Anasazi

Steak Diablo

2	tablespoons olive oil
1	medium yellow onion, finely diced
½	cup fresh garlic, finely chopped
2	cups green chile peppers, roasted, peeled, seeded and chopped
2	teaspoons dried Mexican oregano
	salt *(or to taste)*
8	6-ounce New York strip steaks
12	slices provolone cheese, cut in half

Preheat the oven broiler.

In a medium sauté pan place the olive oil and heat it on medium until it is hot. Add the yellow onions and garlic. Sauté them for 5 to 7 minutes, or until the onions are translucent.

Add the green chile peppers, Mexican oregano, and salt. Sauté the ingredients for 5 minutes. Remove the pan from the heat and set it aside.

Grill the steaks for 5 minutes on each side, or until the desired doneness is almost achieved *(they should be two-thirds done)*.

On a broiler pan place the steaks. Spoon the green chile mixture on each steak. Place the provolone slices on top.

Broil the steaks for 1 to 2 minutes, or until the cheese is melted and bubbly, and the steaks are done.

serves 8

"Most people unconsciously base their taste in foods on what their mothers fed them as children. For instance, my mother always cooked steaks very well done, which is how I always used to order them. Now I eat steak medium rare, and can't imagine having them any other way."

Rustin Newton
Staab House

La Tertulia's Green Chile Stew

⅓	**cup flour**
1	**teaspoon salt** *(or to taste)*
⅛	**teaspoon black pepper** *(or to taste)*
2	**pounds lean beef, cut into bite-size pieces**
¼	**cup vegetable oil**
1	**medium yellow onion, diced medium**
2	**bay leaves**
1	**teaspoon Worcestershire sauce**
1	**teaspoon lemon juice, freshly squeezed**
2	**quarts hot water**
2	**teaspoons salt** *(or to taste)*
½	**teaspoon black pepper** *(or to taste)*
1	**cup green chile peppers, roasted, peeled, seeded and diced medium**
½	**cup flour**
1	**cup water**

In a large bowl place the ⅓ cup of flour, the 1 teaspoon of salt, and the ⅛ teaspoon of black pepper. Mix the ingredients together.

Add the beef pieces and toss them in so that they are well coated.

In a large saucepan place the vegetable oil and heat it on medium high until it is hot. Add the coated beef and sauté it for 10 minutes, or until it is browned.

Add the yellow onions, bay leaves, Worcestershire sauce, lemon juice, the 2 quarts of hot water, the 2 teaspoons of salt, and the ½ teaspoon of black pepper. Stir the ingredients together.

Simmer the stew for 6 to 8 hours *(add more water if needed)*, or until the beef is very tender.

Add the green chile peppers and stir them in.

In a small bowl place the ½ cup of flour and the 1 cup of water, and whisk them together. Add the mixture to the stew and stir it in well. Cook the stew for 5 minutes, or until it thickens.

serves 6 to 8

"When I was first married I lived in Chicago for two years. There was no green chile there and I absolutely craved it! So my mother would air express frozen chile to me and I would use it in my dishes. This recipe is one of those creations. It's spicy and very flavorful. We serve it at the restaurant for lunch on a regular basis."

"La Tertulia is a family owned and run restaurant. The name means 'The Gathering Place'. Everyone who works here is part of our family.....not by blood necessarily, but by commitment and loyalty. Some of our people have been with us for twenty years. We have a private joke amongst us, and say that we are all characters in our own soap opera called 'As La Tertulia Turns'. We know each other so well that we follow each other's lives on a day to day basis."

Joy Ortiz-Nashan
La Tertulia

Cayenne New York Strip
with Marinated Wild Mushrooms
& Grilled Tomatoes

"We serve this steak at the restaurant and people really love it. The wild mushrooms are what make the dish so delicious. You may use any kind that you find fresh in your grocery store, such as portabellas, chanterelles, or tree oysters. Regular button mushrooms will do in a pinch, although they won't have the deep, rich earthy flavor of the wild ones. Some people may even want to pick their own during mushroom season. Only experts should do this, however, because it is very easy to make a mistake.....and a mistake could be lethal."

¼	cup olive oil
2	tablespoons lemon juice, freshly squeezed
1	tablespoon fresh thyme, chopped
1	teaspoon chile pequin *(hot red chile flakes)*
	salt and black pepper *(to taste)*
4	large wild mushrooms
1	tablespoon cayenne pepper *(or to taste)*
4	12-ounce New York strip steaks
2	Roma tomatoes, sliced in half lengthwise

In a medium bowl place the olive oil, lemon juice, thyme, chile pequin, salt, and black pepper. Whisk the ingredients together.

Add the mushrooms and let them marinate for 30 minutes.

Rub the steaks on both sides with the cayenne pepper.

Grill the steaks for 5 minutes on each side, or until the desired doneness is achieved.

Brush the Roma tomatoes with the marinade. Sprinkle them with some more of the salt and black pepper.

Grill the Roma tomatoes *(flesh side down)* and marinated mushrooms for 1 to 2 minutes, or until they have grill marks.

On each of 4 individual serving plates place a steak. Serve the mushrooms and tomatoes on the side.

serves 4

"Grilling is a wonderful way to prepare vegetables, because it gives them an excellent flavor and it is very healthy. Toss them in some olive oil with some lemon juice, and put them on the grill until you get marks. Some vegetables like peppers, zucchini, onions, or leeks should first be blanched in boiling water for one minute and then plunged into ice water."

Steven Lemon
Pranzo Italian Grill

Carmelita's Green Chile Stew

4	**cups water**
½	**pound pork, diced small**
½	**pound green chile peppers, roasted, peeled, seeded and chopped**
½	**medium yellow onion, chopped**
2	**cloves fresh garlic, minced**
	salt *(to taste)*
½	**cup cornstarch**
2	**cups water**
4	**cups tomatoes, diced**

In a large, heavy stockpot place the 4 cups of water and the pork. Simmer it for 2 hours on medium low heat.

Add the green chile peppers, yellow onions, and garlic. Simmer the ingredients for 30 minutes.

Add the salt.

In a medium bowl place the cornstarch and water. Mix them together so that there are no lumps.

Add the cornstarch mixture to the stew and stir it in well. Simmer the stew for 5 minutes, or until it thickens.

Add the tomatoes and stir them in. Simmer the stew for 5 minutes more, or until it is heated through.

makes approximately 2½ quarts

"I learned how to cook classic Northern New Mexico dishes from my grandmother, who was a wonderful cook. She would roast her own chiles, remove the skins and seeds, chop them up, and add a little garlic and salt. We kids would spread the chiles on tortillas, or mix them in with our beans, potatoes, and eggs. To us, that was heaven!"

"I call for cornstarch and water as a thickener in this recipe, because a lot of people don't know how to make a roux, or else they consider it to be too much trouble. If you do want to make a roux, however, you should take equal amounts of fat and flour, and cook them very slowly over low heat for ten minutes while stirring constantly."

"My personal joy in being a chef is to watch the smiles of pleasure on peoples' faces as they eat the food I have prepared."

Randy Mondragon
Staab House

Blue Corn Soft Tacos
with Carne Adovada

2½	**pounds lean pork** (shoulder or butt), **cut into ½" cubes**
4	**cups Pasqual's Red Chile Sauce** (recipe on page 110)
3	**dried New Mexico red chile peppers, stemmed and crumbled**
4	**teaspoons chile pequin** (hot red chile flakes)
2	**sticks canela** (cinnamon)
1	**teaspoon kosher salt**
12	**blue corn tortillas**
¾	**cup white onions, finely chopped**
1	**cup sour cream**
½	**cup fresh cilantro, chopped**

In a large, glass bowl place the pork, Pasqual's Red Chile Sauce, red chile peppers, chile pequin, canela, and kosher salt. Cover the bowl with plastic wrap and let the meat marinate in the refrigerator for 2 days (turn it occasionally). Remove the canela sticks.

Preheat the oven to 350°.

In a large saucepan place the pork and the marinade, and bring them to a boil over medium heat.

Transfer the mixture to a casserole dish with a lid. Cover it and bake the meat for 2 hours, or until it is very tender (stir it several times).

Heat a lightly oiled cast iron skillet on low until it is hot. Cook each tortilla for 30 to 60 seconds on each side, or until it is soft and warm.

In the center of each tortilla place ½ cup of the pork adovada mixture. Add some of the white onions, sour cream, and cilantro. Fold the tortilla over.

serves 6

Chile Caribe, Sage & Mint Marinated Pork Loin

1	medium yellow onion, quartered
2	tablespoons fresh garlic, finely chopped
¼	cup fresh sage, chopped
¼	cup fresh mint, chopped
¼	cup fresh oregano, chopped
2	tablespoons chile caribe *(crushed red chile peppers)*
½	cup canola oil
½	cup olive oil
5	limes, freshly squeezed, pulp removed and chopped
2	oranges, freshly squeezed, pulp removed and chopped
¼	cup apple cider vinegar
1	tablespoon salt *(or to taste)*
1	teaspoon black pepper *(or to taste)*
1	4-pound pork loin, sliced into ½" wide strips

In a large bowl place all of the ingredients *(except for the pork loin pieces)* and stir them together.

Add the pork loin pieces and cover the bowl with plastic wrap. Marinate the pork in the refrigerator for 48 to 72 hours *(turn the pork over in the marinade several times during this process)*.

Remove the pork from the marinade.

Grill the pork for 3 minutes on each side, or until the desired doneness is achieved *(baste the pork occasionally with the marinade)*.

serves 6

"This marinade is very spicy, with a lot of flavor. You can bump the heat up even further by adding fresh jalapeños or hot sauce."

"Chile caribe are fairly large, crushed red chile flakes. They differ from chile pequin, which is hot red chile flakes, in that they have more flavor and they are slightly soft. Chile pequin, on the other hand, is very fiery and the flakes are bone dry."

"I like to marinate the pork for quite a long time, because the flavor only gets better. Sometimes we marinate it for up to a week. You can also use this marinade with fish or chicken."

James Lamoureux
The Evergreen

Carne Adovada Burritos

1	**pound Chimayo red chile powder**
2	**tablespoons ground cumin**
2	**tablespoons garlic powder**
1	**tablespoon ground oregano**
2	**tablespoons salt** *(or to taste)*
	water *(as needed)*
4	**pounds lean pork, cut into ¾" cubes**
8	**flour tortillas**
2	**cups cheddar cheese, freshly grated**

In a large bowl place the red chile powder, cumin, garlic powder, oregano, and salt. While stirring constantly, slowly add enough water so that the sauce has the consistency of peanut butter.

Add the pork cubes and mix them in well. Cover the bowl with plastic wrap and refrigerate the meat overnight.

Preheat the oven to 300°.

In a roasting pan place the pork and the marinade. Cover the pan and bake the pork for 2 hours *(stir it occasionally and add more water if needed)*, or until it is tender.

In the center of each flour tortilla place 1 cup of the cooked pork cubes. Roll the burrito up and place it in a baking dish.

Sprinkle on the cheese. Bake the burritos for 15 minutes, or until the cheese is melted.

serves 8

"This recipe is just unbelievable. It seems so simple, and yet the end result is incredible. The flavor of the Chimayo chile powder is the key. We like to drive through Chimayo, talk to the growers, and buy the highest quality of peppers possible."

"When tourists come to our restaurant and want to order the best New Mexican dish we have, I always recommend our carne adovada."

Patricia Helmick
Peppers

"You don't have to make burritos with this carne adovada. You can eat it plain, or serve it for breakfast with scrambled eggs. Make sure you cook the meat long enough. The sauce should be nice and thick, and the pork should be tender enough to cut with a fork."

Dan Kelley
Peppers

"We own the Burrito Company in downtown Santa Fe, and this carne adovada dish is the same that we serve there. I believe it has contributed to making the Burrito Company and Peppers the success that they are."

Rick Helmick
Peppers

Garlic Pork with Hot Chinese Sauce

Garlic Pork

2	tablespoons soy sauce
2	tablespoons cornstarch
2	tablespoons water
1¼	pounds pork tenderloin, thinly sliced
¼	cup vegetable oil
4	teaspoons fresh garlic, finely chopped
2	teaspoons fresh ginger root, peeled and finely chopped
12	water chestnuts, thinly sliced
4	tablespoons black wood ear mushrooms, soaked in warm water for 15 minutes, stems removed, and thinly sliced
	Hot Chinese Sauce *(recipe on next page)*

In a medium bowl place the soy sauce, cornstarch, and water. Whisk the ingredients together. Add the pork strips and toss them in so that they are well coated with the mixture.

Cover the bowl with plastic wrap and marinate the pork for 30 minutes at room temperature.

In a wok place the vegetable oil and heat it on high until it is very hot. Add the pork and stir-fry it for 30 seconds. Remove the pork and set it aside.

Add the garlic and ginger, and stir-fry them for 1 minute.

Add the pork, water chestnuts, and mushrooms. Stir-fry the ingredients for 2 minutes.

Add the Hot Chinese Sauce. Simmer the ingredients for 2 minutes.

serves 4

"This is a classic dish that is served in restaurants and homes in China. It's very easy to make, and it is virtually impossible for you to ruin. Chicken or eggplant may be substituted for the pork. Most Chinese dishes come with a bowl of hot, steamed rice on the side."

"Black wood ear mushrooms are also known as black fungus, but that name sounds very unappealing to me! You buy them dried, and then soften them in warm water. They have an excellent flavor."

"I was born and raised in Taiwan. We had maids, cooks, and chauffeurs, and I never had to do anything for myself. All I did was go to school and play. I came to the United States when I was eighteen and lived with my husband in San Francisco. All of a sudden I had to do everything..... cook, clean, drive, shop..... it was a shock! My mother-in-law was a good cook, so I watched her to learn what I should be doing in the kitchen."

Marta Hung
Imperial Wok

Hot Chinese Sauce

2	**tablespoons scallions, thinly sliced**
2	**tablespoons hot bean paste** *(see chef's comments on this page)*
2	**teaspoons cornstarch**
2	**teaspoons sugar**
2	**tablespoons cider vinegar**
2	**tablespoons soy sauce**
1	**tablespoon white wine**
2	**teaspoons toasted sesame oil**
1	**teaspoon salt** *(or to taste)*
½	**teaspoon black pepper** *(or to taste)*

In a small bowl place all the ingredients and whisk them together.

makes approximately ⅔ cup

Tacos de Carnitas

6	**pounds pork butt roast**
½	**cup vegetable oil** *(or as needed)*
18	**corn tortillas**
4	**tomatoes, thinly sliced**
2	**cups green cabbage, shredded**
8	**ounces pickled jalapeño chile peppers, thinly sliced**
1	**bunch scallions, chopped**
1	**bunch fresh cilantro, chopped**

Preheat the oven to 275°.

In a dutch oven place the pork roast and cook it for 6 hours, or until the meat is very tender.

Shred the pork and place it in a serving dish.

In a large sauté pan place the vegetable oil and heat it on medium high until it is hot. Place each tortilla in the hot oil for 15 seconds, or until it softens. Drain the tortillas on paper towels.

In the center of each tortilla place some of the pork, tomatoes, green cabbage, pickled jalapeño chile peppers, scallions, and cilantro. Roll the tortilla up.

serves 6 to 8

Spicy Pork Medallions with Bloody Mary Mix

Spicy Pork Medallions

2	eggs
¼	cup milk
2	pounds pork tenderloin, cut into 12 medallions and butterflied
½	cup flour
2	cups dried bread crumbs
3	tablespoons clarified butter *(or as needed)*
1	cup Bloody Mary Mix *(recipe on next page)*, **heated**
1	stalk celery, thinly sliced
1	carrot, grated

In a small bowl place the eggs and milk, and mix them together.

One at a time, dredge each pork medallion in the flour, dip it in the egg wash, and then dredge it in the bread crumbs.

Place a heavy, large skillet *(cast iron, if possible)* on medium high heat, and heat it for 2 minutes, or until water sizzles in the pan. Add the clarified butter and heat it so that it is hot. Sauté the medallions for 3 minutes on each side, or until they are slightly pink in the center, golden brown on the outside, and firm to the touch.

On each of 4 individual serving plates place the pork medallions. Pour the heated Bloody Mary Mix on top. Garnish the dish with the celery and carrots.

serves 4

"There is a bartender in La Posada here in Santa Fe named Hap. One day I went in and had his Bloody Mary, and it was the best one I had ever tasted. It was so good that I ended up having three of them. During this time I got the idea of using a Blood Mary mix for a sauce with pork. I went home and concocted my own recipe, but Hap's was definitely better. So I went back to La Posada and got him to trade his recipe in exchange for my Spicy Pork Medallions recipe. He likes to cook and was happy to do it."

"People really love this dish. The breading on the pork soaks up the Bloody Mary mix, and it's just delicious!"

"I originally called this recipe 'Aunt Hazel's After the Party Pork Chops', but everybody here at the restaurant thought that sounded kind of corny."

Rocky Durham
Zia Diner

Bloody Mary Mix

2	cups tomato juice
1	tablespoon Worcestershire sauce
1	tablespoon tabasco sauce
1	tablespoon lime juice, freshly squeezed
2	tablespoons vodka
¼	teaspoon horseradish
½	teaspoon dill
¼	teaspoon celery salt
½	teaspoon black pepper

In a medium saucepan place all of the ingredients and mix them together. Simmer the sauce on medium heat for 6 to 8 minutes, or until it is reduced by ⅓.

makes 2 cups

"This mix makes great Bloody Marys, without heating and reducing it. The sauce would be good with any poultry or meat that is breaded."

Rocky Durham
Zia Diner

Green Chile Pork Chops

2	tablespoons vegetable oil
4	pork loin chops
½	cup yellow onions, chopped medium
4	cloves fresh garlic, finely chopped
1	teaspoon fresh oregano, chopped
¾	pound green chile peppers, roasted, peeled, seeded and diced medium
2	tomatoes, diced medium
2	cups water
	salt *(to taste)*

In a large sauté pan place the vegetable oil and heat it on medium high until it is hot. Add the pork chops, yellow onions, garlic, and oregano. Sauté the ingredients for 5 minutes, or until the onions are translucent and the pork chops are browned.

Add the green chile peppers, tomatoes, water, and salt. Bring the ingredients to a boil. Reduce the heat to low.

Cover the pan and simmer the pork chops for 30 minutes, or until they are tender.

serves 4

"When I was growing up in Santa Fe our family always had green chile with pork. We very seldom ate chile with any other kind of meat. The leaner the pork the better, and a bone in the meat will give it an even richer flavor. I prefer to use a mild green chile with this dish so that it doesn't overpower the taste of the other ingredients."

"My grandmother was a very wise person. She told me that I needed to learn to take care of myself, and that if I could cook my own food I would always be okay."

Gus Macias
Tortilla Flats

Red Chile Ribs

8	**dried red chile peppers, soaked in 4 cups hot water until soft** (reserve the water)
¼	**medium yellow onion, chopped**
2	**cloves fresh garlic, chopped**
1	**teaspoon chile pequin** (hot red chile flakes)
1½	**teaspoons dried Mexican oregano**
½	**teaspoon cumin seeds, ground**
1	**teaspoon salt**
	salt and black pepper (to taste)
3	**pounds pork baby back ribs**

In a food processor place the softened chile peppers and 2 cups of the reserved water, and purée them.

Add the yellow onions, garlic, chile pequin, Mexican oregano, cumin, and the 1 teaspoon of salt. Purée the ingredients so that they are smooth.

Add 1½ cups of the reserved water to the purée and pulse it in.

Sprinkle the salt and black pepper on both sides of the ribs. Place them in a baking pan and pour the red chile purée on top. Cover the pan with plastic wrap and refrigerate the ribs overnight.

Preheat the oven to 325°.

Remove the plastic wrap from the pan and bake the ribs for 2½ hours, or until they are tender (baste the ribs occasionally and add a little water if they begin to dry out).

serves 6

"My wife and I came up with this recipe. She doesn't like barbeque sauce, which I love, but she is crazy about chile.....the hotter the better. One day we were making spareribs and I decided to throw some chile on them. The kids and my wife ate all of them, while I finished off the barbecued ribs. So from now on we always make two different batches of ribs, and everyone is happy!"

"Don't let the ribs dry out. You have to watch them closely and keep the temperature down to 325°. When you open the oven door to check on them, stand back a bit because of the fumes from the chile. They can really make you cough. I'm pretty used to the fumes, because I grew up with my grandmother, who cooked with chile every day. You knew it was good chile when it would choke you!"

"My grandmother's cooking was Mexican in style, and my mother's was more influenced by American Indian cooking. As a kid I was really nosy, and wanted to sample everything in the kitchen. They were always kicking me out, because I was a boy and was supposed to be doing my chores, not hanging out with the women."

Gus Macias
Tortilla Flats

Harry's Chorizo

2	pounds lean pork, ground
2	serrano chile peppers, finely chopped
1	bunch fresh cilantro, chopped
1	tablespoon red chile powder
1	teaspoon ground cumin
½	teaspoon cumin seeds
¼	teaspoon ground coriander
1	tablespoon paprika
½	teaspoon cayenne pepper
¼	cup red wine vinegar
2	teaspoons salt *(or to taste)*

Note: *The chorizo is best if it is made one day in advance.*

In a large bowl place all the ingredients and mix them together well.

makes approximately 2 pounds

Peppers' Green Chile Stew

¼	cup vegetable oil
2	pounds lean pork, cut into 1" cubes
1	medium white onion, chopped medium
4	medium baking potatoes, peeled and diced medium
4	medium tomatoes, diced medium
1	cup green chile peppers, roasted, peeled, seeded and diced medium
¼	teaspoon ground oregano
½	tablespoon garlic powder
3	quarts water
1	tablespoon salt *(or to taste)*
2	teaspoons pepper *(or to taste)*

In a large heavy pan place the vegetable oil and heat it on medium high until it is hot. Add the pork and sauté it for 10 minutes, or until it is brown. Add the white onions, potatoes, tomatoes, green chile peppers, oregano, garlic powder, water, salt, and pepper.

Simmer the ingredients for 1 to 1½ hours, or until the pork is tender.

serves 6

Seared Pork Loin
with Chile Roasted Pears
& Pumpkin Seeds

1	**3-pound boneless pork loin, cut into 3 pieces**
¼	**cup red chile powder**
½	**cup olive oil**
2	**pears, peeled, cored and finely diced**
½	**cup pumpkin seeds**
½	**teaspoon fresh garlic, finely chopped**
1	**teaspoon fresh cilantro, chopped**
1	**teaspoon red chile powder**
2	**cups tomato juice**

Rub the pork loin pieces all over with the ¼ cup of the red chile powder.

In a large sauté pan place the olive oil and heat it on medium high until it is hot. Add the pork loins and cook them for 5 to 7 minutes on each side, or until they are just done.

Add the pears, pumpkin seeds, garlic, cilantro, and the 1 teaspoon of red chile powder. Stir the ingredients together and cook them for 5 minutes.

Add the tomato juice and deglaze the pan.

Simmer the ingredients for 5 minutes.

Slice the pork and serve it with the pears and sauce on top.

serves 4

"Every time we make this recipe we sell out of it. The ingredients may sound a little unusual, but not so much so that people don't order it. It's exotic and easy to make, and your guests will think you are really a gourmet cook if you serve it."

"I was born and raised in Mexico City, where my family owned a restaurant. My older brother moved to Los Angeles and got a job as a cook, so I followed in his footsteps and got a job as a dishwasher. Now both of us are executive chefs of large hotels. Our parents still live in Mexico, but they come here to visit us. They are very proud of us and think that we have achieved a lot for how young we are."

Martin Rios
Old House

Seared Ginger Pork Tenderloin with Toasted Sesame Curry Sauce & Asparagus

¼	cup ground ginger *(or as needed)*
24	ounces pork tenderloin, cut at an angle into 12 slices
2	tablespoons toasted sesame oil *(or as needed)*
1	tablespoon curry powder
1½	teaspoons cayenne pepper
¼	cup white wine
1	pound asparagus, tough ends cut off
2	tablespoons soy sauce
½	lime, freshly squeezed
½	stick butter

In a small bowl place the ginger. Dredge the pork slices in it so that they are well coated.

In a large sauté pan place the sesame oil and heat it on high until it is very hot. Add the coated pork slices and sear them for 2 minutes on each side, or until they are browned.

Reduce the heat to medium. Sprinkle on the curry and cayenne pepper. Cook the ingredients for 2 minutes more.

Add the white wine to deglaze the pan. Add the asparagus. Cook the ingredients for 5 minutes, or until the sauce starts to bind.

Add the soy sauce and cook the ingredients for 5 minutes, or until the sauce thickens. Add the lime juice and stir it in.

Add the butter. Cook the ingredients for 2 minutes more, or until the butter is melted and the sauce is creamy.

serves 4

Thai Pork Brochettes
with Saus Prik Dipping Sauce

Thai Pork Brochettes

2	tablespoons fresh garlic, chopped
1½	tablespoons ground coriander
1½	tablespoons ground cumin
¼	cup brown sugar
¼	cup Thai fish sauce *(see chef's comments on page 113)*
¾	cup tamarind water *(see chef's comments on page 28)*
¼	cup peanut oil
2	pounds lean pork, cut into thin strips 3" long and 1" wide
	Saus Prik Dipping Sauce *(recipe follows)*

In a medium bowl place all of the ingredients *(except the pork)* and mix them together. Add the pork and marinate it overnight in the refrigerator.

Soak 8 bamboo skewers in water for 15 minutes.

Skewer on the marinated pork.

Grill the pork brochettes for 3 minutes on each side, or until they are lightly caramelized.

Serve the pork with the Saus Prik Dipping Sauce on the side.

serves 4

Saus Prik Dipping Sauce

½	medium tomato, seeded and coarsely chopped
¾	cup golden raisins
¾	cup plums, blanched, skins removed, pitted and chopped
1	serrano chile pepper, coarsely chopped
½	tablespoon chile pequin *(hot red chile flakes)*
2	tablespoons palm sugar *(see chef's comments on this page)*
½	cup apple juice
2½	tablespoons white vinegar
½	teaspoon salt *(or to taste)*

In a food processor place all of the ingredients and purée them.

makes approximately 3 cups

"Patrick runs the kitchen in such a nice manner that it is a pleasure to be back there, watching him work. He prepares the food with love, and this is evident in his dishes. I think that people can tell, at least on a subconscious level, if food has been handled with care or not."

Paul Rochford
Restaurant Thao

"The Saus Prik Dipping Sauce is wonderful with grilled chicken, shellfish, or beef. It's also great with egg rolls or fried won-tons. The flavor is sweet, sour, and mildly spicy."

"Palm sugar is made from 'palm berries' that grow on palm trees. The flavor is quite fruity and is very important to the sauce. Natural food stores carry it because it is a healthy alternative to sugar."

Ron Messick
Restaurant Thao

Breakfast Burritos with Peppers' Chorizo

Breakfast Burritos

4   flour tortillas
6   eggs, scrambled
     Peppers' Chorizo *(recipe follows)*
1   cup cheddar cheese, grated
2   cups Green Chile Sauce *(recipe on page 116)*

Preheat the oven to 350°.

In the center of each flour tortilla place the scrambled eggs and Pepper's Chorizo. Roll the tortilla up.

In a medium baking dish place the burritos. Sprinkle the cheddar cheese on top. Bake the burritos for 10 minutes, or until the cheese is melted.

Serve the burritos with the Green Chile Sauce on the side.

serves 4

Peppers' Chorizo

2½   pounds lean pork, ground
1   tablespoon fresh cilantro, finely chopped
¾   cup Chimayo red chile powder
2   tablespoons chile pequin *(hot red chile flakes)*
2   tablespoons ground cumin
2   teaspoons ground oregano
1   tablespoon ground coriander
4   tablespoons garlic powder
2   tablespoons salt *(or to taste)*

In a large saucepan place the ground pork and sauté it on medium high for 15 minutes, or until it is done. Drain the oil off the meat.

Add the rest of the ingredients and stir them together. Simmer the mixture for 30 minutes *(stir it occasionally)*.

Note: The chorizo may be frozen.

serves 8

"I call these breakfast burritos because they have scrambled eggs in them, but they really are the kind of thing that would be good any time of the day."

Dan Kelley
Peppers

"I wait all week to have this dish, when we serve it as a weekday special. It's really wonderful! Our homemade chorizo is what makes it so delicious."

"Not too many people make their own chorizo. The store-bought kind tends to be very greasy, with gristle and yukky stuff in it. This chorizo is made with pure meat, and you can really taste the difference."

Patricia Helmick
Peppers

"A little bit of this chorizo will go a long way, because it is very spicy! It's a wonderful thing to add to soups, or to use in enchiladas."

Rick Helmick
Peppers

Hot Sausage & Peppers with Polenta & Spicy Tomato Sauce

Hot Sausage & Peppers

12	4-ounce hot Italian sausage links
¼	cup olive oil
2	red bell peppers, seeded and thinly sliced
2	yellow bell peppers, seeded and thinly sliced
1	medium yellow onion, thinly sliced
3	cups Polenta *(recipe on next page)*, **heated**
1½	cups Spicy Tomato Sauce *(recipe on next page)*, **heated**

Preheat the oven to 475°.

On a baking sheet place the sausage links and roast them for 15 minutes, or until they are done.

In a large sauté pan place the olive oil and heat it on medium high until it is hot. Add the red bell peppers, yellow bell peppers, and yellow onions. Sauté the ingredients for 5 minutes, or until the onions are translucent.

In each of 6 individual serving bowls place the Polenta, two sausage links, and the sautéed vegetables. Spoon the Spicy Tomato Sauce on top.

serves 6

"The combination of sausage, peppers, polenta, and tomato sauce is classically Italian. The blend of these flavors is just perfect."

Steven Lemon
Pranzo Italian Grill

"There is a lot of freedom in being a chef. For one thing, you don't have to wear high heels and pantyhose! Also, you can eat whatever and when-ever you want.....a great fringe benefit. One of the things that I really like about cooking, though, is that it gives me a sense of control. Within specific parameters, I have the feeling that I can influence the way things come out. To me this is very satisfying. Also, I enjoy the direct result of seeing people happy and satisfied by my efforts."

Marta Mueller
Pranzo Italian Grill

Polenta

7	**cups water**
	salt *(to taste)*
1⅔	**cups cornmeal** *(coarse ground)*
¼	**cup parmesan cheese, freshly grated**
¼	**cup Fontina cheese, grated**
6	**tablespoons butter**

In a large saucepan place the water and salt, and heat them on medium high until the water boils. While whisking constantly, slowly add the cornmeal.

Reduce the heat to low. Simmer the ingredients for 20 minutes, or until the polenta comes away from the sides of the pan *(stir it occasionally)*.

Add the parmesan cheese, Fontina cheese, and butter. Stir the ingredients together.

serves 6

Spicy Tomato Sauce

¼	**cup olive oil**
3	**cloves fresh garlic, finely chopped**
2	**teaspoons chile pequin** *(hot red chile flakes)*
2	**teaspoons fresh oregano, chopped**
2	**teaspoons fresh basil, chopped**
2	**teaspoons fresh parsley, chopped**
6	**tablespoons white wine**
2	**tablespoons lemon juice, freshly squeezed**
4	**cups canned plum tomatoes, chopped medium**
	salt and black pepper *(to taste)*

In a large saucepan place the olive oil and heat it on medium high until it is hot. Add the garlic and sauté it for 2 minutes, or until it begins to brown.

Add the chile pequin, oregano, basil, parsley, white wine, and lemon juice. Stir the ingredients together and cook them for 1 minute.

Add the tomatoes, salt, and black pepper. Simmer the mixture for 15 minutes.

makes approximately 1 quart

"Polenta is made from cornmeal. It's very versatile because you can add so many different things to it and you also can cook it in so many different ways. In this recipe you serve it soft. If you have some left over, spread it out on a greased cookie sheet and then refrigerate it. After it is cold, cut it into shapes, which you can deep-fry, grill, sauté, or bake."

"I like to make dishes that are fairly simple, straight-forward, and quick to assemble. My cooking has an immediacy to it. I put the ingredients together, and BAM, they're served! One of the secrets to delicious food is to always use the freshest and best ingredients you can possibly find and afford."

"This is a basic tomato sauce that is flavored with herbs and chile pequin. It's wonderful with pasta dishes, and you can adjust the heat as you like."

Steven Lemon
Pranzo Italian Grill

Marinated Lamb Chops with Minted Sweet & Hot Pepper Salsa

Marinated Lamb Chops

¾   **cup dry white wine**
½   **cup lemon juice, freshly squeezed**
1½   **cups olive oil**
1   **small red onion, quartered**
5   **cloves fresh garlic**
4   **sprigs fresh mint**
1   **teaspoon fresh oregano leaves**
2   **teaspoons coriander seeds**
12   **whole cloves**
4   **cinnamon sticks**
4   **bay leaves**
2   **teaspoons black peppercorns**
1   **teaspoon salt**
12   **3-ounce lamb chops**
       Minted Sweet & Hot Pepper Salsa (recipe on next page)

In a medium bowl place the white wine and lemon juice, and whisk them together. While whisking constantly, slowly dribble in the olive oil.

Add the red onions, garlic, mint, oregano, coriander, cloves, cinnamon sticks, bay leaves, black peppercorns, and salt. Stir the ingredients together.

Place the lamb chops in the marinade. Cover the bowl with plastic wrap and let the lamb marinate in the refrigerator overnight.

Grill the lamb chops for 3 to 4 minutes on each side, or until the desired doneness is achieved (medium rare is best).

On each of 4 individual serving plates place 3 of the lamb chops. Place the Minted Sweet & Hot Pepper Salsa on top of each chop.

serves 4

"I love lamb, and this dish is truly one of my favorite ways to eat it. The flavor of the marinade comes through very subtly. I really urge you to try this recipe, because it is outstanding."

"Eat any leftover lamb and salsa wrapped up in a burrito."

"When I cook I always try to please myself. Then I just hope that other people will have similar tastes, and like what I like."

Darrell Hedgecoke
Mañana

"When I was growing up, I spent no time in the kitchen, even though my mother was an excellent cook. All of my energy was spent on school and studying. In spite of that, I ended up being quite a good cook."

Charlotte Silva
Mañana

Minted Sweet & Hot Pepper Salsa

1   green bell pepper, seeded and diced medium
1   red bell pepper, seeded and diced medium
1   yellow bell pepper, seeded and diced medium
1   bunch scallions, chopped
1   green jalapeño chile pepper, seeded and finely diced
1   yellow jalapeño chile pepper, seeded and finely diced
6   sprigs fresh mint, finely chopped
2   limes, freshly squeezed
1   teaspoon granulated garlic
     salt *(to taste)*

In a medium bowl place all the ingredients and stir them together.

makes approximately 2 cups

Pranzo's Grilled Lamb Chops with Polenta & Spicy Tomato Sauce

3   tablespoons capers, rinsed
2   tablespoons caper juice
2   tablespoons fresh oregano, chopped
2   tablespoons olive oil
8   4-ounce lamb chops
     Polenta *(recipe on page 267)*
     Spicy Tomato Sauce *(recipe on page 267)*

In a large bowl place the capers, caper juice, oregano, and olive oil. Stir the ingredients together. Place the lamb chops in the bowl and cover them well with the marinade. Let them sit at room temperature for 30 minutes.

Grill the lamb chops on medium high heat for 3 to 4 minutes on each side, or until the desired doneness is achieved.

On each of 4 individual serving plates place the lamb chops. Serve them with the Polenta on the side and the Spicy Tomato Sauce on top.

serves 4

"The green and yellow jalapeño peppers make this salsa quite spicy. The mint curbs the heat somewhat, and gives it a wonderful, cool flavor."

Darrell Hedgecoke
Mañana

"We have excellent domestic lamb here in New Mexico. One day I was playing around in the kitchen, trying to come up with a new way to fix lamb, and the idea for this just came to me. It's kind of different tasting, but really good. Don't let the lamb marinate too long, or else it will be too salty. You can use any cut of lamb that you like, including a rack."

"Rick Post is one of the owners of Pranzo, and he is a true gentleman. He cares deeply about his restaurant and has a strong commitment to keeping the food and service at a consistently high level."

Steven Lemon
Pranzo Italian Grill

Savory Broiled Lamb with Eggplant Poblano Compote

Savory Broiled Lamb

2	**racks of lamb**
2	**cloves fresh garlic, finely chopped**
2	**tablespoons fresh rosemary, chopped**
2	**tablespoons extra virgin olive oil**
	salt and black pepper *(to taste)*
	Eggplant Poblano Compote *(recipe on next page)*

In a shallow pan place the lamb racks and sprinkle them with the garlic and rosemary. Dribble the olive oil over the lamb. Season the racks with the salt and black pepper.

Cover the lamb with plastic wrap and refrigerate it for 24 hours.

Grill the lamb for 4 to 5 minutes on each side, or until the desired doneness is achieved.

Slice the racks between the bones.

On each of 4 individual serving plates place the Eggplant Poblano Compote. Place the lamb on top.

serves 4

"This is an easy, flavorful way to prepare lamb. By marinating it with the simple ingredients of garlic, rosemary, and olive oil, you give it a subtle flavor that you would not achieve otherwise. And the Eggplant Poblano Compote is the perfect complement. Serve this for an elegant dinner party and you will blow your guests away!"

"Bishop's Lodge is a luxury resort that's set on two thousand acres about three miles north of Santa Fe. It's really nice because we are in the mountains, and yet it takes only five minutes to get to town."

Jim Makinson
Bishop's Lodge

Eggplant Poblano Compote

2	large eggplants, sliced in half lengthwise
1	tablespoon light sesame oil
2	tablespoons extra virgin olive oil
2	poblano chile peppers, roasted, peeled, seeded and diced medium
1	red bell pepper, roasted, peeled, seeded and diced medium
1	yellow bell pepper, roasted, peeled, seeded and diced medium
2	shallots, finely chopped
1	clove fresh garlic, finely chopped
2	teaspoons chile pequin *(hot red chile flakes)*

Preheat the oven to 325°.

Brush the cut sides of the eggplant halves with the sesame oil. On a flat baking sheet place the eggplants with the cut sides down. Bake the eggplants for 20 minutes, or until they are tender.

When the eggplants are cooled, scoop out the meat with a large spoon. Dice the eggplant into ¼" pieces and set them aside.

In a large sauté pan place the olive oil and heat it on medium high until it is hot. Add the poblano chile peppers, red and yellow bell peppers, shallots, and garlic. Sauté the ingredients for 5 minutes, or until the peppers are tender.

Add the eggplant pieces and chile pequin. Stir the ingredients together.

makes approximately 2 cups

"Eggplant and bell peppers complement each other very well. Together with the chiles, garlic, sesame and olive oils, you have a wonderful, spicy, flavorful vegetable mixture that can be served with any kind of fish, meat, or poultry entrée. It tastes very rich although there is no butter or cream."

"To me, the best part of being a chef is the creativity involved in the cooking and the gratification from the people who eat the food. Our guests are always wandering into the kitchen to chat, or visiting with us while we tend to our herb garden."

Jim Makinson
Bishop's Lodge

Anasazi Rack of Lamb
with Indian Succotash

Anasazi Rack of Lamb

2	whole racks of Colorado lamb, split
1	cup dried bread crumbs
3	tablespoons chile pequin *(hot red chile flakes)*
1	tablespoon fresh thyme, finely chopped
¼	cup Dijon mustard
	Indian Succotash *(recipe on next page)*

Preheat the oven to 400°.

Grill the racks of lamb for 3 to 5 minutes on each side, or until they are seared.

In a medium bowl place the bread crumbs, chile pequin, and thyme. Mix the ingredients together.

Brush each split lamb rack with the Dijon mustard. Dredge them in the bread crumb mixture so that they are completely covered.

Place the racks on a sheet pan and bake them for 10 to 15 minutes, or until the desired doneness is achieved. Slice the lamb between the bones.

On each of 4 individual serving plates place the Indian Succotash. Place the lamb on top.

serves 4

"This is a unique dish that will definitely impress your guests. The beauty of the recipe is that there is very little skill required to put it together."

"If for some reason you don't want to fire up the grill, then you can sear the lamb in a skillet instead. When I use the grill I try to think ahead a couple of days and figure out what other things I can grill at the same time for future use. For instance, if I were grilling this lamb I might also grill some tomatoes for a pasta sauce, and some chicken for a chicken salad."

Pete Zimmer
Inn of the Anasazi

Indian Succotash

1	tablespoon olive oil
2	medium red onions, diced medium
4	cloves fresh garlic, roasted *(see chef's comments on this page)* **and chopped**
2	sprigs fresh rosemary, chopped
1	cup Burgundy wine
3	cups veal stock *(see chef's comments on this page)*
2	yellow squash, diced medium
3	carrots, diced small
2	Roma tomatoes, diced medium
1	cup cooked black beans
2/3	cup cooked lima beans
1/4	cup cooked Anasazi beans *(see chef's comments on this page)*
4	limes, juiced
1	teaspoon cayenne pepper *(or to taste)*
	salt and white pepper *(to taste)*

In a large saucepan place the olive oil and heat it on medium high until it is hot. Add the red onions and garlic. Sauté them for 5 minutes, or until the onions are translucent.

Add the rosemary, wine, and veal stock. Simmer the ingredients for 10 to 15 minutes, or until the liquid is reduced by 1/3.

Add the summer squash, yellow squash, carrots, Roma tomatoes, black beans, lima beans, Anasazi beans, and lime juice. Cook the ingredients for 5 minutes more, or until the vegetables are just tender.

Season the vegetables with the cayenne pepper, salt, and white pepper.

serves 4

"Succotash is an old campfire kind of dish. It is like a vegetable goulash, where everything is cooked in the same pot, which is the way cowboys cooked while out on the trail. There also is an Indian influence to the recipe with the squash and Anasazi beans. By the way, Anasazi beans are very similar to pinto beans, so feel free to substitute them."

"I roast garlic by tossing the cloves in some olive oil and then roasting them in the oven at 350° for ten to fifteen minutes, or until they become dark golden brown."

"Veal stock is probably the most difficult and time consuming thing to make in this recipe. A high grade beef stock or bouillon, like Knorr's, can be used."

"Succotash goes really well with other meats. It is especially good with New York Strips. Also, you can double the amount of wine and stock, add a game meat such as rabbit, and stew it."

Pete Zimmer
Inn of the Anasazi

Pasqual's Rack of Lamb with Tomato Mint Salsa

Pasqual's Rack of Lamb

1	cup olive oil
3	cloves fresh garlic, chopped
1	bay leaf
2	racks of lamb
2	tablespoons Chimayo red chile powder
	Tomato Mint Salsa *(recipe follows)*

In a large glass bowl place the olive oil, garlic, and bay leaf. Add the racks of lamb and coat them well with the mixture. Cover the bowl with plastic wrap and marinate the lamb at room temperature for 1 hour *(turn it occasionally)*.

Rub the lamb all over with the red chile powder.

Grill the lamb for 10 to 15 minutes, or until the desired doneness is achieved.

Slice the lamb between the ribs. Serve it with the Tomato Mint Salsa on the side.

serves 4

Tomato Mint Salsa

2	jalapeño chile peppers, seeded and finely diced
¼	small red onion, finely diced
2½	large tomatoes, diced into ¼" pieces
1½	teaspoons fresh mint leaves, finely chopped
1	tablespoon orange juice, freshly squeezed
2	tablespoons dark Mexican beer
½	teaspoon olive oil
2	teaspoons white wine vinegar
¼	teaspoon kosher salt

In a medium bowl place all of the ingredients. Toss them together well.

makes approximately 1½ cups

"We serve emphatic food at Cafe Pasqual's with bold flavors from all over the world. And, we are not shy about using chiles. We listen to what our patrons tell us, and together we explore a cuisine that will lead us to a fabulous, memorable experience at the table!"

"I encourage people not to feel daunted about cooking, but to realize that it's an exciting adventure. It's like a flower garden with all the different blooms in it, and you pick and choose as you see fit to create your own unique and beautiful bouquet. And, don't be afraid if you mess up.....it's no big deal! You usually can adjust things to make them right."

"This salsa is very fresh tasting, with a wonderful, zingy flavor. The dark beer gives it an added dimension. I love it with chicken, beef, and even chips."

Katharine Kagel
Cafe Pasqual's

Mushroom & Lamb Alambre with Japone Chile Sauce

Mushroom & Lamb Alambre

2	pounds lamb, fat and bones removed, and cut into 2" cubes
20	shiitake mushrooms, washed
1	cup olive oil
¼	cup balsamic vinegar
¼	teaspoon cayenne pepper
1	tablespoon black pepper, freshly ground
	Japone Chile Sauce (recipe follows), heated

On each of four 8" bamboo skewers place, in an alternating manner, the lamb cubes and shiitake mushrooms. Place the skewers in a shallow glass pan.

In a small bowl place the olive oil, balsamic vinegar, cayenne pepper, and black pepper. Whisk the ingredients together. Pour the marinade over the lamb skewers and let them sit for 6 to 8 hours (or overnight).

Grill the lamb for 2 to 3 minutes on each side, or until the desired doneness is achieved.

Serve the lamb with the Japone Chile Sauce poured on top.

serves 4

Japone Chile Sauce

4	medium tomatoes
3	cloves fresh garlic
8	dried japone chile peppers (see chef's comments on this page), coarsely chopped
1	cup water

Preheat the oven to 400°.

Place the tomatoes on a flat sheet and bake them for 30 minutes, or until they are very soft.

In a food processor place the roasted tomatoes and the rest of the ingredients. Purée everything so that a smooth sauce is achieved.

makes approximately 2 cups

"The word 'alambre' means 'skewered' or 'on a stick'. This is a very popular dish that lamb lovers enjoy. Most people like their lamb medium rare, so watch your cooking time."

"This appetizer is a favorite of mine, as well as our customers. Lamb has a unique flavor and the way it is prepared here really accentuates it."

"My preference is for food to be straightforward and not too complicated. But at the same time I like food that will make your taste buds jump up and down! I was raised on spicy food and I really love it. But, unfortunately I now have an ulcer and so I can't eat it too often."

"There are eight chile peppers in this sauce, so it is very, very spicy. Japone chiles are dried red peppers that have their own unique heat. If you can't find them, you can use other hot kinds that are available, such as chile pequins."

Tim Lopez
Rancho Encantado

Chimayo Marinated Lamb Chops

2	tablespoons fresh rosemary, chopped
2	tablespoons fresh thyme, chopped
½	cup Chimayo red chile powder
1	teaspoon ground fennel seeds
1	teaspoon ground mace
1	teaspoon ground allspice
1	teaspoon ground cinnamon
1	teaspoon ground cloves
1	cup orange juice, freshly squeezed
¼	cup balsamic vinegar
	salt and black pepper *(to taste)*
3½	cups vegetable oil
16	lamb chops

In a food processor place the rosemary, thyme, Chimayo red chile powder, fennel, mace, allspice, cinnamon, cloves, orange juice, balsamic vinegar, salt, and black pepper. Blend the ingredients together.

With the food processor constantly running, slowly dribble in the vegetable oil.

In a large, shallow pan place the puréed mixture. Add the lamb chops and coat them well with the marinade. Cover the dish with plastic wrap and refrigerate the lamb chops for 24 hours.

Grill the lamb for 3 minutes on each side, or until the desired doneness is achieved.

serves 4

"When you put the lamb on the grill, the marinade almost caramelizes, and it really tastes delicious. This is a great way to prepare lamb. People love it and it's very simple to make. Try to find the very best lamb possible, because that will make a big difference in the end result."

"Whenever I travel in different countries, I eat from street vendors, and luckily I never get sick. I go to farmer's markets, try different restaurants, and eventually get invited to people's homes. Cooking is universal and it surpasses all language barriers."

Dakota
Piñon Grill

Buffalo Chili

1	pound dried blackeyed peas
1	medium carrot, peeled and diced medium
1	large yellow onion, diced medium
1	celery stalk, diced medium
6	juniper berries *(see chef's comments on page 36)*
2	bay leaves
8	cups water *(or as needed)*
3	tablespoons vegetable oil
3	fennel bulbs, thinly sliced
5	shallots, finely chopped
3	cloves fresh garlic, finely chopped
2	pounds ground buffalo meat, browned and drained
6	dried ancho chile peppers, seeded and crushed
6	dried guajillo chile peppers, seeded and crushed
½	teaspoon ground cloves
1	tablespoon ground cumin
1	teaspoon ground allspice
1	teaspoon ground cinnamon
1	teaspoon ground mace
2	quarts beef stock

In a large stockpot place the blackeyed peas, carrots, yellow onions, celery, juniper berries, bay leaves, and water. Bring the ingredients to a boil and then simmer them for 2 hours, or until the peas are tender.

Drain the peas and remove the bay leaves. Return the peas to the stockpot.

In a large sauté pan place the vegetable oil and heat it on medium high until it is hot. Add the fennel, shallots, and garlic, and sauté them for 5 minutes. Place them in the stockpot with the peas.

Add the browned buffalo meat, ancho and guajillo chile peppers, cloves, cumin, allspice, cinnamon, mace, and beef stock. Simmer the ingredients for 30 minutes.

serves 8

"The great thing about this dish is that you can make it with any kind of meat that you want.....beef, lamb, veal, pork, or whatever. There is a lot of leeway in the recipe, and you can use your own creativity. The fennel gives it a unique flavor and the blackeyed peas make it creamy."

"I rarely have days off, but when I do I like to go hiking and camping. It's fun to grill in the outdoors. I haven't figured out how to grill pasta yet, but I'm working on it!"

"Although I have no problem cooking for hundreds of people, I seem to have difficulty preparing a dinner for two at home. Whenever I try, I end up with leftovers for eight days."

Dakota
Piñon Grill

Piñon & Pumpkin Seed Crusted Rabbit Loin with Pineapple Corn Salsa

Piñon & Pumpkin Seed Crusted Rabbit Loin

¼ **cup piñon nuts** *(pine nuts)*, **finely chopped**
½ **cup pumpkin seeds, finely chopped**
2 **tablespoons chile pequin** *(hot red chile flakes)*
2 **tablespoons fresh sage, chopped**
1 **tablespoon fresh thyme, chopped**
6 **rabbit loins, cleaned**
½ **cup flour**
2 **eggs, lightly beaten**
2 **tablespoons olive oil**
 salt and black pepper *(to taste)*
 Pineapple Corn Salsa *(recipe on next page)*

In a medium bowl place the piñon nuts, pumpkin seeds, chile pequin, sage, and thyme. Mix the ingredients together.

Dredge the rabbit loins in the flour and then dip them in the beaten eggs. Dredge them in the nut mixture so that they are well coated.

In a large skillet place the olive oil and heat it on medium high until it is hot. Sear the loins for 2 to 3 minutes on each side, or until they are firm and the crust is golden brown. Season them with the salt and black pepper.

Serve the loins with the Pineapple Corn Salsa on the side.

serves 6

"I'm really fascinated with textures in food, and especially like to experiment with crusts. A lot of people think that I go overboard with this. However, I believe that it is possible to take your palate to its farthest extremes and still taste the great flavor of the meat you are coating. My mission in life is to come up with the most bizarre crust possible for food, and have it be sensational!"

"Rabbits have a bad rap as a food to eat, because a lot of people think of them as being adorable little bunnies that are too cute to consume. In reality, however, they are just like any animal in our food chain. The meat is white and similar to chicken, except that it is ten times as flavorful and much healthier."

Pete Zimmer
Inn of the Anasazi

Pineapple Corn Salsa

1	fresh pineapple, cleaned, sliced into discs, grilled and diced medium
1	red bell pepper, grilled, seeded and diced medium
1	yellow bell pepper, grilled, seeded and diced medium
4	ears corn, grilled, shucked and kernels removed
1	medium red onion, grilled and diced medium
4	jalapeño chile peppers, grilled, seeded and finely chopped
2	tablespoons fresh cilantro, coarsely chopped
3	limes, freshly squeezed
¼	cup extra virgin olive oil
	salt and black pepper *(to taste)*

In a medium bowl place all of the ingredients and gently mix them together. Chill the salsa before serving it.

makes approximately 1 quart

"Fresh, healthy, and spicy is the way I would describe this salsa. By grilling the pineapple and vegetables you get a fantastic flavor. You can eat this salsa straight, like a salad, or serve it with any fish, chicken, or meat entrée."

Pete Zimmer
Inn of the Anasazi

Veal Chops with Smoked Chile Roasted Tomato Sauce

12	Roma tomatoes, roasted *(see chef's comments on page 72)*
½	medium red onion, chopped medium
8	cloves fresh garlic, roasted *(see chef's comments on page 60)*
1	chipotle chile pepper *(in adobo sauce)*
3	limes, freshly squeezed
	salt and black pepper *(to taste)*
4	8-ounce veal chops
2	teaspoons ground cumin
2	teaspoons salt *(or to taste)*

In a food processor place the Roma tomatoes, red onions, garlic, chipotle chile pepper, and lime juice. Coarsely purée the ingredients.

Season the sauce with the salt and black pepper.

Rub the veal chops with the cumin and salt.

Grill the veal chops for 4 minutes on each side, or until the desired doneness is achieved.

On each of 4 individual serving plates place the veal chops. Spoon the sauce on top.

serves 4

"I tried to imagine what would taste good with veal and came up with this recipe. It's light, but substantial, and the sauce really complements the veal. If you can grill the veal over smoking chips, it will taste all the better."

"When I plan a menu I read my favorite cookbooks and look at pictures. Then I make a list of what I want to use, like different herbs, pastas, meats, or duck. Then I slowly form my thoughts into recipes. I imagine the flavors and everything evolves."

Gina Ziluca
Geronimo

Southwestern Venison Chili

"This is a rich, earthy chili that Mark Miller and I developed. It is spicy and has a strong flavor, which is rounded out by the tomatoes and beer. Sometimes we add some nuts and fruit to give it a more complex flavor."

"Here in Santa Fe we have a certain palate for hot chiles, and this recipe would satisfy most locals. Our accountant, who is Asian, would think that it's too mild, but someone from the Midwest might feel his mouth was on fire. So go easy with the chipotle chile peppers, and keep tasting it."

"The texture of this should be thick when it is finished, not soupy. As the beans cook they will release their starch and naturally thicken it. Also, taste the chili for the salt content. As people quit smoking they can taste the food more, and so they require less salt."

"Venison is very healthy. It's lean and has no hormones, and unless the deer has been shot in the wild, it does not taste gamey. If you can't find it, top round or another cut of beef can be used."

Mark Kiffin
Coyote Cafe

6	**tablespoons olive oil**
2	**pounds lean venison, diced large**
1	**large yellow onion, chopped medium**
6	**cloves fresh garlic, finely chopped**
8	**Roma tomatoes, chopped medium**
3	**tablespoons chipotle chile peppers** *(in adobo sauce)*, **puréed**
2	**teaspoons dried Mexican oregano, toasted** *(see chef's comments on page 96)*
2	**teaspoons cumin seeds, toasted** *(see chef's comments on page 68)* **and ground**
1½	**cups dark beer**
1½	**cups dried black beans, cooked and drained**
3	**cups water**
1½	**tablespoons fresh marjoram, chopped**
1½	**tablespoons fresh thyme, chopped**
½	**tablespoon salt** *(or to taste)*
6	**tablespoons sour cream**
6	**scallions, chopped**

In a large sauté pan place the olive oil and heat it on medium high until it is hot. Add the venison and sauté it for 10 minutes, or until it is browned.

Add the yellow onions and garlic, and sauté them for 5 minutes, or until the onions are translucent.

Add the Roma tomatoes, puréed chipotle chile peppers, Mexican oregano, and cumin. Stir the ingredients together.

Add the beer and stir it in well to deglaze the pan.

Add the cooked beans and water, and simmer them for 20 minutes, or until the desired consistency is achieved.

Add the marjoram, thyme, and salt. Stir the ingredients together.

Serve the chili garnished with a dollop of sour cream and a sprinkling of the scallions.

serves 6

Side Dishes

Green Chile Mashed Potatoes

5	large russet potatoes, peeled, diced large, boiled and drained
¼	pound butter, room temperature
¼	cup sour cream
⅛	cup heavy cream
¼	cup mild green chile peppers, roasted, peeled, seeded and diced medium
	salt and white pepper *(to taste)*

Place all of the ingredients *(except for the salt and white pepper)* in a large mixing bowl and beat them until the desired consistency is achieved.

Adjust the seasoning with the salt and white pepper.

serves 4

Jalapeño & Sausage Cornbread

2	pounds spicy Italian sausage, crumbled, cooked and drained
1	large yellow onion, finely chopped
1	cup sharp cheddar cheese, grated
3	jalapeño chile peppers, seeded and finely chopped
1½	cups creamed corn
1½	cups self-rising cornmeal
2	eggs, beaten
1½	cups evaporated milk.

Preheat the oven to 375°.

In a large bowl place all of the ingredients and mix them together.

In a lightly greased, large baking pan place the mixture. Bake the cornbread for 30 minutes, or until a toothpick inserted in the center comes out clean.

serves 8 to 10

"Several times we have tried to remove this dish from our menu, and our customers put up such a terrible fuss that we just gave in and decided to leave it on forever. This is what I call the 'AT&T Syndrome'.....don't bust up something that is working."

Judy Ebbinghaus
Santacafe

"Be careful not to overcook the potatoes, because they will become watery. Cut a large potato into about ten pieces, and cook them until they are tender but still slightly firm."

Laszlo Gyermek
Santacafe

"This recipe is much more interesting than a plain cornbread, which can be rather boring. I find it to be a great thing to serve at parties or pot-luck dinners."

"My grandmother was an excellent cook. Every morning she would get up at 5:30 and bake her bread. Then she would prepare her chile. If you stopped by her house at 4:00 in the afternoon there was always something to eat, but if you waited till 7:00, everything was all gone. She was only four feet and five inches tall, but she was a real spit-fire. She was the definite boss in the family, and everyone had great respect for her."

Joy Ortiz-Nashan
La Tertulia

Grilled Corn on the Cob with Ancho Chile Butter

"We developed this recipe one summer when we had a ton of corn to use up. The butter is red and exciting, and the sweet, mild flavor of the ancho chiles is really compatible with the sweetness of the corn."

"We are mammals and have to eat every day to live. So, my philosophy is.....why not make eating as delicious and sensual an experience as possible! Our lives as human beings will be that much richer."

"This butter is very versatile. It's good on a grilled chicken sandwich, slathered on tortillas, with noodles, or served with fresh bread at dinner. It also would be fun to serve this at breakfast with cornbread or corn pancakes."

*"I have written a cookbook titled **Cafe Pasqual's Cookbook - Spirited Recipes from Santa Fe**. It is being published by Chronicle Books and will be out in the fall of 1993."*

Katharine Kagel
Cafe Pasqual's

Grilled Corn on the Cob

6   ears fresh corn
       Ancho Chile Butter *(recipe follows)*

For each ear of corn pull the husks back but leave them intact. Remove the silks. Pull the husks back up to cover the corn.

Grill the corn for 5 to 7 minutes *(turn it frequently)* so that it is lightly charred and done.

Serve the corn with the Ancho Chile Butter.

serves 6

Ancho Chile Butter

4   **dried ancho chile peppers, stems and seeds removed**
2   **cloves fresh garlic**
2   **cups water**
       salt *(to taste)*
¼   **pound unsalted butter, softened**

In a medium saucepan place the ancho chile peppers, garlic, and water. Heat the ingredients on medium low and bring them to a simmer. Cook them for 15 to 20 minutes, or until the chiles are softened. Strain the chiles *(reserve the liquid)*.

Place the chiles and garlic in a food processor and purée them so that a paste is formed *(add some of the reserved liquid if necessary)*. Add the salt and mix it in.

In a medium small bowl place the butter. Using an electric mixer fitted with the paddle attachment, whip the butter on medium speed until it is smooth and soft. Add the chile paste and mix it in so that it is completely blended with the butter.

Let the chile butter sit at room temperature so that it warms *(but doesn't melt)* before serving it.

makes approximately 1 cup

Calabacitas con Queso & Chile Verde

¼   **pound butter**
3   **medium zucchini, diced medium**
3   **medium yellow squash, diced medium**
3   **ears fresh corn, kernels only**
½   **pound green chile peppers, roasted, peeled, seeded and diced medium**
⅓   **cup Monterey Jack cheese, grated**
⅓   **cup cheddar cheese, grated**

Preheat the oven to 350°.

In a large sauté pan place the butter and heat it on medium high until it is melted and hot. Add the zucchini, yellow squash, and corn. Sauté the ingredients for 2 minutes, or until they are barely warm.

Add the green chile peppers and stir them in. Cook the ingredients for 5 minutes.

Place the mixture in a large baking dish. Sprinkle the Monterey Jack and cheddar cheeses on top.

Bake the calabacitas for 10 to 15 minutes, or until the cheese is melted.

serves 6

"When I was a young boy growing up in Santa Fe, squash and corn were our main vegetables. Everybody grew them in their backyard. It was such a treat in July and August to go to the vegetable garden and pick fresh squash and sweet corn, and then sauté them with cheese."

"You can leave out the green chile, which will give it a fresher taste. That's how we serve it at Tortilla Flats, with the chile on the side."

Gus Macias
Tortilla Flats

"I have wonderful childhood memories of all the delicious aromas of food cooking in our kitchen. I savored the smells when I was playing outside, because I knew they meant it was almost time for lunch or dinner. My mother always served us a fresh, home cooked meal. Sometimes I was jealous of my friends who got to eat bologna sandwiches on white bread and Twinkies, but now I realize how lucky I was. We were poor, but rich in other ways. I try to cook delicious, nutritious meals for my own children. I want them to see and smell, and eventually remember how precious these times are."

Ivan Macias
Tortilla Flats

Green Chile Piñon
Cornbread Dressing

"This is a recipe I came up with for one of our Thanksgiving dinners. Corn and green chile always go well together, so I thought I would try that combination. It came out really good, and the toasted piñon nuts are the crowning touch. I like to bake my dressing rather than stuff it in the turkey, because then it doesn't come out soggy."

"During the early years of my marriage I made one almost fatal mistake. Because of my intense involvement with cooking, I tended to be critical of my wife's endeavors in the kitchen. Maybe not critical, exactly, but I always had a suggestion for improvement. Finally, she blew up. She took off her apron, handed it over to me, and said 'That's it! I quit! From now on you do the cooking!' I guess I wasn't very sensitive. The story ends happily, though, because now I do all of the cooking at home, and I really enjoy it. She's happy and I'm happy!"

Courtney Carswell
The Shed

1	tablespoon butter
½	medium yellow onion, chopped medium
1	celery stalk, chopped medium
1	cup mushrooms, thinly sliced
6	cups day-old cornbread, cut into 1" cubes
1	cup piñon nuts *(pine nuts)*, **toasted** *(see chef's comments on page 317)*
1	cup green chile peppers, roasted, peeled, seeded and chopped medium
1	jalapeño chile pepper, seeded and finely chopped
⅓	cup fresh parsley, chopped
1	teaspoon poultry seasoning
1	cup turkey stock *(use the chicken stock recipe on page 311 and substitute turkey for the chicken)*
	salt *(to taste)*

Preheat the oven to 325°.

In a large saucepan place the butter and heat it on medium high until it is melted and hot. Add the yellow onions, celery, and mushrooms, and sauté them for 2 minutes.

Add the cornbread, piñon nuts, green and jalapeño chile peppers, parsley, poultry seasoning, turkey stock, and salt. Mix the ingredients together well.

In a lightly greased baking dish place the dressing. Cover the dish and bake it for 30 minutes.

serves 6

Tortilla Flats Black Beans

2	cups dried black beans, soaked in hot water for 30 minutes, drained and rinsed until the water is clear
1	carrot, cut into 3 pieces
1	celery stalk, cut into 3 pieces
1	small yellow onion, peeled
2	jalapeño chile peppers, seeded and halved
1	small green bell pepper, halved and seeded
1	clove fresh garlic
½	bunch fresh cilantro, tied together with kitchen string
1	teaspoon fresh oregano, chopped
¼	teaspoon cumin seeds, ground
1½	teaspoons salt
2	quarts water *(or as needed)*

In a large stockpot place the beans, carrots, celery, yellow onion, jalapeño chile peppers, green bell peppers, garlic, cilantro, oregano, cumin, salt, and water. Bring the ingredients to a boil and then reduce them to a simmer.

Cook the beans for 2 hours, or until they are tender *(add more water as needed)*.

Remove the pieces of carrot, celery, onion, jalapeño chile peppers, green bell pepper, garlic, and cilantro before serving the beans.

serves 8

"This dish evolved from a recipe for black bean patties, which we made at another restaurant I used to work for. To me, pinto beans require bacon, but black beans are wonderful without any meat at all. They make a great vegetarian dish. These are not too spicy.....they have just a hint of heat. At Tortilla Flats this is our most requested recipe."

"My grandmother was a 'curandera'.....a kind of healer. She used herbs and foods to heal the local people. Every time she put a spice in the soup she would say something like, 'This is so you won't get a stomach ache', or 'I'm making this stew with my special herbs, because some of you sound like you are coming down with a cough'. I remember she made really hot green chile to clear our sinuses."

Gus Macias
Tortilla Flats

Chile Cheese Bread Sticks

<table>
<tr><td>6</td><td>5" puff pastry squares</td></tr>
<tr><td>4</td><td>tablespoons Dijon mustard</td></tr>
<tr><td>6</td><td>slices bacon, cooked and crumbled</td></tr>
<tr><td>¼</td><td>cup green chile peppers, roasted, peeled, seeded and diced</td></tr>
<tr><td>¼</td><td>cup parmesan cheese, freshly grated</td></tr>
<tr><td>1</td><td>tablespoon fresh cilantro, chopped</td></tr>
<tr><td>1</td><td>egg, lightly beaten</td></tr>
</table>

Preheat the oven to 350°.

Brush the Dijon mustard on both sides of each pastry square. In the middle of each square sprinkle on the bacon, green chile peppers, parmesan cheese, and cilantro.

Place one pastry square on top of the other, with the ingredients on the inside *(like a sandwich)*. Press the squares together to hold the filling in place.

Cut each set of double pastry squares into 8 equal strips. Twist each piece so that it forms a medium tight spiral.

Place the bread sticks on a non-stick baking sheet and press their ends down tightly. Brush the beaten egg on top. Bake the bread sticks for 10 to 12 minutes, or until they are golden brown.

makes 24 bread sticks

"I really love these bread sticks! We serve them with our dinner salads, and customers are always asking for more. The combination of the Dijon mustard with the parmesan cheese is striking, and the bacon gives them a subtle tasting richness."

Lela Cross
La Plazuela

"The reason you press the ends of the bread sticks down tightly on the pan is to attach them to the pan so that they will shrink less."

Tomas Cross
La Plazuela

Winter Squash with Roasted Green Chile

2	**tablespoons butter**
1½	**pounds hubbard** *(or acorn)* **squash, peeled, sliced in half, seeded and cut into 1" cubes**
½	**cup yellow onions, diced medium**
2	**cloves fresh garlic, finely chopped**
1	**cup green chile peppers, roasted, peeled, seeded and diced medium**
	salt and black pepper *(to taste)*

In a large sauté pan place the butter and heat it on medium high until it is melted and hot. Add the squash, yellow onions, and garlic. Sauté the ingredients for 5 minutes, or until the onions are translucent.

Reduce the heat to low. Cover the pan and simmer the ingredients for 20 minutes.

Add the green chile peppers, salt, and black pepper, and stir them in. Simmer the ingredients for 10 minutes, or until the squash is tender.

serves 6

"One day a friend brought me a giant hubbard squash. I cut it up and cooked it with some onions, garlic, and herbs. It was good, but nothing outstanding. The next day there was some left over, so I decided to add some green chile to it.....and BINGO, it came alive! This recipe is very simple, but so often simple things are wonderful."

"The quality of the green chile that you use in your recipes is the key to their success. You can buy green chile that is frozen in the store, but it is not nearly as good as if you roasted your own fresh chile, and then froze it. The easiest thing to do in New Mexico is to wait until the chile harvest happens, and then have the people at the stores roast it for you. Put the whole chiles in zip-lock baggies and freeze them. At the time of use, remove the skin and seeds."

Courtney Carswell
The Shed

Red Chile Mashed Potatoes

2	**pounds baking potatoes, peeled and diced large**
2	**tablespoons red chile powder**
½	**cup water, warm**
2	**tablespoons chipotle chile peppers** *(in adobo sauce)*, **puréed**
2	**tablespoons butter** *(unsalted)*
1	**teaspoon salt** *(or to taste)*

In a large saucepan place the potatoes and cover them with water. Bring the potatoes to a boil and cook them for 20 minutes, or until they are tender. Drain the potatoes.

In a large bowl place the red chile powder and the ½ cup of warm water. Stir them together so that the chile powder dissolves.

Add the potatoes, puréed chipotle chile peppers, butter, and salt. Mash the potatoes so that they are smooth.

serves 6

Szechwan Cucumbers

2½ pounds cucumbers, peeled, seeded and cut into matchsticks
    that are 2" long and ¼" thick
2   tablespoons salt
6   cloves fresh garlic, thinly sliced
2   teaspoons hot bean paste *(see chef's comments on page 257)*
2   teaspoons brown peppercorns *(see chef's comments on page 203)*
4   teaspoons sugar
4   tablespoons toasted sesame oil
4   tablespoons hot red pepper oil
2   tablespoons cider vinegar

In a large bowl place the cucumbers and sprinkle them with the salt. Let the cucumbers sit for 2 hours. Rinse them with cool water and drain them well.

Return the cucumbers to the bowl.

Add the garlic, hot bean paste, brown peppercorns, sugar, toasted sesame oil, hot red pepper oil, and cider vinegar. Toss the ingredients together.

Cover the bowl with plastic wrap and refrigerate the cucumbers for 3 hours.

serves 4

"You can serve this as a salad or appetizer. It's very refreshing and is wonderful in the summer. We use small, Oriental cucumbers when we can get them."

"I don't like Chinese buffets. Most Chinese food is cooked quickly in a wok, and must be served and eaten immediately."

Marta Hung
Imperial Wok

Spicy Posole

"This is a traditional Northern New Mexican recipe that I got from my grandmother. She was from Chama, New Mexico, and raised me from the age of six. Every morning she would get up at five o'clock and make a big stack of fresh tortillas, along with a pot of green chile. I could smell the aromas in my bedroom and knew that when I got up and walked into the kitchen, there would be a wonderful breakfast waiting for me. She was a great woman."

Randy Mondragon
Staab House

1	pound dried posole
2	quarts water
4	ounces dried red chile peppers, crushed
1	medium yellow onion, diced medium
5	cloves garlic, chopped
1	teaspoon dried oregano
½	cup lime juice, freshly squeezed
2	quarts water
	salt *(to taste)*
1	bunch fresh cilantro, chopped
1	medium yellow onion, minced
4	limes, quartered

In a large, heavy stockpot place the posole and the first 2 quarts of water. Let the posole sit over night.

Add the crushed red chile peppers, diced yellow onions, garlic, oregano, lime juice, and the second 2 quarts of water. Bring the ingredients to a boil on high heat. Reduce the heat to low and simmer the ingredients for 4 hours, or until the posole pops open. Season it with the salt.

Serve the posole garnished with the cilantro, minced yellow onions, and lime pieces.

serves 8 to 10

Refried Jalapeño Black Beans

2	tablespoons olive oil
1	pound dried black beans, cooked and drained
¼	cup hot water
1	tomato, seeded and diced medium
2	jalapeño chile peppers, seeded and finely diced
2	cloves fresh garlic, finely chopped
1	bunch scallions, finely chopped
½	bunch fresh cilantro, chopped
	salt and white pepper *(to taste)*

In a large sauté pan place the olive oil and heat it on medium high until it is hot. Add the black beans and hot water. Sauté them for 15 minutes, or until the beans have a creamy consistency.

Mash the beans in the pan.

Add the tomatoes, jalapeño chile peppers, garlic, scallions, cilantro, salt, and white pepper. While stirring occasionally, sauté the ingredients for 5 minutes.

serves 8

"Refried beans are very popular in Mexico, which is where I learned how to make them. Usually they are made without the jalapeños, tomatoes, scallions, and cilantro, which I have added to give them more flavor. The beans are a wonderful addition to enchiladas or tacos, or any dish with tortillas."

"Cooking has always come easy to me. I've been working in restaurants since I was thirteen, and have always loved it. There is no way I can sit behind a desk. I've always got to be moving, working with my hands, and creating."

Scott Shampine
El Nido

"Owning a restaurant is really a fun and exciting way to live, although the long hours can sometimes be difficult. Don (the other owner) and I both wait tables, along with our waitstaff. This keeps us humble and we get a sense of what's really going on with our customers."

Dennis Dampf
El Nido

Chipotle Cream Potato Gratin

2	chipotle chile peppers *(in adobo sauce)*
8	ounces cream cheese, softened
1	pint heavy cream
¼	teaspoon nutmeg, freshly grated
1½	teaspoons salt
½	cup butter, melted
6	large baking potatoes, peeled and thinly sliced
6	shallots, peeled and finely chopped
½	cup scallions *(or chives)*, finely chopped

Preheat the oven to 375°.

In a food processor place the chipotle chile peppers and cream cheese. Purée the ingredients so that they are well blended. With the processor constantly running, slowly add the heavy cream. Add the nutmeg and salt, and blend them in. Set the sauce aside.

Coat a medium casserole dish with some of the melted butter. Add a thin layer of the sliced potatoes, sprinkle on some of the chopped shallots, and dribble on some more of the melted butter. Repeat this layering process until the dish is full. Pour the sauce on top.

Cover the dish and bake it for 1 hour, or until the potatoes are tender. Garnish the dish with the scallions.

serves 8

"This is one of my favorite potato recipes. Because it is very rich you only need to serve a small amount. It's a perfect complement to a vegetable and a piece of grilled meat."

"The only tricky part to this recipe is slicing the potatoes paper thin. I recommend buying a mandolin for such chores, which is a vegetable slicer that comes with various blades that are adjustable. You can find them at gourmet cook stores, and sometimes you see them on those hokey T.V. advertisements."

"I like food that is simply prepared with the freshest, best ingredients possible. I use herbs and spices to enhance the natural flavors of food, but I don't like to get too complicated or heavy handed with the seasonings."

Jonathan Horst
Adobo Catering

Potpourri

Ancho Black Bean Bread

1½	**ounces dried ancho chile peppers soaked in warm water for 30 minutes** *(reserve the liquid)*
1	**medium dried chipotle chile pepper soaked in warm water for 30 minutes** *(reserve the liquid)*
1½	**cups dried black beans, cooked and drained** *(reserve the cooking liquid)*
1	**teaspoon cumin seeds, toasted** *(see chef's comments on page 68)* **and ground**
2	**teaspoons salt**
2½	**tablespoons peanut oil**
1½	**tablespoons molasses**
1	**tablespoon dry yeast**
2¼	**cups whole wheat flour**
2¼	**cups white bread flour**
2	**tablespoons cornmeal**
1	**egg, lightly beaten**

In a food processor place the rehydrated ancho and chipotle chile peppers. Purée them so that they are smooth and then set them aside.

Place the cooked black beans, ½ cup of the reserved black bean cooking liquid, cumin, salt, and peanut oil in the food processor. Purée the ingredients so that they are smooth, and then set them aside.

In a large mixing bowl place the molasses and ½ cup of the reserved liquid from the chile peppers, and stir them together. While whisking constantly, slowly add the yeast.

While continuing to mix constantly, slowly add ½ of the whole wheat and white flours, until the dough reaches a thick, mud-like consistency *(reserve the remaining flour)*.

Cover the bowl with a damp towel and let the mixture rise at room temperature for 20 minutes.

Add the chile purée and bean purée to the batter, and stir them in. While mixing constantly, slowly add the remaining flour so that a firm dough is formed.

Knead the dough on a floured board for 15 minutes, or until it is soft and supple. Place the dough in an oiled bowl and cover it with a damp cloth. Let the dough rise in a warm, draft free place for 1 hour, or until it is doubled in size.

(continued on next page)

"This typifies some of the flavored breads that we do at the Coyote Cafe. It's very wholesome, but with interest. The ancho chile is not as hot as some, and has a combination of smoke, cherry, chocolate, and tobacco flavors. The black beans are earthy, and the chipotles are very spicy. So all of these ingredients combined make for a wonderful, flavorful dark bread that always generates lots of favorable comments."

"I don't think that there is any difference between men and women as chefs. Once I worked at an excellent restaurant in Denver, where I was the only male. Being a chef is not the most feminine of jobs. It's hot and strenuous, and there is a lot of lifting. But the women I know who are in the business are extremely talented and hard working."

"There is a certain spirituality to Santa Fe. I can drive for twenty minutes in any direction and find solitude."

Mark Kiffin
Coyote Cafe

"If you have never made bread before, please don't be afraid to try this recipe. Just follow the steps and it should turn out fine. Even if you mess up, you can try it again. Bread is one of the more affordable things to make. It's basically just flour, water, and yeast. Most people don't bake bread, but I bet that if they would just try, they would really enjoy it. It's a very satisfying and sensual thing to do."

Mark Kiffin
Coyote Cafe

"As you can see, this biscuit recipe is very simple to make. You just mix every-thing together, splat the dough on a sheet pan, and boom it's done! But don't be fooled by its simplicity, because the end result is fantastic. People say these are the best biscuits they have ever tasted."

"This recipe is designed for a high altitude. See the chef's comments on the next page to alter it for a low altitude. Instead of buckwheat flour you can substitute yellow or blue cornmeal, wholewheat flour, or any one of the many different stone-ground grains. You can use the biscuits for a bread at dinner, for breakfast with jam and butter, for eggs benedict, or even as a sandwich."

Pete Zimmer
Inn of the Anasazi

Punch down the dough and knead it again for 3 minutes. Return the dough to the oiled bowl and cover it with the damp cloth. Let the dough rise again for 20 minutes, or until it is doubled in size.

Preheat the oven to 350°.

Punch down the dough and divide it in half. Form each dough half into a round loaf. Place each dough loaf on a baking sheet that is covered with cornmeal. Cover it with a damp cloth and let it rise for 20 minutes *(or until it does not sink when it is poked)*. Brush the loaves with the beaten egg.

Bake the bread for 25 minutes, or until the loaves sound hollow when they are tapped on the bottom with a bread knife.

Cool the bread on a rack.

makes 2 round loaves

Buckwheat Biscuits

3	cups cake flour
2	cups buckwheat flour
1	tablespoon sugar
¼	teaspoon baking powder
1	pinch salt
1	cup sour cream
2	cups buttermilk
1	cup soft butter
¼	cup honey
1	tablespoon orange zest *(outer orange part grated off)*

Preheat the oven to 325°.

In a large mixing bowl place all of the ingredients. Mix them together until they are just combined.

On a flat baking sheet place 6 equal-size dollops of the dough. Bake them for 7 to 10 minutes, or until they are firm to the touch and lightly brown.

Let the biscuits rest for several minutes and then slice them in half horizontally. Serve the biscuits warm.

makes 6 large biscuits

Blue Corn Red Raspberry Muffins

1	cup blue cornmeal
1¼	cups all purpose flour
¼	cup sugar
1	teaspoon baking powder
½	teaspoon ground cinnamon
¼	teaspoon ground cloves
1	pinch of salt
1	egg, lightly beaten
1	cup milk
6	tablespoons butter, melted
1	cup fresh raspberries
	unsalted butter (as needed)
	Red Chile Honey (recipe on page 304)

Preheat the oven to 400°.

In a large mixing bowl place the blue cornmeal, flour, sugar, baking powder, cinnamon, cloves, and salt. Stir the ingredients together.

Add the egg, milk, and butter, and stir them in. Add the raspberries and gently fold them in.

In a greased and floured muffin tin, fill the cups ⅔ full. Bake the muffins for 20 to 25 minutes, or until a toothpick inserted in the center comes out dry.

Cool the muffins for 5 minutes on a wire rack.

Serve the muffins with the butter and Red Chile Honey.

makes 12 muffins

"We sell a ton of these muffins to our customers. The crunchy sweetness of the blue corn together with the tartness of the red raspberries is very appealing."

Peter Raub
Santa Fe Market

"This recipe is designed for our elevation, which is seven thousand feet. If you are much lower, or at sea level, add two more tablespoons of sugar, one more teaspoon of baking powder, and reduce the flour by two tablespoons."

"I do most of the baking in my partnership with Peter. People look at me when I tell them I am a baker, because I am very thin. The truth is, I don't have a sweet tooth. Rather, I tend to crave things that are salty and sour, like pickles."

Marsha Chobol
Santa Fe Market

Sopapillas

1	cup white flour
1	teaspoon baking powder
¼	teaspoon salt
2	tablespoons lard
⅓	cup water (plus 1 tablespoon, or as needed)
6	cups vegetable oil (or as needed)

(continued on next page)

"The key to making a good sopapilla is to have the oil very, very hot.....about 450°. Use a deep, heavy, heavy pan and heat the oil to the point where a small piece of the dough dropped in rises to the top. It's kind of like cooking donuts."

Isabelle Koomoa
Guadalupe Cafe

In a medium bowl sift together the flour, baking powder, and
salt. Add the lard and work it in well with a pastry cutter. Add the
water and mix it in so that the dough is of a smooth consistency
(not crumbly or sticky).

On a floured cutting board roll out the dough so that it is ⅛"
thick. Cut the dough into 4" triangles.

In a deep saucepan place the vegetable oil so that it is 4" deep.
Heat it to 450°. Very carefully deep-fry the sopapillas for 2 to 3
minutes, or until they are golden brown. Drain them on paper
towels.

makes 8 sopapillas

Green Chile Bread

½	**pound butter, chilled and cut into small pieces**
2	**cups flour**
1	**teaspoon baking soda**
¼	**cup sugar**
1½	**teaspoons fresh garlic, finely chopped**
3	**eggs, beaten**
½	**cup olive oil**
2	**cups green chile peppers, roasted, peeled, seeded and diced**
1½	**teaspoons chile caribe** (crushed red chile peppers)
1	**teaspoon salt** (or to taste)
½	**teaspoon black pepper** (or to taste)

Preheat the oven to 350°.

In a large bowl place the butter, flour, baking soda, and sugar.
Cut and mix the ingredients together (use a pastry cutter) so that
pea-size pieces are formed.

Add the remaining ingredients and stir them in so that they are
just incorporated.

On a floured board place the dough and knead it gently for 2
minutes. Form the dough into a loaf.

Place the dough in a lightly oiled and flour-dusted 9" bread pan.

Bake the bread for 1 hour, or until a toothpick inserted in the
center comes out clean.

makes 1 loaf

Dirty Martinis with Marinated Stuffed Olives

Dirty Martinis

1½   cups Stolcheneya vodka
1½   tablespoons olive juice
2   cups ice cubes
      Marinated Stuffed Olives (recipe follows)

In a cocktail shaker place the vodka, olive juice, and ice cubes. Shake the ingredients and then strain the liquid into 4 chilled martini glasses.

Garnish each drink with the Marinated Stuffed Olives.

serves 4

Marinated Stuffed Olives

36   pitted Sicilian green olives
1   red bell pepper, roasted, peeled, seeded and cut into thin
      strips
12   cloves fresh garlic, roasted (see chef's comments on page 60)
12   anchovy fillets
1   teaspoon chile pequin (hot red chile flakes)
1   teaspoon fresh oregano, chopped
3   tablespoons olive oil

Stuff 12 olives with the red bell pepper strips, 12 olives with the garlic cloves, and 12 olives with the anchovy fillets. Set the olives aside.

In a medium bowl place the chile pequin, oregano, and olive oil. Stir the ingredients together. Place the olives in the mixture.

Cover the bowl with plastic wrap and let the olives marinate in the refrigerator overnight.

makes 36 stuffed olives

"When I was a child my father taught me how to make these martinis for him. They are called 'dirty' because the olive juice clouds the clear color of the vodka. The olive juice also takes off the sting of the alcohol, so the drink goes down really smooth. In fact, this drink is so good that non-martini drinkers will have up to three, without realizing how potent they are."

"I've been a bartender for over twelve years, so I guess I must like doing it. The fun part is being on stage and performing for the people sitting around the bar. Everything I do can be seen by others. It's also fun to chat and banter with the customers. The depressing part is seeing a lot of sad, lonely people who come in time after time. They have no friends and nowhere to go, so they come here for companionship. I listen to their problems, but I never get involved, and that seems to satisfy them."

Donna Marchesi
Pranzo Italian Grill

"These green olives really give a gourmet touch to your martini. They also are great to serve with an antipasto dish."

Steven Lemon
Pranzo Italian Grill

Sangrita with Tequila

4	dried red chile peppers, roasted, peeled and seeded
4	cups boiling water
¼	cup red onion, chopped medium
1	quart orange juice, freshly squeezed
¼	cup lime juice, freshly squeezed
	salt *(to taste)*
8	shots tequila *(good quality)*
4	limes, quartered

In a large bowl place the red chile peppers and boiling water. Cover the bowl with plastic wrap and let the chiles sit for 30 minutes. Drain the chiles and discard the water.

In a blender place the rehydrated red chile peppers, red onions, orange juice, lime juice, and salt. Purée the ingredients so that they are smooth *(if needed, thin the mixture with additional orange juice)*.

Serve the Sangrita with a shot of tequila, a lime, and some salt on the side.

makes 6 cups

"This is a traditional Mexican drink that you would find in almost any Mexican household. It's similar to a Bloody Mary mix, but with orange juice instead of tomato juice. You should make it pretty spicy so that it counteracts the sting of the tequila. Take a drink of the tequila, then the sangrita, and then eat the lime and salt."

Marsha Chobol
Santa Fe Market

Fajita Marinade

½	medium white onion, coarsely chopped
3½	ounces chipotle chile peppers *(in adobo sauce)*
2	cloves fresh garlic, finely chopped
2	tablespoons black peppercorns
¾	cup dry red wine
1	cup red wine vinegar
1	cup vegetable oil
½	cup Worcestershire sauce

In a food processor place the white onions, chipotle chile peppers, and garlic. Purée the ingredients so that they are smooth.

In a medium bowl place the puréed ingredients, black peppercorns, red wine, red wine vinegar, vegetable oil, and Worcestershire sauce. Mix everything together well.

makes approximately 3 cups

"I don't like food that is extremely hot, where the heat is all you notice. Rather, I look for depth of flavor in food. I want to be able to taste something throughout the whole experience of eating it."

Marc Greene
Old Mexico Grill

Smoked Chile Butter

1	tablespoon olive oil
¼	yellow onion, sliced
1	clove fresh garlic, chopped
1	smoked pasilla negro chile pepper, deep-fried for 7 seconds and stem removed
½	pound tomatillos, husked, washed, peeled and cut into quarters
½	cup water
½	teaspoon salt *(to taste)*
1	pound unsalted butter, room temperature

In a medium sauté pan place the olive oil and heat it on medium high until it is hot. Add the yellow onions and garlic. Sauté them for 7 to 10 minutes, or until the onions are golden brown.

Place the pasilla negro chile pepper on top of the onions and garlic. Remove the pan from the stove and let the ingredients cool.

In a large saucepan place the tomatillos, water, and salt. Bring the ingredients to a boil on medium high heat. Cover the pan, reduce the heat to low, and simmer the tomatillos for 15 minutes.

Drain the tomatillos and let them cool slightly.

In a food processor place the cooled onions, garlic, chile pepper, and tomatillos. Purée the ingredients so that they are smooth. Refrigerate the mixture for 1 hour.

In a medium bowl place the butter and beat it so that it is soft. Add the refrigerated ingredients and mix them together.

Form the butter into a log and wrap it in plastic wrap. Freeze the butter. Slice off pieces as they are needed.

makes 1½ pounds

Red Chile Honey

¾	cup honey
3	tablespoons red chile powder

In a small bowl place the 2 ingredients and mix them together.

makes ¾ cup

"We use pasilla negro chile peppers that have been smoked. They have a great flavor and go well with the sourness of the tomatillos. The butter is green and has some texture to it. It's wonderful with beef tenderloin or with a substantial fish like mahi mahi."

"My biggest critic is my seven-year-old son. I might be able to sneak something past a customer, but nothing gets by him! He knows exactly what he likes and dislikes, and makes no bones about expressing his opinions."

Kelly Rogers
Santacafe

"To be a successful chef takes a lot of special qualities. You must have a palate that appeals to the public. You must have an artistic eye for visual presentation. You must have common sense, patience, a strong work ethic, and good people skills."

Laszlo Gyermek
Santacafe

"This is a nifty thing to do with honey because it turns two common ingredients into something very exotic tasting."

Peter Raub
Santa Fe Market

Chile Paste

2	teaspoons olive oil
2	red bell peppers, seeded and chopped
6	cloves fresh garlic, finely chopped
1	shallot, finely chopped
2	jalapeño chile peppers, seeded and finely chopped
1	bunch fresh cilantro, chopped
1	teaspoon ground cinnamon
1	teaspoon fresh oregano, chopped
2	teaspoons tomato paste

In a large sauté pan place the olive oil and heat it on medium high until it is hot. Add the red bell peppers, garlic, shallots, jalapeño chile peppers, and cilantro. Sauté the ingredients for 5 minutes. Add the cinnamon, oregano, and tomato paste. Stir the ingredients together and sauté them for 10 minutes.

In a food processor place the mixture and purée it so that it is smooth.

Place the purée in a bowl, cover it with plastic wrap, and let it cool to room temperature.

makes approximately 1 cup

"You can't use this chile paste with something that takes very long to cook, because it will burn. It has a wonderful flavor and will keep well in the refrigerator."

"There are two difficult things about being a chef.....the long hours and dealing with the employees. Here in Santa Fe people are more laid back than in California, so I really have to crack the whip to keep the kitchen up to par."

Jim Makinson
Bishop's Lodge

Curry Oil

1	ounce dried red chile peppers
4	cups soybean oil
6	bay leaves
10	black peppercorns
1½	tablespoons ground turmeric
½	cup curry powder

Note: For best results, this must be prepared 48 hours before using.

In a medium saucepan place all of the ingredients. While stirring occasionally, simmer them for 10 minutes.

Strain the oil through a fine sieve lined with 3 layers of cheesecloth.

Place the Curry Oil in an airtight glass container and refrigerate it.

makes 4 cups

"The curry oil will keep in the refrigerator indefinitely. We make this in the restaurant by the gallon and keep it for over a month. Use it to baste seafood or other items when you are grilling them. Just be warned that the oil will permanently stain your clothes and utensils because of the yellow turmeric and curry powder in it."

Kit Baum
El Farol

Cornmeal Crêpes

½   **cup cornmeal**
½   **cup flour**
2   **eggs, lightly beaten**
½   **cup milk**
¼   **cup vegetable oil**

In a medium bowl place the cornmeal, flour, eggs, and milk. Whisk the ingredients together. Let the batter rest for 20 minutes.

In a crêpe pan place a few drops of the vegetable oil and heat it on medium high until it is hot.

For each crêpe pour 2 tablespoons of the batter into the pan and swirl it around quickly so that it coats the bottom. Cook the crêpe on one side for 30 seconds. Turn the crepe over and cook it for another 20 seconds.

Remove the crêpe from the pan.

Repeat the process with the rest of the batter.

makes approximately 10 crêpes

"Crêpes are easy to make and the cornmeal in this recipe gives them an interesting twist. If you are not used to making crêpes you may have to practice making a couple before you get the hang of it."

"I view the kitchen as a laboratory, and give my people a lot of liberty in experimenting as much as they wish. If they learn one new thing a day I am happy."

Martin Rios
Old House

Beer Batter

8   **egg yolks**
1   **12-ounce bottle of beer**
2   **cups flour**
¼   **teaspoon sugar**
1   **pinch salt**
8   **egg whites, beaten to stiff peaks**

In a medium bowl place the egg yolks and the beer, and whisk them together.

Add the flour, sugar, and salt. Stir the ingredients together.

Add the beaten egg whites and gently fold them into the other ingredients.

makes approximately 3 cups

"This batter comes out light and fluffy with a crisp crust after you deep-fry it. You can use it to coat shrimp, vegetables, or whatever you want."

Tim Lopez
Rancho Encantado

Crêpes

2	**eggs, lightly beaten**
1	**pinch salt** *(or to taste)*
1	**cup all purpose flour**
1	**cup milk**
2	**tablespoons butter, melted**

In a medium bowl place the eggs and salt, and stir them together.

Add the flour and milk in small amounts and beat them in so that the mixture is smooth.

Cover the bowl with plastic wrap and refrigerate the batter for 1 hour.

Heat a 6" nonstick sauté pan on medium until it is hot.

Lightly wipe the inside of the pan with a paper towel dipped in oil *(or use a vegetable spray)*.

Pour approximately ¼ cup of the batter into the pan. Tilt the pan in all directions so that the batter completely covers the bottom. Cook it for 30 to 60 seconds, or until the edges start to color. Turn the crêpe over and cook the other side for 10 seconds. Flip the crêpe out onto a towel and let it cool.

Repeat this process until all of the batter is used. Stack the crêpes and cover them with another towel *(the crêpes must be cool before they are stacked)*.

makes approximately 16 crêpes

Pizza Dough

1¼	cups warm water
1	tablespoon dry yeast
1½	tablespoons olive oil
1	tablespoon honey
¾	tablespoon salt
1¼	cups semolina flour
1¼	cups all purpose flour
1¼	cups hi-gluten flour

In a small bowl place the warm water. Sprinkle in the yeast so that it dissolves.

In a large mixing bowl place the dissolved yeast, olive oil, honey, and salt. Stir the ingredients together.

In a medium bowl place the 3 flours and mix them together.

While mixing constantly *(use the dough hook with an electric mixer)*, gradually add the 3 flours to the olive oil-honey mixture.

Place the dough on a flat, floured surface. Knead the dough for 5 to 7 minutes, or until a stiff, smooth consistency is achieved.

Place the dough in an oiled bowl and cover it with a damp towel. Let it rise for 1 hour, or until it is doubled in size.

Roll out the dough so that it forms two 12" rounds.

makes two 12" rounds

"This is a great pizza dough recipe that was given to me by a friend. You can keep it in the refrigerator for up to five days. The yeast will ferment with the passage of time, and the flavor gets better and better. Also, the dough freezes well."

"Hi-gluten flour can be found in any bulk food store."

"Some people are intimidated by making doughs, but this recipe is really easy. It's straight-forward and there is no way you can mess up."

"I love to eat out in restaurants, but I am very critical. I am classified as a bad customer because if something is wrong with the food or service, I won't complain. I will just pay the bill and then never come back. This is a real business killer, and I hope that most people aren't like me!"

James Lamoureux
The Evergreen

Tart Dough

2½	cups all purpose flour
½	cup cocoa
¾	cup sugar
½	teaspoon salt
½	pound butter
1	cup pecans, finely chopped
¼	cup milk

In a medium bowl sift together the flour, cocoa, sugar, and salt. Add the butter and cut it in *(use a pastry cutter)* so that pea-size pieces are formed.

Add the chopped pecans and milk, and mix them in so that they are just incorporated.

Carefully form the dough into a ball. Place the dough back into the bowl, cover it with a damp cloth and refrigerate it for two hours.

Divide the dough into 2 equal balls. Roll each one out on a floured surface to form a 16" diameter round.

makes two 16" diameter rounds

"The pecans in this dough give it a little excitement and texture. You prepare it like you would any pie dough, and it freezes very well."

James Lamoureux
The Evergreen

Gordita Shells

2½ **cups masa harina** *(ground corn flour)*
1½ **cups water** *(or as needed)*
4 **dried ancho chile peppers, seeded, soaked in water overnight
and drained**
4 **cloves fresh garlic, coarsely chopped**
salt and black pepper *(to taste)*
2 **tablespoons vegetable oil** *(or as needed)*

In a medium bowl place the masa harina. Mix in enough of the water so that a dry dough is formed.

In a food processor place the ancho chile peppers, garlic, and the rest of the water. Purée the ingredients together.

With the processor constantly running, slowly add small pieces of the dough so that it is well combined with the chile purée.

Add the salt and black pepper, and mix them in.

Roll the dough into 12 balls *(about 2" in diameter)*. Carefully roll out each ball between 2 pieces of wax paper *(or use a tortilla press)* so that a ⅛" thick circle is formed.

In a large skillet place the vegetable oil and heat it on medium high until it is hot. Gently fry the shells for 30 to 40 seconds on each side, or until they start to get crisp and darken slightly.

makes 12 shells

"These gordita shells have an excellent, robust flavor. You can fill them with ingredients of your choice, or use them as a great accompaniment for an entrée. I like to leave the seeds in the ancho chiles because they look great in the shells."

"Don't be afraid to taste the raw dough for the correct spice and seasonings. We all remember tasting our mom's cookie dough as kids.....and this is no different. There are no eggs in it so you don't have to be afraid of salmonella. The texture of the dough should be just damp enough to hold it together."

"I have found that women make better cooks than men. They are naturally more intuitive and respectful of the food, and they have much greater patience than men. In fact, I think that overall women are far more mature than men."

Pete Zimmer
Inn of the Anasazi

Chicken Stock

3	**pounds chicken pieces** *(backs, wings, necks, and bones)*
1	**large yellow onion, coarsely chopped**
1	**large carrot, coarsely chopped**
1	**stalk celery, coarsely chopped**
¼	**bunch fresh parsley**

In a large stockpot place the chicken pieces, yellow onions, carrots, celery, and parsley. Cover the ingredients with water.

Bring the ingredients to a boil and then reduce them to a simmer. Simmer the stock for 1½ hours.

Strain the stock into a bowl. Place it in the refrigerator so that the fat congeals on top. Skim off the fat.

Pour the stock into ice cube trays and freeze it. Transfer the frozen cubes to plastic bags.

makes approximately 2 quarts

Crème Fraîche

1	**cup heavy cream**
2	**tablespoons buttermilk**

In a medium bowl place the heavy cream and buttermilk. Place the bowl in a medium warm place. Let it sit overnight, or until the cream thickens so that it is the consistency of a lightly whipped cream.

makes approximately 1 cup

LP CALDWELL

Desserts

Green Chile Pecan Apple Pie

⅓	cup clarified unsalted butter
6	cups Golden Delicious apples *(or enough to fill a 10" pie shell with a gentle mound)*, **peeled, cored and sliced**
1	tablespoon lemon juice, freshly squeezed
1	tablespoon ground cinnamon
1	pinch salt
1	cup green chile peppers, roasted, peeled, seeded, diced and strained
1¼	cups sugar
⅓	cup cornstarch
1	tablespoon ground cinnamon
1	tablespoon lemon juice, freshly squeezed
1	pinch salt
1¾	cups flour
¾	cup sugar
1¾	sticks cold unsalted butter, cut into small pieces
¾	cup pecan pieces
1	tablespoon ground cinnamon
1	10" unbaked pie shell

In a medium saucepan place the clarified butter, apples, the first tablespoon of lemon juice, the first tablespoon of cinnamon, and the first pinch of salt. Heat the ingredients on medium high and then cover the pan with a lid. Simmer them for 15 to 20 minutes, or until the apples are almost cooked and the juices in the pan are nearly evaporated. Let the apples cool to room temperature.

Preheat the oven to 350°.

To the cooked apples add the green chile peppers, the 1¼ cups of sugar, the cornstarch, the second tablespoon of cinnamon, the second tablespoon of lemon juice, and the second pinch of salt. Stir the ingredients together and set the mixture aside.

In a medium bowl place the flour and the ¾ cup of sugar, and mix them together. Add the cold butter a few pieces at a time and cut it in *(use the paddle attachment with an electric mixer, or use a pastry cutter)* so that the ingredients are incorporated and the mixture is crumbly *(pea-size pieces)*.

Add the pecans and the third tablespoon of cinnamon to the flour mixture, and stir them in.

(continued on next page)

"This is an exciting pie, with many complex flavors. It is sweet, hot, salty, and nutty, and it stimulates all of the areas of your tongue. I call it a real thrill pie! It is especially delicious with a scoop of vanilla ice cream."

"People say that green chile really gets your endorphins going. Maybe that's why so many people are addicted to it."

"Don't be afraid of the combination of apples and green chile. If you like East Indian foods, such as chutney, you will love this pie!"

"If you have any leftover pie do not store it in the refrigerator. Just cover it loosely with plastic wrap and place it in your cupboard or on your kitchen counter. Years ago people had 'pie safes' .....small cabinets with louvered doors to allow for air circulation, in which the daily pies were stored."

"If your pie crust starts to get too dark when you are baking it, fashion an aluminum foil 'collar' around the pie dish. Fold the edges of the foil over the crust and pinch the foil closed."

Maggie Faralla
Zia Diner

Place the apple mixture in the pie shell. Place the crumbled butter-pecan mixture on top and spread it around evenly all the way to the edge of the crust *(to "seal" the pie)*.

Bake the pie for 1 hour, or until the top puffs up and is golden brown. Let the pie cool to room temperature.

serves 10 to 12

Walnut Brownie Pie

1	cup Hershey's chocolate syrup
3	eggs, lightly beaten
1½	cups walnuts, chopped
½	cup sugar
¼	cup cocoa powder
2	tablespoons flour
1	tablespoon vanilla extract
¼	cup butter, melted
1	pinch salt
1	9" unbaked pie shell

Preheat the oven to 375°.

In a medium bowl place all of the ingredients *(except for the pie shell)* and mix them together well.

Pour the mixture into the pie shell. Bake the pie for 1 hour, or until the crust is brown and the filling is set.

serves 8

Green Chile Pumpkin Tart
with Roasted Almond Sauce

Green Chile Pumpkin Tart

2   cups pumpkin purée
½   cup green chile peppers, roasted, peeled, seeded and chopped
3   eggs, lightly beaten
1½ cups sugar
½   cup heavy cream
1   teaspoon ground cinnamon
1   teaspoon ground nutmeg
1   teaspoon vanilla extract
1   9" unbaked pie shell
      Roasted Almond Sauce *(recipe on next page)*

Preheat the oven to 375°.

In a medium bowl place the pumpkin purée, green chile peppers, eggs, sugar, heavy cream, cinnamon, nutmeg, and vanilla extract. Mix the ingredients together.

Pour the mixture in the pie shell and bake it for 30 minutes, or until the pumpkin is set.

Pour the Roasted Almond Sauce on top of each serving.

serves 6

"One night we needed a dessert special at the restaurant. It was close to Thanksgiving, and the idea of pumpkin with green chile just popped into my mind. Strange as it seems, the combination is excellent. You don't really taste the green chile.....you just get a hint of a peppery heat."

"My philosophy of cooking changes from month to month. Basically, I think that cooking should be uncomplicated. People think that cooking is harder than it actually is. There is no major secret to wonderful food. In fact, some of the best dishes in the world have incredibly simple recipes. For example, we make a cheesecake that has only three ingredients in it.....cream cheese, whipped cream, and sugar. I think it's the best dessert in town, and everyone who tastes it absolutely loves it."

Paul Hunsicker
Paul's Restaurant

Roasted Almond Sauce

2	**cups heavy cream**
¼	**cup sugar**
1	**teaspoon vanilla extract**
3	**egg yolks**
¼	**cup sliced blanched almonds, roasted**

In a medium saucepan place the heavy cream and heat it on medium until it is hot. Add the sugar and vanilla extract, and bring the ingredients to a boil.

In a medium small stainless steel bowl place the egg yolks and whisk them. While whisking rapidly, add 3 ladles of the hot cream mixture.

Pour the egg yolk-cream mixture back into the saucepan and mix it in. Simmer the sauce for 5 minutes.

Let the sauce cool. Place it in the refrigerator and chill it.

Add the almonds and stir them in.

Purée the sauce in a blender so that it is smooth.

makes 2½ cups

Italian Cheesecake

1½	cups flour
⅓	cup sugar
½	cup butter, chilled and coarsely chopped
1	egg, lightly beaten
2	egg yolks, lightly beaten
1½	pounds cream cheese
¾	cup sugar
1	cup marscapone cheese
3	eggs, lightly beaten
4	egg yolks, lightly beaten
½	cup piñon nuts *(pine nuts)*
½	cup golden raisins
2	tablespoons flour
1	tablespoon lemon zest *(outer yellow part grated off)*
1	tablespoon vanilla extract

In a food processor place the 1½ cups of flour, the ⅓ cup of sugar, and butter. Pulse the ingredients so that they have a cornmeal-like consistency. Place the mixture in a medium large mixing bowl.

Add the 1 egg and the 2 egg yolks. Mix the ingredients together so that the dough forms a ball.

Wrap the dough in plastic wrap and place it in the refrigerator for 1 hour.

On a floured board roll out ¾ of the dough so that it forms a 12" circle. Place the dough in a 9" springform pan and gently press it in to form a crust *(the dough should come up the sides by 2")*.

Roll out the remaining dough. Cut it into strips that are ¾" wide and 10" long. Set the strips of dough aside.

In another medium mixing bowl place the cream cheese and the ¾ cup of sugar. Beat the mixture for 5 minutes, or until it is light and fluffy.

Add the marscapone, and mix it in.

Add the 3 eggs and 4 egg yolks, and beat them in so that they are well combined *(do not overbeat)*.

Add the piñon nuts, golden raisins, the 2 tablespoons of flour, lemon zest, and vanilla extract. Mix the ingredients together well.

(continued on next page)

"I used to make a classic Italian lemon ricotta cheesecake that we served at the restaurant. People liked it, but they were really funny about its texture, and complained that it was too dry. I realized that most Americans' vision of a true cheesecake was something that was moist and creamy, such as the Sara Lee Cheesecakes you can buy in the supermarket. So I decided to use the same recipe of the lemon ricotta cheesecake and substitute marscapone for the ricotta, which made it much creamier. Now all of our customers love it, even though I personally prefer the original version."

"This is a very straight-forward recipe that takes no particular baking skills. The cheesecake freezes very well and also will keep in the fridge for up to five days if it is well covered."

Jane Stacey
Pranzo Italian Grill

Pour the batter into the crust. Lay the reserved strips of dough across the top of the batter to form a lattice design. Tuck the edges of the strips down the sides of the pan into the batter.

Bake the cheesecake for 45 minutes, or until the filling is set in the center. Let the cake cool before serving.

serves 10

El Diablo Tart

Tart Dough *(recipe on page 309)*, **refrigerated**
1¼ **cups raspberry jam**
1 **cup red chile jelly** *(see chef's comments this page)*
1 **teaspoon chile caribe** *(crushed red chile peppers)*

Preheat the oven to 350°.

Divide the refrigerated tart dough into 2 equal pieces.

On a floured board roll out both pieces of dough into circles that are approximately 18" in diameter and ⅛" thick. Place one of the circles of dough in a 16" tart pan.

In a small bowl place the raspberry jam and the red chile jelly, and stir the ingredients together. Pour the mixture into the tart shell. Sprinkle on the chile caribe.

Cut the second circle of dough into ½" wide strips. Arrange the strips of dough on top of the filling in a lattice pattern. Seal the edges of the strips of dough and the tart crust by pinching them together.

Bake the tart for 45 minutes, or until it is golden brown.

serves 8

Chocolate Pound Cake
with Ibarra Chocolate Glaze

Chocolate Pound Cake

1½	cups butter
3	cups sugar
5	eggs
1½	tablespoons almond extract
1	cup cocoa powder
2	cups all purpose flour
1	tablespoon ground cinnamon
½	teaspoon baking powder
1	teaspoon salt
1	cup milk
¼	cup water
4	ounces sliced blanched almonds
	Ibarra Chocolate Glaze *(recipe on next page)*

Preheat the oven to 350°.

In a large mixing bowl place the butter and sugar. Cream them together with an electric mixer *(use the paddle attachment)* for 2 minutes, or until the mixture is light and fluffy.

Add the eggs and almond extract, and beat them in well.

In another medium bowl sift together the cocoa, flour, cinnamon, baking powder, and salt.

In a small bowl place the milk and water.

Add ⅓ of the milk mixture and ⅓ of the dry ingredients to the creamed butter mixture, and mix them together. Repeat this process until all of the ingredients are thoroughly incorporated.

Add the almonds and stir them in.

Pour the batter into a 9" oiled and floured tube pan. Bake the cake for 1 hour, or until a toothpick inserted into the center comes out dry. Let the cake cool.

Remove the cake from the pan. Spread the Ibarra Chocolate Glaze on the top and sides.

serves 10 to 12

"So many people love chocolate, and this recipe is a great way to satisfy their craving. You can make it ahead of time because it holds very well. Also, it freezes nicely. Suzy Dayton, our incredibly talented pastry chef, developed this recipe."

"One reason why a restaurant such as the Coyote Cafe is successful is that the staff is like a family working together. Each employee truly cares about the customers. We are truly grateful to them, and we show our gratitude by being attentive to details and thanking them."

Mark Kiffin
Coyote Cafe

Ibarra Chocolate Glaze

½   **cup heavy cream**
3   **ounces Ibarra** (*Mexican*) **chocolate**
1   **ounce bittersweet chocolate**
3   **tablespoons butter**
1   **tablespoon honey**
1   **tablespoon corn syrup**
3   **tablespoons sliced, blanched almonds, toasted** (*see chef's comments on page 317*)

In a small saucepan place the heavy cream and heat it on medium for 5 minutes, or until it is slightly scalded. Set the cream aside.

In the top of a simmering double boiler place the Ibarra chocolate, bittersweet chocolate, butter, honey, corn syrup, and almonds. Heat the ingredients for 5 minutes, or until the chocolate and butter are melted.

Add the scalded cream and stir it in. Remove the pan from the heat and let it cool for 10 minutes.

makes approximately 1½ cups

Warm Fruit Compote
with Buckwheat Biscuits &
White Chocolate Chile Ice Cream

Warm Fruit Compote

2	tablespoons butter
2	tablespoons sugar
1	tablespoon vanilla extract
2	tablespoons water
4	fresh peaches, peeled, pitted and quartered
2	pints blackberries, washed
1	lemon, freshly squeezed
½	teaspoon fresh mint, minced
6	**Buckwheat Biscuits** *(recipe on page 299),* **halved and warm** **White Chocolate Chile Ice Cream** *(recipe on next page)*

In a medium saucepan place the butter and heat it on medium until it is melted. Add the sugar, vanilla extract, and water. Simmer the ingredients for 2 minutes, or until the sugar is dissolved.

Add and fold in the peaches, blackberries, and lemon juice. Simmer the ingredients for 3 to 5 minutes, or until the fruit is slightly wilted.

Add the mint and fold it in.

On each of 6 individual dessert plates place the bottom half of a Buckwheat Biscuit. Place the fruit compote on top. Place the top half of the biscuit on the fruit. Place a scoop of the White Chocolate Chile Ice Cream next to the biscuit.

serves 6

"I love this recipe because it is not one of those fancy, chi-chi desserts that is delicious, but pretentious. Rather, it is short, sweet, simple, and right to the point.....full of character and yet humble. The combination of the fruit, biscuits, and ice cream is really outstanding. And, once each component is made, it takes only seconds to put it together. The visual presentation and the wonderful contrasts of tastes and textures will blow your guests away!"

Pete Zimmer
Inn of the Anasazi

White Chocolate Chile Ice Cream

¼	**cup sugar**
2	**egg yolks**
4	**cups heavy cream**
1	**cup honey**
1	**vanilla bean, meat scraped off**
2	**cups white chocolate, chopped small**
1	**tablespoon chile molido** *(ground red chile peppers)*

In a medium large mixing bowl place the sugar and egg yolks. Mix them together for 1 minute.

Add the heavy cream, honey, and vanilla bean meat. Fold the mixture into the egg yolks.

Freeze the mixture in an ice cream machine for 7 to 10 minutes, or until a semi-soft consistency is achieved.

Fold in the white chocolate and chile molido.

Place the mixture in an airtight container and freeze it for 24 hours.

makes 2 quarts

"Some people might get a little freaked out at the thought of putting white chocolate and chile together. I admit that this combination is probably one of the most unusual flavors you will ever experience, but it also will be one of the most interesting.....and, it's delicious! First you taste the vanilla and butter, and then this beautiful flavor of the white chocolate comes forward. Then, at the last second, the hot chile kicks in to give you some heat.....not enough to put you on fire, but just enough to really complement the dish."

"With this ice cream being so unique you want something very simple to accompany it. Of course it is excellent with fruit, and it also is delicious with a heated butterscotch-caramel sauce served on top. Or, you could serve it plain with some crushed pecans and shaved white chocolate. Another idea is to eliminate the chile and add some crumbled brittle chips and toasted almonds to the ice cream when you are making it. The basic recipe is extremely versatile, so use your imagination!"

Pete Zimmer
Inn of the Anasazi

Creamy Vanilla Ice Cream with Piñon Brittle

Creamy Vanilla Ice Cream

2	cups heavy cream
1	cup light cream
⅔	cup sugar
1	vanilla bean, split
6	egg yolks, lightly beaten
1	cup Piñon Brittle *(recipe on next page)*

In a large saucepan place the heavy cream, light cream, sugar, and split vanilla bean. Stir the ingredients together. Heat them on medium for 5 minutes, or until the sugar is dissolved.

In a medium bowl place the egg yolks. While whisking constantly, pour in half of the hot cream mixture. Return this mixture to the saucepan and continue to whisk it until the temperature reaches 165° *(use a candy thermometer)*.

Strain the mixture through a sieve into a bowl. Cover the bowl with plastic wrap and refrigerate it for 2 hours.

Place the mixture in an ice cream freezer and freeze it according to the manufacturer's instructions.

Add the Piñon Brittle pieces and stir them in.

makes approximately 1 quart

"This is a very rich ice cream that is first cooked like a French-style custard. The egg yolks are what make it taste so yummy. Usually a commercial French vanilla ice cream won't have egg yolks.....it's only the old-fashioned, homemade kind that does."

"You can use this basic ice cream recipe as a foil for lots of other fruits or candies. For Valentine's Day I made a strawberry swirl ice cream by cooking fresh berries with a little sugar and lemon juice, and then swirling them in. It was delicious!"

"The piñon brittle in this ice cream tastes divine. You can use store-bought brittle if you prefer, although I don't think it comes close in comparison to my homemade version."

Sylvia Johnson
Celebrations

Piñon Brittle

2	**cups sugar**
1	**cup corn syrup**
½	**cup water**
2	**cups piñon nuts** *(pine nuts)*, **toasted** *(see chef's comments on this page)*
2	**tablespoons butter**
2	**teaspoons baking soda**
1	**teaspoon vanilla extract**

In a medium heavy saucepan place the sugar, corn syrup, and water. Stir the ingredients together. Cook them on medium high heat until they come to a boil and the temperature reaches 230° *(use a candy thermometer)*.

Add the toasted piñon nuts and the butter, and stir them in. Cook the mixture until it reaches 300°.

Take the pan off the heat. Add the baking soda and vanilla extract, and stir them in well.

Pour the mixture on a buttered, flat baking sheet. Spread it out with a rubber spatula so a thin layer is formed.

When the candy is cool, break it into large pieces. Store it in an airtight container.

makes 1 pound

White Chocolate Mousse

½   **pound white chocolate**
4   **egg yolks, lightly beaten**
2   **eggs, lightly beaten**
4   **egg whites, beaten to soft peaks**
3   **cups heavy cream**
¼   **cup piñon nuts** *(pine nuts)*, **toasted** *(see chef's comments on page 325)*
12 **fresh mint leaves**

In the top of a simmering double boiler place the white chocolate. Heat it for 5 minutes, or until it is melted.

In a small bowl place the 4 egg yolks and 2 whole eggs, and whisk them together. Pour a small amount of the hot, melted chocolate into the eggs and stir it in. While constantly stirring, slowly add the remaining chocolate.

Add the egg whites and fold them in.

Add the heavy cream. Whip the ingredients together so that the mixture thickens.

In each of 6 individual goblets place the mixture. Chill the mousse for 12 hours in the refrigerator.

Garnish each serving with the piñon nuts and mint leaves.

serves 6

"This recipe won the 'Taste of Santa Fe' grand prize several years ago, so you know that it is going to taste really, really delicious."

"When I was ten years old I knew I wanted to be a cook. Friends would come over and I would make them sandwiches and fresh soup with chopped parsley on top to make it look nice. I have a friend who tells me that once when we were kids I made him a steak sandwich and some soup from scratch, and it was the best meal he has ever had in his life. He said it even looked good!"

"Not only do I do all of the cooking at home, I also do all of the cleaning and laundry. All I ask of my wife is that she take good care of our two little girls. My wife tells me that a lot of women would love to have a husband like me, and she appreciates everything I do for her. The truth is though, I do all of these things for myself, as well as for her, because I am a perfectionist. No one else can do things the way I want them done, except for me."

Tony Trujillo
Inn at Loretto

Tres Chocolate Bizcochitos with Red Chile

2	tablespoons butter
2	ounces unsweetened chocolate
6	ounces semisweet chocolate
2	eggs, lightly beaten
3	tablespoons instant espresso powder
¾	cup sugar
1	teaspoon vanilla extract
⅓	cup flour
2	tablespoons red chile powder
⅛	teaspoon baking powder
¼	teaspoon salt *(or to taste)*
1	cup chocolate chips
1½	cups pecans, chopped

Preheat the oven to 350°.

In a simmering double boiler place the butter, unsweetened chocolate, and semisweet chocolate. Slowly melt the ingredients together *(stir them occasionally)*. Set the chocolate aside to cool.

In a medium mixing bowl place the eggs, espresso powder, sugar, and vanilla extract. Beat the ingredients on high speed for 2 minutes, or until they are light and fluffy.

Add the cooled melted chocolate and stir it in.

Add the flour, red chile powder, baking powder, and salt. Mix the ingredients together so that they are well combined.

Add the chocolate chips and pecans, and stir them in well.

Place a piece of parchment paper on a flat baking sheet. Drop quarter-size dollops of the dough on top *(they should be 2 inches apart from each other)*.

Bake the cookies for 5 minutes. Turn the baking sheet halfway around. Bake the cookies for another 5 minutes. Cool them on a wire rack.

makes approximately 30 cookies

Piñon Shortbread Cookies

½	**pound butter, softened**
½	**cup brown sugar**
¼	**cup piñon nuts** *(pine nuts)*, **toasted** *(see chef's comments on page 325),* **crushed and ground**
2	**cups flour**
¼	**teaspoon salt**

Preheat the oven to 325°.

In a medium bowl place the butter and beat it with an electric mixer for 2 minutes, or until it is smooth and creamy.

Add the brown sugar and beat it in so that it is well incorporated.

In another medium bowl place the piñon nuts, flour, and salt. Mix the ingredients together.

With the electric mixer constantly running, slowly add the flour mixture to the butter so that a dough is formed.

Place the dough on a floured surface and roll it out so that it is ½" thick. Cut the dough into 2" shapes and place them on an ungreased cookie sheet.

Bake the cookies for 20 to 25 minutes, or until the edges are slightly brown.

makes approximately 24 cookies.

"This is a gourmet shortbread cookie recipe that lends itself to creative cookie cutting. We make stars, hearts, bunnies, or whatever shape is the symbol of our current holiday. I like to dip half of each cookie into melted chocolate, so you get a two-toned look. It's also fun to press your thumb into the center of each cookie before you bake it, and then later fill it with jam."

"When I was a child I was fascinated with baking. I used to experiment in the kitchen all of the time, without having the slightest idea of what I was doing. I would make things completely from scratch, and they would come out horrible. Or I would put a cake in the oven and then go outside and play for four hours, completely forgetting it. In retrospect, I guess my mom was pretty tolerant."

"I really believe that when you bake you can't be unhappy, bitter, or angry. To be a truly good baker you must be at peace with yourself."

Suzanne Chavez
The Galisteo Inn

Chocolate Piñon Tart

¾	**pound butter, cut into chunks**
½	**cup sugar**
1	**egg yolk**
2	**cups unbleached white flour**
1	**teaspoon vanilla extract**
⅛	**teaspoon ground cloves**
¼	**teaspoon salt**
4	**tablespoons cold water** *(or as needed)*
12	**ounces bittersweet chocolate, finely chopped**
½	**cup piñon nuts** *(pine nuts)*
8	**eggs, lightly beaten**
¾	**cup sugar**
1	**cup heavy cream**
1	**orange, zested** *(outer orange part grated off)*

Preheat the oven to 350°.

In a food processor place the butter, the ½ cup of sugar, egg yolk, flour, vanilla extract, cloves, and salt. Blend the ingredients together.

With the food processor constantly running, add the water a tablespoon at a time, so that the dough forms a ball.

On a lightly floured surface roll out the dough into a thin disc. Place it in a 10" tart pan.

Place a piece of foil on top of the dough and weight it down with dried beans *(or pie weights)*.

Bake the crust for 20 minutes. Remove the dried beans and the foil. Let the crust cool on a wire rack.

Sprinkle the chocolate pieces and the piñon nuts in the bottom of the tart shell.

In a large bowl place the eggs, the ¾ cup of sugar, heavy cream, and orange zest. Mix the ingredients together well.

Pour the mixture into the tart shell.

Bake the tart for 30 minutes, or until it is firm.

serves 10

Mexican Brownies

10	ounces baking chocolate
2½	cups butter
12	medium eggs
5	cups sugar
2½	cups all purpose flour
1	tablespoon vanilla extract
1	teaspoon salt
1¼	cups margarine
4½	cups powdered sugar
⅔	cup heavy cream
⅔	cup sherry
2	cups pecans, finely chopped
2	pounds chocolate chips
1¼	cups unsalted butter
1	cup water

Preheat the oven to 325°.

In the top of a simmering double boiler place the baking chocolate and the 2½ cups of butter. Heat the ingredients so that they are melted. Stir them together.

In a large bowl place the eggs and beat them for 3 minutes, or until they lighten in color. With the mixer constantly running, gradually add the sugar.

Add the melted chocolate mixture, flour, vanilla extract, and salt. Mix the ingredients together well.

In a greased jelly roll pan place the brownie mixture and spread it out evenly.

Bake the brownies for 30 minutes. Remove the pan from the oven and place it on a wire rack to cool.

In a medium mixing bowl place the margarine and the powdered sugar, and cream them together.

Add the heavy cream and sherry, and beat them in so that the mixture is light and fluffy. Add the pecans and stir them in.

Spread the mixture on top of the cooled brownies.

Cover the brownies with plastic wrap and refrigerate them.

(continued on next page)

"These are wonderful, richly decadent brownies. However, anyone who has a cholesterol problem shouldn't be eating these, or at the very least margarine should be substituted for the butter. As the president of the Santa Fe division of the American Heart Association and co-author of the world's first low cholesterol cookbook, I am always trying to educate people about food that is healthy for the heart. We had an employee who had a coronary. Later we found out that he had been eating a dozen scrambled eggs every morning. He was unaware that this might cause problems with his heart."

"Casa Sena means the 'House of Sena'. The whole building surrounding the plaza used to be the home of Major Jose Sena, where he lived with his wife and twenty-eight children."

Gordon Heiss
Casa Sena

In the top of the simmering double boiler place the chocolate chips, the 1¼ cups of unsalted butter, and the water. Heat the ingredients so that they are melted. Mix them together well.

Spread the chocolate mixture on top of the cold brownies.

Cover the brownies with plastic wrap and refrigerate them again for 1 hour. Cut the brownies into squares.

makes approximately 3 dozen brownies

Chocolate Amaretto Mousse Cake

2	packages Pepperidge Farm chocolate cookies, crushed
⅓	cup butter, melted
1½	pounds semisweet chocolate, cut up
½	cup amaretto liqueur
½	cup strong coffee
4	egg yolks
2	cups heavy cream, whipped until stiff
½	cup sliced almonds

In a medium bowl place the crushed cookies and melted butter, and mix them together. Press the mixture evenly on the bottom and sides of a 10" springform pan to make a crust.

In a medium glass bowl place the chocolate and heat it in the microwave for 3 minutes, or until it is melted.

Add the amaretto and coffee, and stir them in. Let the chocolate cool.

One at a time, add the egg yolks and beat them in.

Fold in the whipped cream.

Pour the mixture into the prepared crust. Sprinkle the almonds on top.

Chill the mousse for 2 hours *(minimum)* before serving it.

serves 10 to 12

Red Chile Wedding Cake Cookies

1	pound butter, room temperature
2½	cups brown sugar
1	teaspoon vanilla extract
1	teaspoon red chile powder
5	cups unbleached white flour
2	cups walnuts, chopped
½	cup powdered sugar
1	teaspoon red chile powder

Preheat the oven to 350°.

In a large mixing bowl place the butter and brown sugar. Cream the ingredients together for 3 minutes.

Add the vanilla extract and the first teaspoon of red chile powder, and mix them together.

With the mixer constantly running, sprinkle in the flour *(the batter will be stiff)*.

Add the walnuts and mix them in.

Roll the dough into small balls *(the size of golf balls)* and place them on a baking sheet.

Bake the cookies for 15 minutes.

In a small bowl place the powdered sugar and the second teaspoon of red chile powder. Stir the ingredients together.

Roll each cookie in the powdered sugar mixture so that it is coated all over. Set the cookies on a wire rack to cool.

Sprinkle the remaining powdered sugar-chile mixture on top of the cooled cookies.

makes approximately 36 cookies

"Wedding cake cookies are traditional at special events, festivals, and weddings. They are like a shortbread cookie with nuts. I wanted to give a Southwestern twist to the recipe, so I added the chile powder. I like the idea of having something hot and spicy at the end of a meal, as well as in the middle. The richness of the butter goes very well with sweet and hot tastes. By the way, this is a foolproof recipe.....it comes out perfect every time."

Gretchen Rymes
Santacafe

"When Gretchen first started making these cookies she used only a tiny amount of the red chile powder. We kept tasting them and asking her to add more and more, until finally she ended up with these proportions."

Kelly Rogers
Santacafe

Coconut Milk Crème Brûlée

2	**cans coconut milk** *(see chef's comments on page 113)*
7	**tablespoons sugar**
8	**egg yolks, lightly beaten**
1	**teaspoon vanilla extract**
1	**tablespoon rosewater**
¼	**teaspoon salt** *(or to taste)*
½	**cup brown sugar**

In a large saucepan place the coconut milk and bring it to a boil. Remove the pan from the heat.

In a small bowl place the sugar, egg yolks, vanilla extract, rosewater, and salt. Mix the ingredients together.

While stirring constantly, place a small amount of the hot coconut milk into the sugar-egg yolk mixture.

Add the tempered mixture back to the rest of the coconut milk and stir it in well.

Pour the custard mixture in the custard cups. Place them in a large baking pan that is filled with 1" of water. Cover the pan.

Bake the brûlées for 15 minutes, or until the centers are just set.

Sprinkle the brown sugar on top of each serving and then caramelize it with a flame *(such as a blowtorch)*.

Remove the custard cups from the pan of water and let them cool for 3 hours.

serves 6

Rancho Encantado Torte with Macadamia Golden Raisin Cream

Rancho Encantado Torte

¼	pound butter, softened
1½	cups sugar
3	egg yolks
½	teaspoon vanilla extract
2½	cups all purpose flour
1½	cups macadamia nuts, finely chopped
1	teaspoon baking powder
¼	teaspoon salt
1	cup milk
3	egg whites, beaten to soft peaks
	Macadamia Golden Raisin Cream *(recipe on next page)*
1	cup macadamia nuts, finely chopped

Preheat the oven to 350°.

In a large bowl place the butter, sugar, egg yolks, and vanilla extract. Cream the ingredients together with an electric mixer *(use the paddle attachment)* for 2 minutes, or until the mixture is light and fluffy.

In a medium bowl place the flour, the 1½ cups of chopped macadamia nuts, baking powder, and salt. Mix the ingredients together.

While mixing constantly, slowly add the flour mixture to the butter-egg yolk mixture. Slowly add the milk and mix it in.

Add the egg whites and gently fold them in.

Pour the batter into an oiled and floured 8" round cake pan that has been lined with parchment paper.

Bake the cake for 25 to 30 minutes, or until a toothpick inserted in the center comes out clean.

Cool the cake on a wire rack for 15 minutes. Remove the cake from the pan and place it in the refrigerator for 1 hour.

Slice the cake in half, horizontally. Place the bottom half of the cake on a decorative plate, with the cut side up.

Spread the cake with ⅓ of the Macadamia Golden Raisin Cream.

(continued on next page)

"This is an outrageous recipe that I developed during a time when we did not have a pastry chef. I've always loved to bake, and will do it whenever I get the chance."

"Last year I spent some time in Hawaii and was able to see a lot of the native cooking. Some of the food was delicious, but other things weren't too palatable, such as the poi (cooked taro root). I took the good parts and tried to incorporate them with Southwestern ingredients in some of my dishes."

Tim Lopez
Rancho Encantado

"I have a real sweet tooth, so I really do love this dessert. Luckily, my sweet tooth has never caused me to gain extra weight. I guess that's due to genes and too many hours working."

John Litton
Rancho Encantado

"Tim is a wonderful chef. I have complete confidence in him and know that anything he produces will be something I can be proud of. Much of his knowledge comes from his mother, who also is an excellent cook. He has recipes that have been in his family for many generations. Tim's cooking comes from the heart, and I think that is one reason why he is so successful."

"Rancho Encantado is a beautiful, luxury resort nestled in the foothills of the Sangre de Cristo mountains. We have hiking trails, tennis, horseback riding, and swimming, but our specialty is relaxation. Many of our guests are famous, and we give them the sense of anonymity that they desire. All of our guests are treated as special individuals, and I think that's why seventy-five percent of them return for repeat visits."

John Litton
Rancho Encantado

Place the other half of the cake on top. Spread the rest of the Cream on the sides and top of the cake. Sprinkle on the 1 cup of macadamia nuts.

serves 8 to 10

Macadamia Golden Raisin Cream

1   **pint heavy cream, very cold**
1   **cup powdered sugar**
½   **teaspoon vanilla extract**
1½   **cups macadamia nuts, coarsely chopped**
1   **cup golden raisins, coarsely chopped**

In a medium mixing bowl place the heavy cream, powdered sugar, and vanilla extract. Beat the ingredients for 5 to 6 minutes, or until they form soft peaks.

Add the nuts and golden raisins, and fold them in.

makes 4 cups

Apple-Green Chile Clafouti

¼   **cup sugar**
4   **eggs, lightly beaten**
1½   **cups half & half**
½   **teaspoon vanilla extract**
¼   **teaspoon salt**
1⅓   **cups unbleached white flour**
1   **tablespoon butter**
¾   **cup green chile peppers, roasted, peeled, seeded and finely diced**
1½   **cups Granny Smith apples, peeled, cored and thinly sliced**
¾   **teaspoon ground cinnamon**

Preheat the oven to 350°.

In a large bowl place the sugar, eggs, half & half, vanilla, salt, and flour. Whisk the ingredients together and set them aside.

In a 9"x13" baking pan place the butter and heat it in the oven until it is melted. Spread the melted butter over the bottom and sides of the pan.

Spread the green chile peppers evenly on the bottom of the pan. Layer the apple slices on top. Sprinkle the cinnamon on top of the apples.

Pour the custard mixture on top.

Bake the clafouti for 30 minutes, or until it is puffy, golden brown, and firm in the center.

Serve the clafouti while it is still warm.

serves 4 to 6

"Clafouti is a kind of French custard that was traditionally made with black cherries. The pits were left in because they added flavor during the cooking. There are numerous variations on the original dish, and this is my unique Southwestern version. I got the idea to use the green chiles with apples from a friend who gave me some homemade apple-green chile jelly. I thought it sounded really awful, but the flavors were wonderful!"

"People are very impressed with this dish. It's light and not terribly rich, and is quite easy to prepare."

Gretchen Rymes
Santacafe

Natillas Ice Cream

3	cups milk
1	vanilla bean, split lengthwise
3	cinnamon sticks
1	teaspoon nutmeg
8	egg yolks
1½	cups sugar

In a medium saucepan place the milk, vanilla bean halves, cinnamon sticks, and nutmeg. Heat the milk on medium high for 5 to 10 minutes, or until it is scalding *(stir it occasionally)*. Remove the pieces of vanilla bean and cinnamon sticks.

In a medium bowl place the egg yolks and sugar. Beat them together for 2 minutes, or until ribbons are formed.

Add a small amount of the scalded milk to the egg yolk mixture and stir it. While stirring constantly, very slowly add the rest of the milk.

Transfer the mixture back to the saucepan. While stirring occasionally, heat it on medium low for 5 to 10 minutes, or until the mixture thickens so that it will coat a wooden spoon.

Freeze the custard in an ice cream machine according to the manufacturer's instructions.

makes approximately 2 quarts

Pumpkin Cheesecake in Pecan Crust

3	8-ounce packages cream cheese
1	cup sugar
3	eggs
1½	cups pumpkin purée
1	teaspoon vanilla extract
1	teaspoon orange extract
1	teaspoon ground cinnamon
1	teaspoon ground ginger
1	teaspoon pumpkin pie spice
1	tablespoon cornstarch
1	cup pecan pieces
1	stick butter, melted
½	cup brown sugar
1	cup flour

Preheat the oven to 350°.

In a medium bowl place the cream cheese and sugar. Beat them with an electric mixer for 3 to 4 minutes, or until the mixture is light and creamy.

Add the eggs and beat them in well.

Add the pumpkin purée, vanilla extract, orange extract, cinnamon, ginger, pumpkin pie spice, and cornstarch. Mix the ingredients together so that they are very well blended.

In a food processor place the pecan pieces, melted butter, brown sugar, and flour. Blend the ingredients together. Press the mixture into a springform pan (reserve ¼ cup) to form a crust. Pour in the pumpkin mixture. Sprinkle the reserved crust mixture on top.

Bake the cake for 60 minutes, or until the top is golden brown and slightly cracked.

Let the cheesecake cool and then refrigerate it overnight.

serves 16

"This is the most outrageously delicious cheesecake I have ever eaten. It is a perfect balance of the pumpkin and cheesecake flavors. We serve it during the holidays and people absolutely rave about it. And yes, it is as fattening as it sounds, but it's worth every calorie!"

Joanna Kaufman
The Galisteo Inn

"I have a basic cheesecake recipe that has only four ingredients in it.....cream cheese, eggs, sugar, and vanilla. One day around Thanksgiving time I was trying to come up with a dessert other than my traditional pumpkin pie recipe, and got the idea to combine the two. It's been a real success."

Suzanne Chavez
The Galisteo Inn

"My earliest memory of cooking is baking pies with my grandmother. I had my little miniature pie pans and rolling pin, so I could bake my own little pies. My grandmother was an incredible gardener and cook, and she taught me invaluable lessons in the kitchen."

Dorothy Charles
The Galisteo Inn

Karen's Ice Cream Sandwich

"When I first bought this restaurant I interviewed a lot of bakers, trying to find someone who would make desserts that would fit in with our concept of food.....simple, good, and hearty. Everyone wanted to make things like tirami-su, or whatever the current vogue in town was. Then I met Karen English, a very creative woman, who was just what I was looking for. She used to be the Pie Lady in Martha's Vineyard. She suggested that we make and serve our own homemade ice cream sandwich. After I tasted one, I knew it would be perfect for our restaurant. It's one of our most popular items."

Harry Shapiro
Harry's Road House

2	ounces semisweet chocolate
3	tablespoons cocoa
3	tablespoons water
6	tablespoons butter, softened
6	tablespoons brown sugar
5	tablespoons white sugar
1	egg
1	tablespoon vanilla extract
¾	cup flour
½	teaspoon baking soda
½	teaspoon boiling water
4	cups premium ice cream *(your favorite)*, softened

Preheat the oven to 325°.

In the top of a simmering double boiler place the chocolate and heat it for 5 minutes, or until it is melted. Add the cocoa and the 3 tablespoons of water, and whisk them together so that they are smooth. Remove the pan from the heat.

In a medium mixing bowl place the butter, brown sugar, and white sugar. Cream the ingredients together for 3 to 5 minutes, or until the mixture is light and fluffy.

In a small bowl place the egg and vanilla extract, and beat them together. Add the egg to the butter mixture and beat the ingredients together. Add the melted chocolate and stir it in. Add ½ of the flour and stir it in. Mix the baking soda with the boiling water. Add it to the batter and stir it in. Add the rest of the flour and mix it in.

Place a sheet of wax paper on a small, greased baking pan. Grease the top of the wax paper with butter. Place the batter on the wax paper and spread it out evenly.

Bake the cookie dough for 8 to 10 minutes *(the dough may not seem completely cooked)*, or until it is barely done.

Place the cookie in the freezer for 3 hours, or until it is completely frozen. Remove the cookie from the freezer and cut it in half, horizontally *(to make 2 cookie halves)*.

Spread the ice cream on the inside of one of the cookie halves. Place the other cookie half on top. Wrap the sandwich in plastic wrap. Place the sandwich in the freezer for 2 hours, or until the ice cream is hard. Cut the sandwich into 8 pieces.

serves 8

Oreo Piñon Kahlua Cheesecake

1½	pounds Oreo cookies, finely crushed
½	pound butter, room temperature
2½	pounds cream cheese, room temperature
6	eggs
1⅛	cups sugar
2	tablespoons Kahlua liqueur
2	cups sour cream
¼	cup sugar
1	tablespoon Kahlua liqueur
¼	cup piñon nuts *(pine nuts)*, **toasted** *(see chef's comments on page 325)*

Preheat the oven to 350°.

In a large bowl place the cookie crumbs *(reserve ¼ cup)* and the butter. Mix the ingredients together so that they are well blended.

Place the mixture in a 10" springform pan and press it evenly on the bottom and the sides of the pan *(to form a crust)*.

In another large mixing bowl place the cream cheese and beat it for 2 minutes, or until it is smooth.

One at a time, add the eggs to the cream cheese and beat them in so that the mixture is smooth.

Add the 1⅛ cups of sugar and the 2 tablespoons of Kahlua, and beat them on high speed for 5 minutes.

Pour the mixture into the crust.

Bake the cheesecake for 35 minutes, or until the center is set *(leave the oven on)*.

In a medium bowl place the sour cream, the ¼ cup of sugar, and the 1 tablespoon of Kahlua. Stir the ingredients together.

Spread the mixture evenly over the top of the cheesecake.

Sprinkle the reserved ¼ cup of cookie crumbs and the piñon nuts on top. Bake the cheesecake for 10 minutes more, or until a toothpick inserted in the center comes out clean.

serves 12 to 16

"I love this dessert, but it's sinfully decadent! Make it when you want to serve something really special, and you are willing to splurge with calories."

"If you don't have a springform pan you can make this in a regular pan, or even as cupcakes. Sprinkle more cookie crumbs and piñon nuts on top, if you want to add something extra. Or, use your imagination. Add whipped cream, fresh berries, or whatever you like. Do what you want in the kitchen, without fear of getting into trouble."

Lela Cross
La Plazuela

"It's important not to overcook or undercook the cheesecake. The center should be a little bit jiggly, but also a toothpick inserted should come out clean. Ovens vary in their temperature, so watch it closely. You don't want to ruin such a spectacular dessert."

Tomas Cross
La Plazuela

Mexican Chocolate Crème Brûlée

1	2-ounce Ibarra *(Mexican)* chocolate bar, melted
2	cups heavy cream
2	cups half & half
6	tablespoons cocoa powder
1	stick canela *(cinnamon)*
1¼	cups sugar
8	egg yolks

Preheat the oven to 350°.

In the top of a simmering double boiler place the Mexican chocolate and melt it.

In a large saucepan place the melted chocolate, heavy cream, half & half, cocoa powder, and canela stick. Stir the ingredients together and bring them to a boil.

Remove the pan from the heat and set it aside. Remove the stick of canela.

In a medium mixing bowl place the sugar and egg yolks. Beat the ingredients with an electric mixer until they become a very pale yellow.

Place a small amount of the melted chocolate mixture into the egg yolks and mix them together.

Add the egg yolk mixture to the melted chocolate. Stir the ingredients together so that they are well combined.

In a medium roasting pan place 4 ramekins. Ladle the brûlée mixture into the ramekins. Pour water into the roasting pan so that it is 1" deep *(to make a water bath)*.

Bake the crème brûlées for 15 minutes, or until they are firm.

Remove the ramekins from the water bath and let them cool on a wire rack.

serves 4

"Once I worked with a chef in Dallas who made the best crème brûlée around. I took that basic recipe and added some Mexican chocolate and cinnamon to give it a Southwest twist. It is not a terribly rich dessert and the flavor is heavenly. Our regular customers get upset if we don't have it, which happens from time to time, because we rotate our desserts."

"I think I'm a pastry chef in the deepest part of me, because whenever I make desserts I feel like I am in heaven. It's such a welcome relief from the pressures of banquets, menus, specials, and paperwork."

Martin Rios
Old House

Avocado Lime Cheesecake

2	cups graham cracker crumbs
1⅓	cups piñon nuts *(pine nuts)*, **ground**
½	cup butter, melted
4	avocados, peeled, pitted and mashed
1	pound cream cheese, room temperature
1	cup sugar
6	eggs
1	tablespoon lime zest *(outer green part grated off)*
¼	cup lime juice, freshly squeezed
2	teaspoons vanilla extract
⅓	cup heavy cream, whipped to soft peaks
3	cups sour cream
2	tablespoons sugar
1	teaspoon vanilla extract
½	cup piñon nuts

Preheat the oven to 350°.

In a medium bowl place the graham cracker crumbs, the 1⅓ cups of ground piñon nuts, and the melted butter. Mix the ingredients together well.

On the bottom and sides of a 9" springform pan place the graham cracker mixture and press it down firmly to make a crust.

In a large mixing bowl place the avocados, cream cheese and the 1 cup of sugar. Cream the ingredients together well.

While mixing constantly, add the eggs one at a time.

Add the lime zest, lime juice, and the 2 teaspoons of vanilla extract. Mix the ingredients together.

Add the whipped cream and fold it in.

Pour the batter into the pan.

Bake the cheesecake for 30 minutes. Remove it from the oven *(leave the oven on)* and let it sit for 10 minutes.

In a small bowl place the sour cream, the 2 tablespoons of sugar, and the 1 teaspoon of vanilla extract. Mix the ingredients together.

Spread the sour cream mixture on top of the cheesecake.

Sprinkle on the ½ cup of piñon nuts.

(continued on next page)

"My wife, Cricket, who is a registered dietician, came up with the idea of using avocados and limes in a cheesecake. I tried several formulas until I came up with one that worked. When I first tried the piñon crust I didn't realize how oily the nuts were, and oil oozed out and flooded the oven. This is an excellent way to use avocados, and they give an interesting flavor to the cheesecake."

*"At Casa Sena we have the Cantina, which is like a dinner theater. The people who wait on your table will suddenly gather by the piano and sing these marvelous show tunes. They all have fantastic voices and are aspiring show business folk. One of our waitstaff was in the opening cast of **A Chorus Line** on Broadway. He eventually got fed up with New York and moved to Santa Fe to write a book. Now he's a singing waiter to pay his bills."*

Gordon Heiss
Casa Sena

Return the cheesecake to the oven and bake it for 5 minutes.

Remove the cheesecake from the oven and let it cool for 6 to 8 hours, or until it is firm.

serves 12

Raspberry Fig Marscapone Tart

1	pound marscapone cheese
½	cup powdered sugar
1	9" baked tart shell
1	cup figs, seeded and quartered
1	cup fresh raspberries

In a food processor place the marscapone cheese and powdered sugar, and blend them together. Press the mixture evenly into the bottom of the tart shell.

Arrange the figs on top. Place the raspberries in the spaces between the figs.

Chill the tart before serving it.

serves 8 to 10

Index

MAIL ORDER SOURCES

The Chile Shop
109 E. Water St.
Santa Fe, NM 87501
(505) 983-6080

Coyote Cafe General Store
132 W. Water St.
Santa Fe, NM 87501
(505) 982-2454

Josie's Best New Mexican Foods
P.O. Box 5525
Santa Fe, NM 87502
(505) 473-3437

The Santa Fe School of Cooking
116 W. San Francisco St.
Santa Fe, NM 87501
(505) 983-4511

Bueno Foods
2001 Fourth St., S.W.
Albuquerque, NM 87102
(505) 243-2722

La Palma
2884 24th St.
San Francisco, CA 94110
(415) 647-1500

Dean & DeLuca
560 Broadway
New York, NY 10012
(212) 431-1691
(Please enclose $3.00 for a catalogue.)

Elizabeth Berry
Gallina Canyon Ranch
144 Camino Escandido
Santa Fe, NM 87501
(505) 982-4149
(Please enclose $1.00 for a catalogue.)

COOKBOOK ORDER FORM

Please send me the book(s) which I have indicated below. For shipping charges I am enclosing $3.00 for the first book, and $1.50 for each additional book.

Quantity	Book Title	Price	Total
____	**Santa Fe Hot & Spicy Recipe** *(softbound)* . . . . *Hot new recipes from Santa Fe chefs* • 392 recipes • 352 pages	$16.95	_____
____	**Santa Fe Lite & Spicy Recipe** *(softbound)* . . . . *Lighter, healthier recipes from Santa Fe chefs* • 350 recipes • 336 pages	$15.95	_____
____	**Santa Fe Recipe** *(softbound)* . . . . *Recipes from favorite local restaurants* • 300 recipes • 305 pages	$14.95	_____
____	**Taos Recipe** *(softbound)* . . . . *Recipes from restaurants in Taos, New Mexico* • 170 recipes • 177 pages	$12.95	_____
____	**Southern California Beach Recipe** *(hardbound)* . . . . *Recipes from favorite coastal restaurants* • 335 recipes • 352 pages	$17.95	_____

Shipping Total: _____

☐ Check here if you would like the book(s) autographed by the author.

TOTAL AMOUNT ENCLOSED: _____

Ship to: _____

Address: _____

City: _____

State: _____ Zip: _____

Make check or money order payable to **Tierra Publications**. Send it to:

Tierra Publications
2801 Rodeo Road, Suite B-612
Santa Fe, New Mexico 87505
(505) 983-6300

(MasterCard and Visa phone orders accepted)

Notes